AF606976

Award-Winning BASKET DESIGNS

Techniques and Patterns for All Levels

PATI ENGLISH

Schiffer Publishing Ltd

4880 Lower Valley Road • Atglen, PA 19310

Other Schiffer Books on Related Subjects:

Ply-Split Braided Baskets: Exploring Sculpture in Plain Oblique Twining, David W. Fraser, ISBN 978-0-7643-4652-1

A Guide to Basket Weaving, Marie Pieroni, ISBN 978-0-7643-4530-2

New and Different Materials for Weaving and Coiling, Marianne Barnes, ISBN 978-0-7643-3992-9

Library of Congress Control Number: 2015951627

Designed by Molly Shields
Type set in AlternateGothic2 BT/Times New Roman

Unless otherwise noted, all photographs by Kelly Hazel.

ISBN: 978-0-7643-4971-3

Printed in China

Published by Schiffer Publishing, Ltd.
4880 Lower Valley Road
Atglen, PA 19310
Phone: (610) 593-1777; Fax: (610) 593-2002
E-mail: Info@schifferbooks.com

For our complete selection of fine books on this and related subjects, please visit our website at www.schifferbooks.com. You may also write for a free catalog.

This book may be purchased from the publisher. Please try your bookstore first.

We are always looking for people to write books on new and related subjects. If you have an idea for a book, please contact us at proposals@schifferbooks.com.

Schiffer Publishing's titles are available at special discounts for bulk purchases for sales promotions or premiums. Special editions, including personalized covers, corporate imprints, and excerpts can be created in large quantities for special needs. For more information, contact the publisher.

DEDICATION

To my very first basket weaving student, my mom, Bertha McMahon Smith. With her encouragement and since her passing, I have embarked on a journey to keep the art of basketry alive by teaching students of all ages.

To my dear friend, Desi Schumacher, who invited me to my first weaving class and with whom I continue to weave.

CONTENTS

Acknowledgments 4
Introduction 5

SECTION 1

Chapter 1
Brief History with an Overview of Basket Weaving in the United States 6

Chapter 2
Weaving Materials, Dyes, and Tools 18

Chapter 3
Base Techniques 26

Chapter 4
Weaving Techniques 31

Chapter 5
Rim Borders 47

Chapter 6
Handles, Wraps, Weaving Hints, and Finishing Touches 54

SECTION 2

Chapter 7
Award-Winning Basket Projects 68
- Shaker Cathead 69
- Double Handle Plaid Carryall 74
- Cozy Wine Cradle 80
- Chasing Diamonds 86
- Diamonds All Around 95
- Becoming Blue Skies 100
- Spirals Change 106
- Ribbons to Remember 111
- Hopi-Inspired Grand Canyon and Rain Clouds 118
- Autumn's Dress 126

SECTION 3

Chapter 8
Juried Exhibit Basket Projects 132
- Wren House Williamsburg Basket 133
- Cotton Laundry Basket with Overlays 136
- Seagrass Egg Basket 140
- Oval Bargello Basket 143
- Rectangle Sampler Basket 147

SECTION 4

Chapter 9
Gallery of Works (JoAnn Kelly Catsos, Flo Hoppe, Billy Owens, Nathan Taylor, Kathy Tessler, Matt Tommey, Laura Lee Zanger, and Judy Zugish) 152

Chapter 10
Display and Care of Baskets 161

Weaving Suppliers 162
Glossary 163
Bibliography 165
Notes 165
Index 166

ACKNOWLEDGMENTS

As a former elementary school library media specialist turned basket maker and teacher for a second career, I especially thank my husband, Glenn D. English; with his love, encouragement, support, and inspiration, I was able to make a change in my career direction, continue my teaching career, and fulfill my dream to one day become an author.

Thank you to author, gourd artist, and friend, Marianne Barnes, who inspired me to embark on this writing journey.

Thank you to Kelly Hazel, a wonderful photographer, who has come to love baskets and see them in many different lights. Her attention to detail and curiosity is apparent in each photograph.

Thank you to Dolores von Rosen, who inspired me to teach at conventions and beyond, and to each artist found in the Gallery section of this book for the photographs and the contributions of their original woven art.

Thanks go to the many weavers who have tested my project patterns.

Thank you to my family: my sons, David and Scott, who lived amidst coils of basket reed in a home filled with works in progress and a basket collection from around the world, and shared in the everyday life of a full-time basket maker and instructor. Thank you to my sister, Cathy, who has continuously encouraged me creatively and who has (thankfully) helped name many of my new creations. Thanks to my dad, Jim Smith, for his love of wrapped handles on baskets. He always says, "It feels like leather in my hands."

Finally, I express thanks and gratitude to my proofreaders Alexa Brandt, Bettina George, Pam Givens, Pat Milz, and Susie Johnson for their dedication to this work in so many ways.

INTRODUCTION

Baskets play a significant part in our heritage. For many centuries, our ancestors from all over the planet have participated in basket weaving as a practical life skill. Weaving has evolved from functional pieces necessary for survival to the popular art form enjoyed today.

This instructional book has broad appeal for weavers at all levels, offering chances to learn, weave, enjoy, and share. It will also provide pleasure for those who have an interest in the visual arts. It is for basket collectors, anyone who has a love of fine craftsmanship, and for those who wish to become familiar with and appreciate this lifelong skill.

Presenting a fascinating selection of basketry styles, this book offers more than the traditional, historical baskets originally created and named according to specific purposes.

To enjoy weaving these award-winning designs, the weaver must first learn the basics, the same sequential steps our ancestors utilized, and then practice these while exploring each new technique presented. The reader can use all or parts of this book to create the projects found within, as well as to experiment to create new, original basket designs. An array of skill-expanding projects is available here whether your interest is in traditional basketry or contemporary art pieces.

Winning designs from a variety of competition venues are presented with instructions, along with a number of designs the author has taught at juried state conventions and seminars. Traditional square and Shaker-style baskets are found, with a new twist to change or update the original design. Contemporary patterns employ more advanced techniques in flat, flat oval, and round reed. Look for plaids, twills, spirals, braids, arrows, lightning bolts or zigzags, diamonds, twining, waling, braiding, and more in these innovative baskets. Handle wraps and rim borders are explored as well.

Looking to the Gallery section of the book, readers can enjoy the artwork of a variety of artisans. Weavers from across the United States bring their unique ideas and artistic talents to this sampling of twenty-first-century woven art.

Utilize the useful reference guides: a list of suppliers, a glossary, and a bibliography. These references will be invaluable in your basket journey. Let's begin…

CHAPTER ONE

BRIEF HISTORY | *with an Overview of Basket Weaving in the United States*

Basket weaving is one of our most ancient art forms. Some anthropologists believe it is the oldest form of all. Archaeologists have found ancient basket fragments in caves and rock formations, dating back more than 10,000 years before pottery. These artifacts discovered in Africa, Asia, and North and South America have been preserved for future generations.

Basketry is a universal art, one practiced around the world in every civilization. The history of the people and their culture, the perspectives expressed by the individual weavers…every basket tells a story. Where was the basket created? Which materials were selected and why? What designs, symbols, accent colors, and techniques were incorporated? Answers to these questions provide clues to the origin and history of each basket.

Baskets are made by hand with the exception of fruit baskets such as commercial apple, peach, and berry baskets, which are stapled together.

Today we employ the same skills utilized many years ago by Native Americans, early settlers, farmers, and our ancestors. These are the skills that have nearly been forgotten and serve as the impetus for this author to keep the art of basketry alive.

Almost every culture in the world made baskets of various sizes and shapes using a myriad of weaving techniques. Geographical location determined the type of basketry practiced since it depended on the natural raw materials available. Many types of plant materials, too numerous to name here, are utilized in basket weaving. However, some of the more common are willow and rush in Europe; and rattan, reed, cane, bamboo, and palm in areas nearer to the equator and to the Far East, China, Japan, and the East Indies. Today these materials are imported to the United States. Other natural materials native to the United States are yucca of the southwest; beargrass and rivercane of the southeastern Cherokee designs; bulrush; and sweetgrass, which is coiled into the Gullah baskets of Charleston, South Carolina. Pine needles, willow, devil's claw, cornhusks, honeysuckle, kudzu, grape, and other vines are also employed. Baskets are also created with white oak, black ash, birch, maple, cedar, pine, walnut, and various other trees found in the United States.

White oak basket with an add-in handle. 7" dia × 3½" h, 9½" with handle. Collection of the author.

Coiled sweetgrass basket. 6" dia. × 2¼" h, 7½" with handle. Collection of the author.

This small oval tray is made with pine needles and raffia; artist unknown. 12" l × 6" w × 1" h.

Large pine needle tray, woven in Florida in the Seminole design. 21" l × 13½" w × 1¾" h.

Throughout history these natural resources were gathered, collected, transported, cleaned, sorted, prepared, dried, and woven into various shapes. Burden baskets, storage baskets with lids, water jars, agricultural and food baskets, winnowing trays, sifters, bowls, mats, and fish traps were made to accomplish daily survival activities. Later cradles, fans, furniture, wool drying and cotton gathering baskets, caskets, drums, masks, bells, hats and head coverings, moccasins, sandals, dolls, rattles, balls, other toys, split-twig animal figures, jewelry, purses, backpacks, and various other containers were created.

This large burden basket from Thailand has a woven strap and is made of reed, processed and smoked, to achieve the deep dark color. 18" dia. × 22" h. Collection of the author.

Hopi wicker plaque from northern Arizona with a striking colorful design. 11½" dia. Collection of the author.

A woven fan from Thailand. 10" w × 10" h, 13" with handle. Collection of the author.

A Native American Papago woven mat, coiled in design. 13" l × 11" w × ⅜" h. Collection of the author.

This piece of furniture made in Thailand is a clothes storage basket with a lid. 6" w × 11" h, 13½" with feet. Collection of the author.

Woven pillows made in Thailand. 10" l × 7" w × 5" h. Collection of the author.

Child's twill woven chair. 6" w × 5" h.

Woven bracelets. The bracelet on the bottom left (3" dia. × ¾" w) is from Hawaii; the center bracelet (3½" dia. × ¾" w) made of reed and cane is by the author; the bracelet on the right (2¾ dia. × ¼" w) is from Thailand.

Woven bells: Tall bell of waxed linen by Helen Stauffer, 2½" dia. × 4" h; center bell of honeysuckle from the Qualla Arts and Crafts Mutual, Cherokee, North Carolina, 2" w × 2" h; bell made of sweetgrass and purchased at the City Market in Charleston, South Carolina, artist unknown, 3" dia. × 3" h. Collection of the author.

The woven rattle pictured on the left (2½" dia. × 2½" h, 3½" with handle) was made in Vietnam; the colorful rattle (8" l × 5" w) was woven in Thailand.

Woven earrings made of rivercane and purchased at the Qualla Arts and Crafts Mutual in Cherokee, North Carolina. ¼" w × ⅜" h, ⅝" with handle.

Ancient patterns were often of geometric designs. Pictorial designs included human figures, lightning bolts, water, whales, horses, deer, coyote tracks, lizards, fish, birds, butterflies, and more locally-specific images.

Natural materials were dyed and woven into these designs. Bloodroot, for example, produced a red dye, while black walnuts and butternuts gave a warm brown. Indigo plants produced a blue dye. Flowers from available plant life, onion skins, and even clay were used to produce warm colors. Berries mashed, strained, and heated also produced dyes. When used with the natural weaving materials, these created a variety of traditional colors.

Pictorial designs are common in Native American baskets. The Alaskan hanging pouch (8½" dia. × 4"–9" h) features geese along the bottom and jumping fish. The two small round trinket baskets with lids are from the Makah tribe, with woven designs of ducks (2⅝" dia. × 2⅝" h) and men in a boat (2⅝" dia. × 1⅝" h). Collection of the author.

This Native American Makah basket from Washington State, a small woven lidded trinket basket, features a woven design of men in a boat. 2" dia. × 1⅝" h. Collection of the author.

Woven fish. Top: 2" w × 2" h. Middle: 5" w × 5" h. Bottom: 3" w × 3" h. Collection of the author.

A man in a maze design is woven into this tray from Pakistan. 11" dia. × 1" h. Collection of the author.

Lightning bolts or zigzag design in a woven bowl made in Botswana, Africa. 7½" dia. × 2" h. Collection of the author.

A bird design is woven in this miniature basket from near the Panama Canal. 3½" dia. × 3" h. Collection of the author.

Baskets were embellished with found materials: feathers, porcupine quills, shells, handmade beads, and handmade leather fringe. These are present on baskets from the northwest coast and the southwest areas of the United States.

Functional artifacts along with ceremonial and aesthetic items were woven and passed down from one generation to the next. Wedding baskets were created in many cultures, ranging from Africa to our Navajo ancestors of Arizona, and these were passed down through families, for use in weddings and other religious ceremonies, sometimes beaten like a drum, or used by the "medicine man" as a bowl for those who became sick. These baskets were so tightly woven that they were able to hold liquids mixed with herbs or roots for various medicinal purposes. In these round, coiled baskets, accents were created in circles or bands of color, representing the circle of life. In Navajo baskets, black represents dark clouds and rain, an important cultural theme since their land was dry and desertlike. Red symbolizes the rising and setting sun, with a black design for the mountains. The circle, not completely closed, features a coil in the center to represent an opening for spirits to find their way out, and during ceremonies, the basket was held with the opening facing east for this spiritual purpose.

A South African wedding basket from the Zulu nation also has bands of color in the traditional colors of rust and brown but is coiled using a different twist technique than the Navajo.

Burden basket with leather fringe and recycled metal cans. 4¼" dia. × 4" h, 16¼" with fringe and hanger. Collection of the author.

Woven of natural materials gathered in Hawaii, these baskets include philodendron sheaths, shells, and beads. Left: 6" dia. × 3½" h. Right: 6½" dia. × 5" h. Collection of the author.

Wedding baskets with bands of color representing the circle of life.

Navajo wedding ceremonial basket purchased at the Sacred Mountain Trading Post in northern Arizona. This was the very first basket I acquired to start my personal collection of Native American baskets. 11" dia. × 3" h. Collection of the author.

Wedding basket made by Zulu weavers in Africa. This is only the second wedding basket I have been able to find for purchase. Kept in the family, a wedding basket may be woven as part of the bride's dowry. 16" dia. × 4" h. Collection of the author.

The connection among the basket maker, the materials, and the natural surroundings was, and is to this day, of great importance. Each weaver brings personal life experiences to the art form as an expression of creativity.

Our North American native tribes numbered in the many hundreds. Using only their hands, these native ancestors, along with settlers in this New World, produced woven vessels using a blend of materials. As a result, considerable borrowing and an intermarriage of weaving ideas occurred, creating a melting pot of basketry in North America. Thus, a rich tradition of weaving art and craftsmanship developed.

A fine example of European influence with regards to our early American basket makers is found in ribbed or egg baskets up and down the East Coast from New England to the Southeast. Split oak or ash ribs were handmade for the frame of this useful and versatile basket also known as the hip basket and fanny basket. The graceful pouches formed by weaving in a continuous technique allow for easy storage and transportation of fresh eggs, flowers, vegetables, and other useful items.

Market baskets, plaited and carried to the nearest trading post or marketplace, were filled with an abundance of crops to barter for services and necessary items.

Sweetgrass baskets, coiled in parts of Africa, were transported to North America with slaves who eventually found their baskets added alongside the prevailing coiled and plaited vessels. Similar grasses growing along the coast of South Carolina, Georgia, and Florida are gathered to this day by local weavers. Our African American ancestors arrived in South Carolina more than three hundred years ago, weaving and coiling agricultural baskets. Today, from the City Market at the corner of Meeting Street and North

Sweetgrass basket made under the instruction of Barbara McCormick of McClellanville, South Carolina. 8" dia. × 2" h.

Seagrass and reed ribbed egg basket, woven by the author. 6" dia. × 4" h, 5" with handle.

At the corner of Meeting and North Market Streets in Charleston, South Carolina, you can purchase sweetgrass baskets at the City Market. *Photography by Glenn English.*

Market Street in Charleston, South Carolina, to roadside stands scattered along Highway 17 north of Mt. Pleasant, South Carolina, tourists can still find the traditional Sweetgrass baskets of yesteryear being created and offered for sale.

Another universal example, the burden basket, twined, plaited, or coiled into a sturdy pack, was used for harvesting, carrying, and storage. It has been a significant part of everyday life for ages in various cultures all around the globe. Most Apache mothers and grandmothers, along with women throughout time in all parts of the world, have carried babies on their backs in burden baskets. More recently, leather fringe with recycled pieces of metal cans were added to this basket to create soft musical sounds to lull the baby to sleep. This basket also had a place in ceremonies and rituals, and often was given as a gift.

Coiled sweetgrass baskets in a variety of shapes and sizes. These baskets were purchased at the City Market, Charleston, South Carolina, and along Highway 17 in Mt. Pleasant, South Carolina. Collection of the author.

With the onset of exploration and immigration in the eighteenth and early nineteenth centuries, basket makers in the United States began to produce more baskets for trade and eventually for tourism.

In the latter half of the nineteenth century and in the early twentieth century, collectors, gallery owners, museum curators, and art and curio shop proprietors became interested in woven designs from across the United States. Native Americans designed "fancy baskets" to meet the tourists' demands. Sewing baskets and purses with more embellishments were created for their newfound customers. Continuing their use of traditional color accents, they expanded their cultural designs, creating the next generation of basketry. With assistance from the Department of the Interior, fine artwork was promoted in various locations to keep our woven heritage alive. The Qualla Arts and Crafts Mutual in Cherokee, North Carolina, is an excellent example of a working co-op and retail sales shop. It was organized to help increase the variety and amount of art and crafts created, to raise awareness and the level of craftsmanship, and to develop a fair market return for the work of individual artists. This is a location for local Cherokee artists to work together; creating weaving, beading, rug making, and other artwork, and market it as a profitable career choice.

Throughout the United States in the last few decades, basketry is recognized and gaining popularity as a cultural tradition and one necessary to keep alive. A renaissance in basketry circles is evident by the increased number of educational opportunities available for weaving.

You will find many basket artists and instructors teaching at art schools such as the John C. Campbell Folk School in Brasstown, North Carolina; The Penland School of Crafts, Penland, North Carolina; Arrowmont School of Arts and Crafts, Gatlinburg, Tennessee; Penobscot Basket School, Searsport, Maine; Sievers School of Fiber Arts, Washington Island, Wisconsin; and Fishsticks Basketry School, Marysville, Washington. Additional art and craft schools include the Adirondack Folk School, Luzerne, New York; Arbutus Folk School, Olympia, Washington; Craft and Folk Art Museum, Los Angeles, California; North House Folk School, Grand Marais, Minnesota; and the Ozark Folk Center, Mountain View, Arkansas.

In addition, numerous state and regional associations have formed to share and keep this art alive well into the twenty-first century. Conventions and seminars are offered throughout the year in a great variety of venues.

Adding to the history and tradition of basket weaving, twenty-first century technology and the incorporation of materials such as copper, wire, leather, film, yarn, plastic, and more, produce functional, serviceable, utilitarian, and decorative baskets in an infinite number of designs. Three-dimensional sculptural art forms are developed from combining traditional basketry with contemporary vision, materials, and techniques. Our possibilities are endless.

Cherokee sewing basket with swing handles and cross overlays is made of white oak and maple, with bloodroot and walnut dyes. I purchased this basket at the Qualla Arts and Crafts Mutual in Cherokee, North Carolina. It bears the official tag from the US Department of the Interior, Indian Arts and Crafts Board. 9" l × 6" w × 7½" h, 11" with handle.

CHAPTER TWO

WEAVING MATERIALS, DYES, AND TOOLS

WEAVING MATERIALS

Two major types of materials are used in weaving in the United States today. One type is termed "naturals": these are materials gathered from our environment, that is, from forests, fields, deserts, roadsides, and so on. This includes bark, wood shavings, grasses, vines, berries, and many other plant-like sources.

The second type of material is reed, a material purchased already processed and ready for use. I choose to create with reed purchased from several suppliers around the United States, such as those listed in the Appendix. Reed is readily available for purchase by mail or online. This reed, the inner core of the rattan palm, originates from rattan grown in the tropical areas of Asia (South China, Malaysia, Indonesia) and in West Africa. Nearly six hundred species of rattan exist; those within the genus Calamus and the genus Daemonorhops of the Palmae family—they can grow up to a few hundred feet[1]—are utilized in the construction of baskets.

Pine needles can be gathered locally in many places in the United States, and are available for purchase commercially.

The honeysuckle vine is best to weave with after it has been boiled, stripped of its bark, and cleaned. When it is completely dry, it can be coiled for future use in place of round reed.

Natural plant materials. From left to right: philodendron sheaths; honeysuckle vine which has been boiled, stripped of the bark, and cleaned; and pine needles, natural and dyed red.

This climbing vine grows rapidly, straight up toward the sun. As its length increases, it climbs with thorns, known as spiny flagella, and uses nearby trees for support. This raw material is pulled and cut down with an axe or large knife and left to dry naturally in the sun for local use. For exporting to other markets, it is gathered into twenty-foot lengths on the same day it is cut and is transported, then sorted and processed. The processing involves exposure to a kerosene and diesel fuel mixture. The inner bark is removed and then split into many widths of cane for use in furniture and basketry. The core of the rattan palm is then cut, bundled, and tied into one-pound coils, which are graded by quality, color, and size. Coils of reed are treated with methyl bromide, an insecticide that is also used on produce before it is shipped to the United States.[2]

Transported from overseas, the reed finally arrives at a local destination in the United States for weavers such as you and me to use.

Reed is divided into types and sizes. Among the types, flat flat is flat on both sides; flat oval is flat on one side and oval or raised on the opposite side; oval oval is oval on both sides; round reed, as its name implies, is completely rounded; and half round is flat on one side and round on the opposite half, and is actually cut lengthwise from round reeds.

Measurements or sizes are given in inches or millimeters. Flat flat reed and flat oval reed are available in widths of 3 mm, 11/64", 3/16", ¼", ⅜", ½", ⅝", and ¾", while flat reed is also available in ⅞" and 1" wide sizes. Oval oval reed is available in 3/16", ¼", and ⅜". Half round reed is available in 3 mm, ¼", ⅜", ½", ⅝", and ¾", and is very stiff and sturdy.

Round reed, which ranges from the smallest size, #00, through #0, #1, #2, #2.5, #3, and #4, is used for fine twine and textural weaving techniques such as waling or braiding. The middle sizes, #5, #6, #7, #8, #9, and #10, are used for ribs in ribbed or egg baskets and as rim filler at the rim of baskets. The larger sizes, #12 and #15, are soaked and then coaxed into various shapes, glued, and pinned to create decorative or sturdy handles. Round reed is measured in millimeters, but the numerical size system used does not match the millimeter width. Use the following for accurate sizing:

#00	1.00 mm
#0	1.25 mm
#1	1.50 mm
#2	1.75 mm
#2.5	2.00 mm
#3	2.25 mm
#3.5	2.50 mm
#4	2.75 mm
#5	3.25–3.50 mm
#6	4.00–4.50 mm
#7	5.00 mm
#8	6.00 mm
#9	7.00 mm
#10	8.00 mm
#12	9.50 mm
#15	12.50 mm

Flat oval reed is available commercially. The ¼" flat oval reed is one of my favorite sizes and styles with which to work. Flat oval reed is found in coils by sizes: 3 mm, 11/64", 3/16", ¼", 7 mm, ⅜", ½", ⅝", and ¾".

Flat reed is available from many commercial suppliers listed in the Appendix. Flat reed is one of the most popular types of reed woven into baskets. Each coil is a full pound of reed, coiled, tagged with size indicated, and tied together for sale. Sizes include: 3 mm, 11/64", 3/16", ¼", 7 mm, ⅜", ½", ⅝", ¾", ⅞", and 1".

Round reed is available in many sizes, from the smallest, #00, through #0, #1, #2, #2.5, #3, #3.5, #4, #5, #6, #7, #8, #9, #10, #12, and the largest, #15. Smaller round reed is woven into many designs for texture and beauty, while the larger sizes can be made into decorative or sturdy handles.

Coils or hanks of reed are tied together in one-pound bundles, often called pound coils. The quality of reed varies and is available in superior, first quality, and second quality grades as well as smoked, which is processed differently and is darker in color. To maintain control of a new coil of reed, carefully cut the ties to loosen it, and immediately bind the ends together with a wide rubber band to avoid the reed becoming tangled and unmanageable. Hang the new coil securely on a post, peg, or doorknob, and gently pull from it the number of reeds to be used.

Some weavers like to sort each new pound coil by quality of pieces: thick for spokes and more flexible reeds for weavers. Sorting is also done by lengths, with groups then held together by separate rubber bands, coiled, and labeled. For example, longest reeds may be marked for use as handle wraps and stored until needed. The reeds pulled from the coil for use as weavers are then placed in cool or warm water to soak briefly. Transfer the reed from water to a towel to keep it moist and ready to weave. Materials that are not used need to dry completely before storing them for future use; if reed is stored when it is damp, it will discolor, darken, or mildew. When the reed is dry, coil it and tie like sizes together. It can be stored in paper bags, plastic totes, boxes, or hung on pegs or dowels. Make certain to keep reed out of the sun and away from any heat source, which would cause it to dry out and become brittle.

Braided seagrass in three sizes is used as an accent weaver for texture in a basket and adds another dimension as the inside and outside rim.

Cane, from the inner bark of the rattan palm, is also available in various widths, including Superfine Carriage, 1.50 mm; Carriage, 1.75 mm; Superfine, 2.00 mm; Fine-fine, 2.25 mm; Fine, 2.50 mm; Narrow-medium, 2.75 mm; Medium, 3.00 mm; and Common, 3.50 mm. Binder cane is a wider and thicker chair cane material available in sizes Small, 4.00 to 4.50 mm; Medium, 5.00 to 5.50 mm; and Large, 6.00 to 6.50 mm. The narrower sizes are used in many baskets for lashing rims, and as weavers in Nantucket-style baskets. They are also used for weaving light fixtures and for chair caning. Binder cane is used in weaving furniture.

Seagrass is a commonly used natural material found growing in tropical areas along shorelines. These marsh grasses are gathered and twisted or braided into a rope-like core. Seagrass is available in several sizes. Size #00 is 2.00 mm; #0 is 2.25 to 2.50 mm; #1 is 2.75 to 3.00 mm; #2 is 3.50 to 4.00 mm; #3 is 4.50 to 5.00 mm; #4 is 5.50 mm; #5 is 6.00 mm. It serves as a rim filler in most baskets and can also be woven as a textural accent.

Braided seagrass in widths of ¼", ⅜", ⅝", and ⅞" and other materials are used alongside reed weavers.

Paper-thin strips of maple or ash create soft curls and other embellishments, while 1½" and wider strips serve as accent design elements where painted or stenciled designs can be applied.

In the United States, natural materials are abundant and commonly used in the weaving process. In the Gallery section of this book, you will find hand-split white oak used in Billy Owens's baskets. Baskets are also being created with black ash by Nathan Taylor, a well-known

Various sizes of seagrass coils, a commercially prepared material, most often used as the rim filler in baskets and as a weaving accent. It is available in sizes #00, #1, #2, #3, #4, and #5. Handwoven braided seagrass coils are available in ⅜", ¼", ⅝", and ¾" widths for rim material and weaving accent also.

Strips of maple and ash are commercially available in various sizes and can be dyed for a fine weaving accent. This material has a sheen to it whether kept natural or dyed.

Shaker and Nantucket-style basket maker. Steve and Joanne Kelly Catsos are also currently preparing and working with black ash. Kathy Tessler weaves with brown ash. Tree bark and cedar roots are gathered and employed by Judy Zugish of Marysville, Washington. Matt Tommey in North Carolina is working with mimosa, poplar, and hickory bark, as well as kudzu and honeysuckle vines. Sweetgrass, long leaf pine needles, and palmetto are the materials of choice for Barbara McCormick of McClellanville, South Carolina, an instructor and sweetgrass basketmaker of the coiled technique. Pine needles are also a popular natural material gathered by many weavers for use in their contemporary woven designs, such as in Marianne Barnes's weaving on gourds.

A variety of trees found in the United States and their by-products have been employed in basket making for hundreds of years, and are still being used today.

Pine needles are sorted by length and then coiled or woven into baskets.

DYES

To add color accent to woven baskets, weavers have used natural dyes for thousands of years. As described in chapter 1, Native Americans and early weavers chose plant life and other natural resources to produce many traditional colors found in their basketry. Today, weavers still utilize natural dyes. I finish most baskets with a natural walnut hull dye or stain made of nuts gathered from our property. I have included the recipe for making this warm brown dye color.

More often, due to their convenience and time-saving qualities, commercially available dyes are used. A rainbow of colors may be found at basket suppliers. Fiber-reactive dyes, along with other powder and liquid dyes that are used for fabric and wood, also work for basketry, and may be found at grocery and department stores.

Most powder and liquid dyes are mixed with water and are then ready to use. Fiber-reactive dyes are prepared over a period of days to achieve the desired color. This type of dye has the advantage of being more colorfast than the others. However, the disadvantage is the exposure to chemicals. Always wear rubber or latex-free gloves when handling dye. Indoors, work in a well-ventilated area with a downdraft fan, or dye materials in an open garage or outdoors on the porch for the best ventilation. Since fumes may be harmful, wear a mask when sensitivity is an issue.

Coils of round reed dyed with various dye colors.

Dye Preparation

Many weavers purchase commercially dyed reed, in colors of their choice, from one of the numerous suppliers. This eliminates the time and work involved in dyeing materials at home. But doing your own dyeing of materials with either natural dyes (nuts, flowers, teas, etc.) or commercial dyes allows you to control color consistency from one size reed to the next and to be sure reed has been rinsed enough to avoid bleeding.

To achieve the various colors in the basket projects in this book, I dye to reach specific colors and use a different enamel roasting pan for each shade. This ensures color consistency and a lack of color bleeding. Remember, once a pan is used for dyeing, it cannot be used for food or any other purpose.

Prepare the dye surface whether you are working indoors or out. I prefer to dye inside at my stove, behind which a plexiglass screen has been installed to protect the wallpaper. Cover countertop or table surfaces with vinyl, plastic, or newspaper. When dyeing materials outdoors, hang dyed materials on tree branches or covered surfaces to dry.

For each pound of reed to be dyed, heat one gallon of water with one cup of distilled white vinegar, and one package of commercial dye in an enamel or stainless steel pan. For larger amounts of reed, add additional water, dye, and vinegar in correct proportions. For smaller amounts of reed, halve the amounts. I find the use of vinegar helps to set the stain to result in less bleeding in your basket.

Loosen the ties on a pound coil of reed to allow the dye to penetrate and be absorbed into the center of the coil. Or pull smaller bundles from the larger coil, secure and wrap them from the ends, and twist-tie them together, keeping the various sizes and lengths separate.

When the water is hot, but not quite boiling, place the coil(s) of reed into the dyebath in the enamel pan. Keep the hot water temperature below its boiling point, 212 degrees Fahrenheit (100 degrees Celsius). Check for color accuracy within a minute. Turn the coil(s) of reed over to the opposite side to achieve consistent results. Wet reed will appear darker than after it is allowed to dry.

When the desired color is reached, remove the reed from the dyebath wearing gloves or with stainless steel tongs. Place the dyed reed on plastic or newspaper, or hang it to dry. Continue to dye batches of reed until ample materials are prepared for the chosen project.

Once the dyed reed is dry, rinse it in a vinegar and water bath consisting of one cup white vinegar and one or more gallons of warm water, in a plastic container or deep sink. Rinse and dry a total of three times. This labor-intensive process eliminates most bleeding without the use of chemicals, and the reed will produce the desired look within your baskets. Vinegar works to prevent most bleeding, while some weavers use several tablespoons of common table salt in their dyebath to help set the stain and eliminate bleeding. Experiment with each technique to find which method works best with the water at your location.

Space dyed reed, also known as tie-dyed reed, is a unique way to add color to any basket. Using the same technique described above, this process employs three or more colors spaced around a coil of reed. Dip one third of the coil in the first color of your choice; allow it to drip dry. Then dip the next third of the coil in color number two, and allow it to drip dry. Finally, dip the last third of the coil into your third color choice. Where each of these colors meet and intersect, a new color is created. Starting with three colors will result in five or six colors blended together. When space dyed reed is woven into a basket, the colors appear in a random fashion creating a truly one-of-a-kind basket.

These processes involve adding color as the basket is woven, but color may also be added when the project is finished and completely dry. After drying is also the time to choose whether to allow the basket to age naturally or to apply a color stain as an overwash.

Many weavers use commercially available stains in spray cans to seal the basket. These contain tung oil and urethane, and are available in several wood colors including oak, maple, walnut, black walnut, driftwood, and clear. Applied to a finished basket, these easy-to-apply sprays are low maintenance and add color and sheen.

Other weavers apply tung oil, linseed oil, or baby oil to finished baskets.

My choice is to finish most baskets with a natural walnut hull dye or stain. The following is a recipe adapted from instructions by Suzanne Moore of North Carolina Basketworks. Have fun staining your baskets naturally.

An enamel roasting pan makes a great dye pan. Other items needed for dyeing reed and natural materials are a ladle, tongs, newspaper, and latex-free gloves.

Natural Black Walnut Stain

Ingredients:

1 cup or more of walnut hulls, crushed in a nylon knee-high stocking or cheesecloth (or place whole walnuts, with dried hulls still intact, in nylon as above)
1 gallon of nearly boiling water in a large enamel or stainless steel pan or pot
1 cup of white distilled vinegar

Directions:

Place the prepared crushed or whole walnut hulls into nearly boiling water. Let this sit, like a teabag, for fifteen minutes or longer. Add the white vinegar and stir gently. For darker stain, steep one hour or overnight.

When the desired color is achieved, strain the liquid mixture. Dip the basket into the pan of walnut stain, being sure to coat all parts of the basket. For a darker finish, allow the basket to dry and then dip it a second time. If the stain seems too dark, rinse the basket in warm water to remove some of the dye. For large baskets, too big for the pan, use a ladle, a sponge, or a paintbrush. Using a funnel, I add the stain to a recycled spray bottle. Then I can spray baskets outdoors or in a large cardboard box; be sure to protect nearby surfaces with newspaper.

Allow the stained basket to air dry overnight, turning the basket upside down to allow the base to receive adequate air circulation and to avoid any mildew or discoloration.

Storage: To store liquid stain for a later use, strain it before storing it in an airtight glass or plastic container (clearly marked Black Walnut Stain). Store it at a cool temperature.

Caution: This is a natural nut substance; however, do not ingest it in powder or liquid form. Keep it in a labeled, securely sealed container, away from children.[3]

Natural walnut hull stain can be made with walnuts gathered and then stored in nylon stockings. When walnut hulls are dry, soak them in hot water or crush into a powder and then heat to produce a warm, brown color to apply to your baskets.

TOOLS

Several items commonly found in the home provide the first basketry tools you need: scissors, a ruler or tape measure, a pencil, clothespins, and a container or sink for water.

Keep tools in good condition by storing them dry, to avoid any rust on metal surfaces.

Store your tools in a favorite basket with dividers, or purchase a canvas tool bag with lots of pockets and compartments. These are found at hardware and home improvement stores.

To these basic tools add:

old towel
apron
spray water bottle
small sponge
2 spoke weights
awl
sharp knife
scarfing or shaving tool
reed gauge
straight and bent tip tools or screwdrivers
lashing tool
needle-nosed pliers
side/diagonal cutters
wire type cutters or heavy duty pruning shears
tapestry needles
waxed linen thread
large clips or clamps
mini clips
wire twist ties
cable ties

An array of tools and other items can be used in basketry. Many of these are available from basketry suppliers listed in the Appendix, while other items can be found around your home and at the local home improvement store. Pictured from back to front, left to right: **Back (Row 1)**: Basketry tools in wooden stand with bent-tip to straight-tip tools in various lengths. **Row 2**: Side cutters, bent-nose pliers, wire cutters, pruning shears. **Row 3**: Wood-handled awl, reed gauge, plane or shaver, gel glue, sponge, plastic pail with metal and fabric spoke weights, latex free gloves. **Row 4**: Plastic round reed bobbins, various clips, pins, clamps, awl, knife, scarfing tool, threading tool with red handle, lashing tools, tapestry needles, sanding blocks, spray water bottle, and green twist tie wire. **Front (Row 5)**: Shave knife and scissors.

CHAPTER THREE

BASE TECHNIQUES

Our ancestral baskets were created with woven bases using the materials available in nearby surroundings. The base, or the bottom foundation of the basket, is an important first step in creating a visually appealing basket.

Open-bottom bases are designed by weaving reed stakes or spokes over and under each other, leaving space between each piece of reed. For many baskets, this open bottom allows flowers, roots, herbs, vegetables, clothing, and other items ample air circulation.

Closed, filled-in, or twilled bases are woven to have a solid base, which keeps even the smallest items secure. These are the bases utilized to start several of the projects in this book.

Wood bases have also found a place in basketry. A solid bottom, with a slot or groove routed approximately ½" deep along the side edge, allows reed spokes or stakes to be inserted and secured to start the basket. Other wood bases have holes drilled near the edge of the base to insert spokes to tuck underneath. As with handles, wood bases are made of various species: ash, cherry, hickory, oak, pine, poplar, walnut, and others. These are also commercially available in many sizes and shapes.

Begin a square open-weave basket base with reed spokes placed horizontally on your work surface and spaced equal distances apart. Weave the center vertical spoke over one spoke, under one spoke, through each original spoke. Line up the center marks.

WOVEN BASE TECHNIQUES

A **square open weave base** is used in this book's first two projects, the Shaker Cathead Basket and the Double Handle Plaid Carryall Basket.

Soak the reed briefly. Then determine the wrong or rough side of the reed and mark each spoke in the center, on that wrong side.

Place all spokes horizontally, on a flat work surface, with the marked wrong sides facing up. Without a handle in the square base of the Shaker Cathead Basket, weave vertical spokes through the original horizontal spokes. Beginning at the center marks, weave over the first spoke closest to you, then under, over, under, over, under, and pull until the center marks line up.

Continue to weave vertical spokes to the right and left of the center spoke, alternating over and under at the start.

Adjust the base measurements to the desired size and place a clothespin in each corner to secure the base.

A finished open weave base for a cathead basket. All horizontal and vertical spokes are lined up, with one row of twine around the perimeter to secure all base spokes.

A **plaid woven base** with two handles is used in the Double Handle Plaid Carryall Basket. Two "D" handles are notched out at the center for 1 inch, or the width of the handle, creating an overlap in the center. The notch is whittled or created by a router to allow the handles to be level. Work for equal depth in the notch, half the thickness of the bottom of the handle. The notch is done on the top side of one handle and the bottom of the other. One handle is placed along with the horizontal spokes and one handle with the vertical spokes.

With 8 horizontal spokes for plaid, place alternating colors, navy, wine, navy, wine, approximately ½" apart on a flat surface.

Next, place handle #1 and then continue alternating the navy and wine horizontal spokes above the handle.

Now you are ready to weave the vertical spokes. Center handle #2 is woven under color accent #1 navy, and over accent #2 wine spokes at the center marks.

Then weave all vertical spokes, alternating accent colors. Begin with accent #2, wine, to the right and left of the center vertical handle, and under accent #2 wine and over accent #1 navy. This begins the plaid.

Continue alternating the dyed, vertical spokes, under and over, until there are four spokes on each side of each handle. This produces an open-weave base with space between each spoke. Place a clothespin in each corner.

A **filled-in base** is another type of woven base that can use either filler spokes or is woven in a twill technique with spokes adjacent or touching each other. This type of base provides a solid foundation that small items cannot fall through, as there are no openings.

To create your first filled-in base, start with the instructions for the Rectangle Sampler Basket.

Cut all spokes as listed in the project's Materials list, and soak them briefly.

Mark them in the center, on the rough side, and place the spokes horizontally on the work surface, alternating one wide spoke with a pair of filler spokes. Two pieces of flat oval reed are treated as one spoke. Use wide spokes horizontally with fillers in between each.

Line up the center marks.

Use two spoke weights to anchor both fillers and spokes.

With the remaining spokes, weave a center vertical spoke at the center marks; begin under the wide spoke and over a pair of filler spokes.

Continue to weave the total number of vertical spokes on each side of the center spoke, alternating over and under from the start. The last vertical spokes are woven the same as the center spoke, under the wide spokes and over pairs of fillers.

Trim and tuck the filler spokes into the second vertical spoke from the end, splitting the pairs so that one piece moves on a diagonal upward while the other is downward, creating "crows' feet," also known as "chicken feet."

Secure the base measurements with a clothespin in each corner.

Wood handles are notched for 1" at the center to accommodate the intersection of the two. This allows the second handle to rest on top. Using a chisel or router, whittle the handle until the additional handle sits level.

The double handle technique provides a sturdy start to the basket. The first handle is included with the horizontal spokes, while the second handle is placed in the prepared notch along with the woven vertical spokes.

A filled-in base can be accomplished in several ways. By using filler spokes, two narrow flat or flat oval reeds together are treated as one spoke. Place a pair of filler spokes between and touching each of the horizontal spokes. Then vertical spokes are woven in.

Trim and tuck the ends of the filler spokes to finish this woven filled in base technique. These create crows' feet, also known as chicken feet.

Rectangular filled-in base with pairs for filler spokes.

A **twill base** is a second technique which produces a closed or solid bottom, and it is used in projects such as Chasing Diamonds and Diamonds All Around.

A larger number of base spokes is used in this style basket to allow the twill design to develop.

The Chasing Diamonds Basket has 72 dyed base spokes, each 36 inches long.

Begin by placing 36 spokes horizontally on the table, rough side facing up, and anchor these with spoke weights.

Put a pencil mark at 13" from each end of the spokes to mark where the twill base begins and ends. If the dyed spokes are a dark color, make marks with a white, dressmaker's pencil for better visibility.

Weave an Over 4 Under 4 Twill Base, also known as Over 2 Under 2, with paired spokes. Begin at the left pencil mark and weave vertical spokes as paired spokes (put 2 spokes together and treat as one). Begin the first pair by weaving over 4 spokes (over 2 pairs) and then under 4 spokes (under 2 pairs).

Paired spokes #2 (spokes 3 and 4) are woven over 2 spokes (one pair), then under 4, over 4, and end under 2 spokes (one pair).

Weave paired spokes #3 (spokes 5 and 6), over 4 spokes (2 pairs), and then under 4 spokes (2 pairs).

Paired spokes #4 (spokes 7 and 8) are woven under 2 spokes (one pair), over 4 spokes, under 4, and finish over 2 spokes (one pair).

Following this pattern of paired spokes, repeat the pattern as above until all 18 pairs (36 vertical spokes) are woven.

Pack each row as it is woven, horizontally and vertically. It is more difficult to pack later.

To secure the twill base, place a clothespin in each corner.

A twill woven base is another example of a filled-in basket base.

WOOD BASE TECHNIQUES

Oak is my favorite species of wood to use as a basket base. A sturdy hardwood with more pronounced growth rings and grain variations, oak adds additional color and interest to the foundation of the basket. Oak is considered a dense wood, and it repels water to help eliminate warping in the base. For darker bases, choose walnut or cherry; ash, maple, pine, and poplar will provide lighter shades. Consider the dyed accent colors to be woven into the basket and use these to assist you in selecting your wood base.

Bases are available commercially in numerous shapes and sizes: round, oval, square, rectangle, triangle, oblong or racetrack, hexagon, and peanut shape. Bases with dividers are also available in several of these shapes.

Wood bases can be finished with stain colors and urethane of your choice to protect their surfaces from water and other substances. This step can be performed prior to weaving the basket or after completion. If you plan ahead to finish this step before weaving, when the basket is complete, the base will be ready as well.

Round wood bases are available from 2" to 12" in diameter and larger by request.

Bases are available with dividers in various shapes. This pair of oblong bases works well for kitchen baskets for salt, pepper, and spices; wine; or oil and vinegar.

Rectangular wood bases are available in a variety of widths and lengths.

These oblong wood bases are also known as racetrack bases.

A sampling of the many sizes and shapes in wood bases: round, square, rectangle, triangle, oblong (racetrack), oval, bases with dividers, and bases with openings. These bases have a slot or groove along the side edge. The groove allows spokes to be secured in the base prior to weaving.

Pre-finish the Wood Base

Lightly sand in the direction of the wood grain and wipe any excess dust from the wood base.

Wear rubber or latex free gloves while working on a covered, protected surface.

Apply stain. Wipe the excess with a clean cloth or paper towel, and allow to dry completely.

Apply the first coat of urethane (matte, satin, or glossy finish). Spray or wipe-on varieties can be used. Wear gloves and use a clean cloth, paper towel, or a paintbrush; apply a light coat of urethane, working with the grain in the wood. Allow this to dry completely before applying more urethane.

Repeat this urethane process for a total of three or more coats, lightly sanding and wiping in between each, until the desired sheen is achieved.

Use very fine sandpaper or steel wool. Always sand the finished base in the direction of the grain. Wipe any residue clean.

Wood bases are the foundation for several projects in this collection. Round wood bases are used in Becoming Blue Skies, Ribbons to Remember, Spirals Change, and Autumn's Dress. An oblong "racetrack" wood base is the start to the Cozy Wine Cradle project. In creating your original basket with a wood base, consider the size of the finished basket when choosing the size of the base.

To determine the number of spokes needed to complete a project, check the Materials list. When creating your original designs, determine the techniques to be used for the number of spokes needed.

All wooden bases, regardless of shape, may be divided into four quadrants or quarters.

Wood Base and Spoke Placement

Divide the wood base into four quadrants or quarters. With a pencil, mark the quadrants' centers near the edge of the base to assist in inserting spokes with equal distance between each spoke within each quadrant.

From paper, cut a template the same size as the wood base. Fold the template in half, then fold it in half once again. Next place the open template on the wood base and mark the four quadrants.

You may also do this by approximating if you choose.

Check the slotted grooved opening before inserting spokes into the base. If the groove is narrow and the spokes fit tight, do not wet them; insert dry spokes, and then spray with water. If the groove is wider and your spokes move about and are loose, wet the spokes briefly and then insert them. When water is absorbed, it will temporarily enlarge the spokes, causing them to stay in place. Or, insert a one-inch piece of cane on top of the spoke then insert into the groove. If these steps do not solve the movement issue, apply a small amount of fast-drying gel glue to the end of the spoke. Insert it into the groove, and hold it there long enough for the gel glue to thoroughly dry.

Insert the first base spoke, rough side up, at or near one of the center marks.

Insert one quarter or one half of the base spokes within the marks. Check your spacing, and then continue to insert all spokes rough side up, creating an equal distance between each one. Push all spokes firmly into the slot or groove. When finished, count the total number of spokes to be sure the accurate number are in place.

A paper template the same size as the round wood base is folded in half and in half again. Unfold and place it on the base to mark the four quadrants to assist when inserting spokes.

An oblong template is placed on this racetrack base to indicate where to mark the four quadrants.

CHAPTER FOUR

WEAVING TECHNIQUES

Numerous weaving techniques are found in the projects within this book. Row builds upon row, creating the sidewalls of the baskets as weavers move around vertical spokes in a horizontal manner. The first two baskets start with the traditional round reed Twining technique. This is the first row of weaving in a woven base basket and is used in many projects. The first two baskets, the Shaker Cathead Basket and the Double Handle Plaid Carryall, begin with the twining technique.

This **Twining technique** starts with one or two wet, flexible round reed weavers. These are needed to secure all woven base spokes in place. This works with any number of spokes.

Match the ends of the round reed; find the middle or the halfway point, and bend or crimp the reed gently. Now loop this around the second or third spoke from the corner of your base, the Starting Spoke. You may also use two shorter pieces, placing one behind each of two consecutive spokes. Notice that you have a weaver on top of the spoke and a weaver under or behind the spoke. Twist the round reed weaver on top of the spoke behind or under the very next spoke and pull it out to the front of the third spoke to the right.

Continue by twining the weaver over the spoke to the right, behind the next spoke, and out to the front. Keep the twined weaver snug around the base of the basket to help control its shape. If the basket has a handle, be sure to include it as a spoke. Add an extra twist in front of the handle to create a tighter weave and to stabilize the handle.

After twining completely around the base and returning to the Starting Spoke, twist, and then tuck both round reed weavers under the loop, or at the two consecutive spokes used; trim both reed ends close to the base.

Start the Twining technique with the round reed folded and crimped in half; then loop around one spoke near the left side of the basket.

Twining is twisting the round reed around each spoke to secure it in place. Alternate over and under as well as alternating the weavers.

Twining at a corner, alternate the over and under sequence for a close, secure corner.

End twining when you reach the starting loop. Twist the round reed weavers before inserting both ends into the loop from the outside facing inside the base. Tuck both ends under the twining at the next spoke. Trim the ends to ½" long.

A **Continuous Weave technique**, using one weaver of #1 or #2 round reed, is woven when your basket has an uneven number of spokes. Weave over and under for several rows to help secure the spokes in the base.

With all spokes inserted, begin with a wet, flexible piece of round reed as close to the wood base as possible. Crimp or bend the end of the round reed and insert it into the routed slot or groove in the base.

Weave over one spoke, then under one spoke, over the next, and again under, all the way around the base.

At the Starting Spoke, continue weaving, but be sure the new row of weaving is the opposite of the first or previous row.

Check for equal spacing between spokes. If there is movement or spokes appear loose, now is the time to use gel glue to secure the spoke(s) for the duration of the project.

Push spokes into the base and use a small tool to push the weaver in close to the wood base.

Weave for a total of two or more rows.

Tuck the end of the round reed weaver under the previous row, and trim it as needed. The use of several rows of Continuous Base Weave enlarges the size of the base and allows for a gentle upsett (bending upright of the spokes) of the basket side walls.

To use the Continuous Weave technique on the side walls of a basket, an uneven number of spoke ends will produce a gentle transition from one row to the next.

Begin by placing a tapered weaver behind any spoke. This becomes the Starting Spoke, "SS." Weave over, under, over, all the way around the basket. Pack each row as you weave it. To end, taper the weaver on the same side as the beginning tapered end.

Continuous Weave technique uses an uneven number of spokes.

End a Continuous Weave under the round reed at the Starting Spoke.

Chase Base Weave is the technique that is used with an even number of spokes in a wood base. Found in the Cozy Wine Cradle Basket and Ribbons to Remember, this method uses two pieces of round reed.

Begin with one piece of #1 or #2 round reed, and work at any place in a round base or on the long side of a rectangular or oval wood base and as close to the base as possible.

Crimp or bend the end of Round Reed Weaver #1 and insert it into the slot in the base between two spokes. This eliminates seeing a loose end later. Weave over, then under, and continue weaving until reaching about halfway around the base.

Check spacing between the spokes and anchor with a spoke weight if necessary.

Push all spokes into the base to keep them in place; use a small, bent tip tool to push the weaver in close to the base.

Chase Weave with Round Reed Weaver #2. Crimp and insert the end of this weaver into the slotted wood base in the space before (to the left of) Round Reed Weaver #1. Weave over and under, opposite the first weaver, around the wood base until you are two spokes away from the first weaver. Pick up Round Reed Weaver #1 and continue to weave over and under around the wood base.

Chase Weave for a total of two or more rows. Round Reed Weaver #2 chases Round Reed Weaver #1, but does not pass it.

Check spacing for equal distance between all spokes. Tuck the ends of the round reed weavers under the previous row at the starting place; trim the ends.

To Chase Weave with wider weavers, 3⁄16" or 1⁄4" flat or flat oval reed, taper the ends of two weavers. Follow the instructions above, but instead of crimping and bending your weaver into the slot of the wood base, tuck your weaver behind any spoke, mark with "SS" for the Starting Spoke.

Over and Under, Start and Stop Weave

When the base is woven and completely twined, upsett the spokes, bend into the correct upright position, and hold with clothespins. Then it is time to weave using one of the many other available techniques.

Over and Under, Start and Stop technique is also known as Randing or Plain Weave. In this technique, the vertical spokes are visible in the basket. Most often, we begin weaving with the rough, or wrong, side of the base spokes facing up and the right, or smooth, side of the base touching the table surface. Begin Over and Under, Start and Stop Weave Row #1 with 11/64", 3/16", 1/4", or wider flat or flat oval reed. From the left side of the basket, place the weaver opposite the base weaving, over (or on top of) one spoke, then under one spoke, over, and continue around the basket adjusting clothespins at corners as needed. When you have woven around the entire basket and are at your Starting Spoke, overlap each row for four spokes, then trim and tuck the end of the reed. An option when using flat oval reed is to shave down the oval rounded edge on one end of the weaver. Doing this creates less bulk, and a less obvious overlap. Now move to the next side of the basket and continue to weave the next row with flat or flat oval reed of your choice, alternating under and over.

Check for equal spacing between all spokes. Use mini clips or clothespins throughout the project.

An exception to the rule of working with the wrong side of the base spokes facing up is the Shaker Cathead base. Begin a Cathead base with the right side of the base spokes facing up. This allows for the intense shaping tactics necessary in creating the Cathead. At each corner, begin the shaping process. Keep four corner spokes together with a clothespin or a small clamp to enhance the Cathead.

Overlap each row for four to six spokes to allow movement in the shaping process, then trim and tuck the reed end.

Begin weaving Over and Under, Start and Stop on the outside of the basket spoke.

Over and Under, Start and Stop weaving ends with a four-spoke overlap. Weave over the starting place, under the next spoke, over the next, and tuck under the fourth spoke. This hides the ends; you do not see them on the inside or the outside of the basket.

Where the weaver overlaps, always place a clip or clothespin to eliminate the weaver coming apart.

Chain Weave is also an Over and Under, Start and Stop Weave as described in the previous technique. For this weave, follow the same starting instructions.

At the point of your choosing, add the Chain design anywhere along the side walls of the basket.

After weaving several rows of natural weavers, select a dyed accent reed and wet it briefly. Wipe any excess dye with towel or paper towel at least three times to reduce the possibility of any color bleeding onto the basket.

Weaving three consecutive rows of start and stop weavers in the same or similar color(s) creates the Chain Weave design. By weaving three consecutive rows, alternating over and under, every other spoke will have two dyed weavers while the next adjacent spoke will have one dyed weaver.

Often Native American baskets display this connecting chain design.

Three consecutive rows of dyed accent weavers create the Chain design.

Plaid Weave, evident in the Double Handle Plaid Carryall Basket project, is another example of Over and Under, Start and Stop Weave. Inspired by the madras plaid of a favorite old shirt, the navy and wine dyed plaid design is achieved by a specific placement of base spokes along with a specific placement in dyed accent weavers. The intersection of these spokes creates the plaid.

Plaid is created with the use of two or more dyed accent colors in the base spokes.

The Double Handle Plaid Carryall starts with a plaid base of 8 spokes each of two colors. (Refer to Plaid Base, chapter 3.)

In the Plaid Weave technique, accent color #1, the navy weavers, will be woven under the vertical spokes of this same color. Weave:

The Plaid design in wine and navy dyed reed has walnut stain applied to mute the colors for an antique appearance.

2 rows -------⅝" or ¾" flat reed, natural
1 row---------⅜" or ½" flat reed, navy or color accent #1, under navy and over wine
1 row---------⅝" flat reed, natural
1 row---------½" flat reed, navy or color accent #1, under navy and over wine
1 row---------½" flat reed, wine or color accent #2, under wine and over navy
1 row---------½" flat reed, navy, with ¼" overlay woven together
1 row---------½" flat reed, wine or color accent #2, under wine and over navy
1 row---------½" flat reed, navy or color accent #1, under navy and over wine
1 row---------⅝" flat reed, natural
1 row---------½" flat reed, navy or color accent #1, under navy and over wine
1 row---------⅝" flat reed, natural

Mix up the colors or add a third or fourth contrasting color, in narrower or wider weavers, for a completely new plaid design.

Twill Weave is also an Over and Under technique; however the main difference in this technique is that the reed will weave over more than one vertical spoke before going under the next vertical spoke. Twill Weave develops into a diagonal design, with many variations and pictorial designs possible: diamonds, triangles, stars, zigzags, spirals, animals, various shapes, and letters of the alphabet. Many Native American and ancestral baskets incorporate twill weave to create a picture. Currently, Laura Lee Zanger of Augusta, Georgia, is experimenting with new and old twill pictorial designs. She has renewed many Native American designs and has written the instructions for several where no written pattern previously existed.

Twill can be woven either as a Start and Stop Weave or as a Continuous Weave technique. Start and Stop Weave is used to maintain level, even design elements. The Cozy Wine Cradle, also known as a Flower Cradle, is completed with a Continuous Twill technique.

Twill Weave Start and Stop technique varies from the traditional over 1, under 1 weave. It can be an over 2, under 2 Twill Weave, an over 3, under 3 Twill Weave, or another amount that creates diamonds, lightning bolts or zigzag lines.

Begin the weaving pattern at the left side of the base. A project in this book, Chasing Diamonds, utilizes a 3, 3 Twill (over 3, under 3), for the most part, with changes on each side which create the design. The twill zigzags around the square basket without a pattern break; no interruption in the pattern.

Make use of the photograph and the graphs for the correct pattern.

To create Diamonds All Around, Twill Weave with a 3, 1, 3, 5 design. This allows the weaver to float, or weave, over 3 spokes, under 1 spoke, over 3 spokes, and under 5 spokes. Reverse this sequence for diamonds.

Create a new design by using graph paper or a computer-generated spreadsheet to illustrate the twill. Fill in squares with a dark color for the float, which is weaving over the spokes, while weaving under spokes is displayed as white.

An increment in a twill design is the number in which the twill grows; add the overs and unders to determine the increment on each side of the basket. For example, a 3, 3 twill has an increment of 6.

The Chasing Diamonds design is a Start and Stop Twill Weave; over 3 spokes, under 3 spokes creates the lightning bolts or zigzag lines.

The Start and Stop Twill Weave technique used in Diamonds All Around is over 3 spokes, under 1 spoke, over 5 spokes, under 3 spokes, over 5 spokes.

Continuous Twill Weave in a 2, 1 pattern is used to create the Cozy Wine Cradle project, weaving Over 2 spokes and Under 1 spoke.

For Rows 1–6, wet ¼" flat oval reed; begin by tapering the weaver for 4" to 6".

Start under the 3rd spoke from the left on the long side of the base.

Twill Weave Over 2 spokes and Under 1 spoke around the basket.

Keep weaver packed and use clothespins to assist in the continuous weave technique.

The Twill Weave will move up and over one spoke to the right (or left) with each row. Check the weaver as it splits the over pair of Over 2 on the previous row; continue weaving Over 2, Under 1.

Add in a new weaver as needed with a three- or four-spoke overlap; shave the end for ease in packing.

Look for the diagonal design as a total of 6 rows is woven.

Adjust all spokes to keep them upright and vertical.

Avoid pulling in too tightly at rounded corners. Pack rows of twill before weaving the next step in this project.

Use clothespins to control tension and assist in shaping.

The Continuous Twill technique starts with a tapered weaver and ends with a tapered weaver to create level sides on the basket. Taper one end of the weaver for 6"; start very narrow and trim to the full width of the weaver.

In this Twill technique, the flat oval weaver moves over 2 spokes and under 1 spoke.

The Cozy Wine Cradle Basket is a Continuous Twill Weave: over 2 spokes, and under 1 spoke.

Braid Weave technique adds a textural finish to many baskets. This Continuous Weave can be woven in round, flat, or flat oval reed. Experiment by varying the number of pieces of reed and colors used as weavers to create different designs. Or, weave an entire basket using Braid Weave.

In the Rectangle Sampler project, weave with ¼" flat oval reed, in two dyed accent colors and one natural weaver, or choose to weave with tri-color, space-dyed reed.

Taper the ends of three weavers for 6 inches.

Place two weavers behind two consecutive spokes on one of the long sides of the basket. Mark the Starting Spoke "SS," the spoke you begin behind.

Weaver #1 moves over two spokes, then under one spoke, and out to the front of the basket.

Weaver #2 now on the left, will also float over two spokes, under one spoke, and out to the front.

Weaver #3 actually begins the braid; it is placed above the first two weavers and behind the third vertical spoke as the third consecutive spoke.

The first two weavers form an arrow. This third weaver weaves over the two vertical spokes, then between the arrow, to divide it, or split the arrow, and then under the third vertical spoke, and out to the front.

This is a Continuous Weave where the weaver on the far left goes over two spokes, divide, or split the arrow formed by the two weavers, then under the third spoke to the right and out to the front of the basket.

After each row of braid, look on the inside of the basket to check for accuracy. The braided weavers will alternate slanting up or down on each base spoke. This diagonal slant will stay the same all the way up the spoke.

Check for correct positioning. In the event a spoke has diagonal slants in both directions, go back and adjust where necessary.

Pack each row of the braid as it is woven to avoid gaps later. To finish the braid pattern, taper the end of each weaver for 6 inches. Complete the braid ending each weaver under its starting spoke on the same side of the basket where it originated.

Double Braid Weave, used in the Autumn's Dress project, pairs two pieces of the same color round reed as one weaver and uses three of these paired weavers to complete the braid named after the double weavers. Experiment with natural and dyed reed as one double weaver or any other combination.

Triple Braid Weave, as its name implies, uses three weavers each made of three pieces of round reed.

The Braid Weave in the Rectangle Sampler Basket uses three ¼" flat oval weavers. This Continuous Weave is over 2 spokes, between the arrow, then under 1 spoke.

In Autumn's Dress, the Double Braid Weave technique is woven in round reed. Place two pieces of round reed together to make one double weaver. Weave with three double weavers in different colors.

The **French Randing Weaving technique** is most often completed with short pieces of flat or flat oval reed. This is a great technique to use up the cut off scrap ends of reed and adds texture as an interesting accent to a basket. Found in the Rectangle Sampler Basket, all one solid color creates consistency, while experimenting with space dyed reed or alternating several colors will produce a completely different effect.

The French Randing Weaving technique creates a slant or diagonal design and is pictured in short 7½" pieces of ¼" flat dyed reed, one short weaver behind every vertical spoke.

Mark a Starting Spoke, "SS." Begin by placing a short weaver behind this spoke and tuck it under the previous row of weaving.

Weave from left to right at a diagonal over 1, under or behind 1, and out to the front.

Place the next diagonal short weaver to the *left* of the Starting Spoke and weave over 1, under 1, and out to the front. Continue French Randing in this way all around the basket, by placing a diagonal weaver to the left of the previous spoke until you reach the Starting Spoke. This completes one row.

Check to be sure you have placed a diagonal weaver behind every vertical spoke, 42 pieces total for this project. The last few will be tight fitting.

French Randing Row 2 also begins at the Starting Spoke.

Continue to weave the short diagonal weaver over 1, under 1, and out to the front as before. Working around the basket, use the next spoke to the left each time. Pack the weavers as needed.

To end, trim each diagonal weaver; be sure it rests on the inside of the basket to the right of vertical spokes.

Each diagonal weaver will be under 1, over 1, under 1, over 1, under 1, over 1. Trim and place the short weaver under 1 and remain on the inside of the basket.

Pack all diagonal weavers for a consistent diagonal design.

Ti-Twine Weave technique is a combination of Over and Under, Start and Stop Plain Weave using a wide, stiff weaver along with a narrow, flexible Continuous Weaver that wraps around the wide reed. Two weavers can be worked at the same time, or you may choose to weave one row with wider, flat reed and then wrap the Ti-Twine with ¼" flat or flat oval dyed accent reed as the flexible, continuous weaver.

Ti-Twining begins with the wide ⅜" flat weaver. Weave over, under, over; and then tuck a ¼" dyed accent weaver under the previous row.

Take the ¼" dyed flexible weaver from inside the basket, work it over, on a diagonal to the right, from top left to bottom right. Weave over the vertical spoke to the right where the ⅜" weaver is in the under position.

The dyed accent weaver is woven to the inside of the basket on a diagonal and around the next vertical spoke to the right.

Continue with the ⅜" weaver, going over, under, over. Repeat the diagonal weave and Ti-Twine with a ¼" dyed accent weaver. Continue to alternate weaving with a ⅜" weaver Over and Under, Start and Stop Weave, and a ¼" accent weaver. Or, you may choose to complete the Over and Under ⅜" weaver, trim and overlap to end, then continue with the Ti-Twine. Choose which technique works best for you.

To finish Row 1, overlap the ⅜" weaver for 4 spokes and trim. Do not trim the ¼" weaver.

Row 2: Start the next ⅜" weaver, over, under, over matching the previous row; continue the ¼" weaver by bringing it up a row on the inside of the basket. On the outside of the basket, the ¼" Ti-Twine weaver is over the vertical spoke that has the ⅜" weaver going under, while the ¼" Ti-Twine weaver is under or inside the basket when the ⅜" weaver is over the vertical spoke.

Weave 3 or more rows of Ti-Twine for a unique accent to any basket.

Be sure all ⅜" weavers match in their over and under sequence. This is opposite the traditional method of alternating over and under with each row.

French Randing creates an interesting diagonal design with short pieces of reed. This is a great technique to recycle your scraps of dyed and natural accent reed.

The Ti-Twine design uses a flexible weaver to wrap around a horizontal weaver. This creates a diagonal weave.

The Twining Technique

Using round reed, as described at the beginning of this chapter as a base weaving technique, is also utilized as a weaving technique on the side walls of baskets. Twining in different numbers of rows or using contrasting colors will produce varying results with the same materials.

Wale or Waling, a twining technique, is woven with more than two weavers to produce a three-dimensional, rope-like textural focal point.

By varying the number of vertical spokes in the basket project, Waling techniques will create a variety of different designs.

Three Rod Wale, also known as Triple Twine, uses three weavers over any number of spokes. See project instructions for the number of spokes to be used to create varying design results. This technique starts several projects featured in this book. These include: Becoming Blue Skies, Ribbons to Remember, and Autumn's Dress.

Weave 3 rows of Three Rod Wale from the right, or outer, side of the basket and gently begin to upsett the spokes to create a slight flare. Pack each row as it is woven.

Place three pieces of round reed, one each behind three consecutive spokes.

Weaver #1 (on the far left side) of the three weavers is under or behind the marked Starting Spoke, SS. Weave over 2 spokes to the right (spoke numbers 2 & 3). Now weave under the 4th spoke, and out to the front of the basket.

Weaver #2, behind the second spoke, (now the left-most weaver), over 2 spokes and under 1 spoke, and out to the front of the basket.

Weaver #3 (the left-most weaver) is woven over 2 spokes, under 1 spoke and out to the front, as above.

Continue around the basket for the desired number of rows.

To begin the Three Rod Wale technique, also known as Triple Twine, place 3 weavers behind 3 consecutive spokes.

In Three Rod Wale, the left-most weaver is over 2 spokes to the right, under 1 spoke, and bring it out to the front of the basket.

Step-up to end this round reed technique. Stop the Three Rod Wale at the space to the left of the Starting Spoke (the last spoke). Weave with the right-most weaver. The round reed farthest to the right will be woven over 2 spokes and under 1 spoke. Trim and place to the inside of the basket.

Continue with the round reed on the right of the two remaining, weaving over 2, under 1, and trim to the inside.

Finish with the last round reed, weaving over 2, under 1, and trim to the inside.

To check for accuracy, the last round reed weaver should be behind the Starting Spoke. This finishes the Step-up and creates a level ending.

To end the Three Rod Wale technique, stop weaving at the space to the left of the Starting Spoke; now you are ready to start the Step-up.

Begin the Step-up with the right-most weaver, over 2 spokes, under 1 spoke and trim the weaver to the inside of the basket.

With the remaining weaver on the right of the two, weave over 2, under 1, and trim to the inside.

The last of the three weavers finishes the Step-up, over 2, under 1 and it ends behind the Starting Spoke.

Double and Triple Three Rod Wale are worked in the same manner as the Three Rod Wale or Triple Twine above. The only difference is the number of pieces of reed for each weaver. Using additional reed results in an even greater three-dimensional effect, creating the look of a dyed rope. This is a very attractive border when used on each side of another accent, or it may stand alone as a design element for one or more rows.

Double Three Rod Wale has two pieces of dyed or natural reed, or a combination of both, to be used as one weaver, so six pieces in all are needed to complete this technique.

Triple Three Rod Wale has three pieces of reed to make one of the three weavers; therefore, nine pieces of reed are necessary.

To create a three-dimensional design resembling dyed rope, put two or three pieces of round reed together to make a double or triple weaver. Triple weaver #1 is inserted behind the Starting Spoke.

Triple weaver #2 is inserted behind the next spoke to the right of the Starting Spoke.

Triple Three Rod Wale has three weavers each made up of three pieces of round reed. Triple Weaver #3 is inserted behind the third consecutive spoke.

In Triple Three Rod Wale, the left-most Weaver #1 moves over 2 spokes, under 1 spoke and out to the front of the basket.

Triple Weaver #2 is now in the left-most position, weave over 2, under 1 and out to the front of the basket.

Each of the three triple weavers in the Triple Three Rod Wale technique are over 2 spokes, under 1 spoke and out to the front.

To end one row of Triple Three Rod Wale, stop with the first weaver that reaches the space to the left of your Starting Spoke.

The Step-up begins with the right-most weaver of the three consecutive weavers. This is the same weaver stopped to the left of the Starting Spoke. Weave over 2 spokes to the right, under 1 spoke, trim and tuck this first weaver to the inside of the basket.

The Triple Three Rod Wale Step-up continues with the next weaver on the right of the remaining two. Weave over 2 spokes, under 1, trim and tuck inside the basket.

The Step-up is finished with the third triple weaver over 2 spokes, under 1 spoke, trim and tuck inside. This last weaver is behind the Starting Spoke, a way to check for accuracy.

Spiral Weave is a Three Rod Wale technique that can be woven with single weavers, double weavers for Double Spiral Weave, or triple weavers for a Triple Spiral Weaving technique. In addition, you may weave with more than one dyed, accent color.

The number of vertical spoke ends in the project will determine the design possibilities. Refer to individual projects for the exact number of spokes to be used.

For an **Outside Spiral** design to appear on the outside or right side of the basket, your project must use a total number of spoke ends that can be divided by three minus one.

The Cozy Wine Cradle, Autumn's Dress, and the Spirals Change all incorporate this weaving technique. For example, Autumn's Dress has 44 spokes. Do the math: a number divisible by 3 is 45. Subtract 1, and you have 44 spokes.

The Outside Spiral technique is a Continuous Three Rod Wale. It requires a total number of spoke ends that can be divided by three; then subtract one from this number to figure the correct number of spokes.

Reverse Spiral is as its name implies. The spiral changes, reverses, and moves in the opposite direction. Weaving left-handed can be a challenge; if you weave slowly, a rhythm will come. If you are left-handed, weave right-handed to create the Reverse Spiral.

Begin this technique by starting three new weavers behind the same three spokes used in the Step-up ending the previous row. Insert the short end on the right and leave the long end to the left. You may choose to crimp and tuck the new weavers, or you may simply place ends behind the three consecutive spokes.

Moving to the left, start with the right-most weaver rather than the left-most weaver as in the regular Three Rod Wale. This right-most weaver is Dyed Weaver #1; it matches the dyed color in the previous row and will move to the left.

Weaver #2, a Natural Weaver, is behind the next spoke to the left and it matches the previous row's natural weaver.

Weaver #3, a Dyed Weaver, is left of these original weavers and matches the dyed reed in the previous row.

The right-most Weaver #1 is woven to the left over 2 spokes and under 1 spoke. Notice that weavers come up from under or below the other two weavers. Continue with the next weaver forming a zigzag or arrow in this first transition row with dyed and natural weavers forming individual matching arrows.

Continue the Reverse Three Rod Wale Spiral for the desired number of rows creating a larger, wider arrow.

Step-up to end the last row of Reverse Spiral that moves to the left.

Work the Step-up with the left-most weaver, opposite the instructions for a Step-up in regular Three Rod Wale, as described previously.

In preparation for a Reverse Spiral, end the Outside Spiral with a Step-up and trim these weavers to the inside. Begin with three new weavers behind the same three spokes used in the Step-up. The ends of these new weavers will be to the left.

In the Reverse Outside Spiral technique, Weaver #1 is inserted behind the Starting spoke with the end to the left.

Weaver #2 for the Reverse Outside Spiral technique is inserted to the left of the Starting Spoke and Weaver #1.

Three weavers are in position to weave to the left for the Reverse Outside Spiral technique. With the right-most weaver, begin the Reverse Spiral; weave to the left, over 2 spokes, under 1 spoke and out to the front of the basket.

Create the arrow design with Three Rod Wale and Reverse Three Rod Wale.

Three Rod Wale Bargello Arrow technique is inspired by embroidery stitches. In basketry this is achieved by a Chase Weave. One row of Three Rod Wale, also known as Triple Twine, is followed by one row of Reverse Three Rod Wale. Each row creates a slight diagonal line upward or downward. When these two meet, an arrow is created.

Continue weaving with alternating rows of Three Rod Wale and Reverse Three Rod Wale to create several rows of arrows.

You may choose to secure one set of three round reed weavers with a wire twist tie while not in use, or you may use round reed bobbins to secure and separate the weavers.

There is no Step-up until the last row of Three Rod Wale is finished and after the desired number of arrows is completed.

Begin at the marked Starting Spoke. Place three weavers behind three consecutive spokes. Weave one row of Three Rod Wale and stop three spokes before reaching the Starting Spoke.

Reverse Three Rod Wale begins with three new pieces of round reed, one each behind three consecutive spokes. Begin one spoke to the left of the Starting Spoke.

The color sequence will change to allow the arrow to form. The color of Weaver #3 in the first row becomes the color of Weaver #1 in the Reverse Three Rod Wale. Weavers will match the color in the previous row.

With the left-most weaver, weave under the two weavers to the right (instead of weaving over these two as in regular Three Rod Wale). Move these two out of the way with your left hand, then continue to weave the left-most weaver over 2 vertical spokes and then under or behind the next vertical spoke, and out to the front. The Reverse Three Rod Wale part of the arrow is a diagonal from the top left down to the right or point of the arrow.

Continue this sequence around the basket until nearly reaching the original set of coiled Three Rod Wale weavers.

Transition to the original weavers and weave one row of Three Rod Wale. Check to be sure individual arrows match in color. The vertical rows of arrows will match in color as well. Every time around the basket, you will change the chase weave in a slightly different place since you stop two or three spokes sooner each time.

To end the arrow and complete the design, finish the last row of Three Rod Wale with a Step-up. Stop weaving the Three Rod Wale at the space to the left of the Starting Spoke (the last spoke). Then weave with the right-most weaver, the round reed farthest to the right, over 2 spokes and under 1 spoke. Trim and place reed to the inside of the basket.

Continue with the round reed on the right of the remaining pairs; weave over 2 and under 1, and trim to the inside.

Finish with the last pair of round reed, weave over 2, under 1 and trim to the inside. Finish the last row of Reverse Three Rod Wale two spokes to the right of the Starting Spoke. This completes the arrow. Leave the ends of the weavers on the inside of the basket and trim them.

There is no Step-up in Reverse Three Rod Wale; weavers will end behind the spokes where they originated.

This Bargello Arrow is a Chase Weave inspired by embroidery stitches. Start with one row of Three Rod Wale for the upward diagonal line of the arrow. Follow this with one row of Reverse Three Rod Wale for the downward diagonal line to complete one arrow stitch.

Single Spiral Weave technique creates diagonal lines or spirals that appear in the background as found in the Ribbons to Remember Basket while Reverse Single Spirals are found near the rim in Spirals Change.

Three rows of Three Rod Wale become a Single Spiral by replacing one weaver for another of a different color.

Insert a new dyed reed in the color of your choice and cut the original weaver out by replacing it with this new one. Continue Three Rod Wale for 3 rows with one weaver of a new color and two of the original color (or natural).

At the Starting Spoke, replace the new color with the original color.

Three Rod Wale for several more rows with all three weavers the same dyed color.

The Single Spiral technique is a variation of Three Rod Wale. By replacing one of the original weavers with one of a contrasting color, create this spiral by weaving three rows with one weaver of the new color and two of the original color or natural reed.

This is an example of Reverse Single Spirals. A Three Rod Wale technique, weave left-handed to create Single Spirals moving to the left near the rim of Spirals Change.

Another waling technique, **Four Rod Wale,** begins with four weavers and uses four vertical spokes. This technique adds a three dimensional textural element to any basket.

Place the round reed weavers near the left side of the basket and behind four consecutive vertical spokes, starting behind the marked Starting Spoke.

Begin with Weaver #1 (on the far left side) under vertical spoke #1, the Starting Spoke. Then weave over the 3 spokes to the right (spoke numbers 2, 3, and 4), under the 5th spoke, and continue out to the front of the basket.

Next, take Weaver #2 (left-most weaver), over 3 spokes, under 1, and bring it out to the front.

Follow with Weaver #3 (left most weaver), over 3 spokes, under 1, and comes out to the front.

Finally, Weaver #4 (left-most weaver), goes over 3 spokes, under 1, and out to the front of the basket. Continue around the basket alternating weavers. Stop one spoke before reaching the Starting Spoke.

Step-up to end the weavers and complete the design element:

Stop the Four Rod Wale at the space to the left of the Starting Spoke. As described previously, weave with the right-most round reed weaver. The round reed farthest to the right is woven over 3 spokes and under 1. Trim and place it to the inside of the basket. Continue with the round reed on the right. Again, weave over 3 spokes, under 1, and trim it to the inside of the basket, until finished with all four round reed weavers.

Four Rod Wale can also be woven as over 2 spokes and under 2 spokes. This will create a different design that is the same on the inside and outside of the basket.

By combining more than one piece of round reed, make a thicker weaver to add additional texture, as in **Double Four Rod Wale.** Two pieces of reed per weaver makes a double weaver. This technique uses four double weavers for a total of eight pieces of round reed. Vary the colors in the weavers for additional design possibilities.

The name **Five Rod Wale** refers to the number of reeds being used as weavers. Hence, Five Rod Wale uses five weavers. Start this technique in the same manner as Three Rod Wale, but place two additional round reed weavers behind or under the next two consecutive spokes to the right of your Starting Spoke and existing spokes.

Begin Five Rod Wale by weaving Weaver #1, (the left-most weaver), over 3 spokes, under 2 spokes, and out to the front of the basket.

Next, take Weaver #2 (left-most weaver) weave over 3 spokes, under 2, and out to the front.

Follow with Weaver #3 (left most weaver) weave over 3 spokes, under 2, and out to the front.

Again, pass Weaver #4 (left-most weaver) over 3 spokes, under 2, and out to the front.

Finally, Weaver #5 (left-most weaver) is woven over 3 spokes, under 2, and out to the front of the basket.

Continue around the basket alternating weavers. Stop when the weaver is at the space before the marked Starting Spoke.

You may Step-up to finish the weaving and complete the design, or you may choose to continue with each of the five round reed weavers in a Continuous Weave. This continuous technique will appear to spiral, while a Step-up in each row causes the rows to stack in horizontal bands.

Pack each row as you weave and end a continuous weave with a Step-up as previously described in the Three Rod Wale technique.

The **Spiraling, Swirls, Becoming, and Blending** technique has several names and is a variation of Five Rod Wale. Many round reed weavers have incorporated this design element into their repertoire of weaving accents. I discovered this in a three-day seminar in Greenville, South Carolina, with Kari Lonning.

Color placement is key to this weaving technique where the beginning accent color changes. With the substitution or blending of a new color in place of one of the original weavers, the design appears to spiral or swirl, almost float along the basket.

Insert Dyed Weaver #1 behind the marked Starting Spoke after the last of the original weavers has finished the over, under rotation.

Trim the original round reed weaver behind the Starting Spoke to have one dyed Weaver #1 with four original natural or accent color weavers. Place a twist tie or small clamp around this Dyed Weaver #1 to be able to count the number of rows.

Weave Five Rod Wale for the desired number of rows.

Insert Dyed Weaver #2 at the beginning of Row 5 for example, mark with a twist tie. Be sure the Dyed Weaver #1 has completed the over 2, under 1.

Then replace the original weaver that comes just after this first dyed weaver.

Weave for additional rows with two dyed weavers and 3 natural or original accent color weavers. Continue in this way until all original weavers are the new dyed accent. This additional color adds to the dramatic finish of this technique that spirals, swirls, and blends into one new color accent.[1]

The Five Rod Wale technique uses five weavers placed behind five consecutive spokes.

In Five Rod Wale, weave with the left-most weaver over 3 spokes and under 2 spokes then out to the front of the basket.

Replace one original weaver with a new dyed weaver to begin the Blending or Becoming technique, a variation of Five Rod Wale.

With the new dyed weaver in the left-most position, weave over 3 spokes, under 2 spokes to begin the Blending Five Rod Wale technique.

CHAPTER FIVE

RIM BORDERS

RIM PREPARATION

The rim of any basket serves as a sturdy finish to the woven vessel. In preparation for the rim, weave three Rim Rows of Twining with #2 round reed around the basket and above the last row of weavers. Or, weave with 7 mm or ⅜" flat reed for one Rim Row, also known as a False Rim.

Pack all weavers for the final time.

Re-wet the spoke ends until flexible. Carefully bend spokes to the inside of the basket. Cut the spoke ends on a diagonal or to a blunt point. Then tuck each spoke, or every other spoke under the third row of weavers on the inside of the basket near the rim.

The spokes to be trimmed are determined by the final row of weaving. When a spoke originates from the inside of the basket and the last weaver is over the spoke, it may be trimmed even or level with the top of the Rim Rows.

Then tuck the remaining spokes, those that have the last row of weaving under the vertical spoke. Use a weaving tool or a flat screwdriver to aid in tucking spokes. Re-wet

Spoke ends are cut on a diagonal or to a point for ease in tucking them to the inside of the basket.

After soaking spoke ends, gently bend and tuck each spoke or every other spoke to the inside.

This spoke end is tucked under the natural weaver, the third row from the rim. It is level with the top of the rim.

these spoke ends as needed to avoid cracking or breaking reed. Crimp wider spokes with crimping tool or needle-nose pliers before tucking.

Depending on the size of the basket, the rim material can be ¼", 7 mm, or ⅜" flat oval for smaller sizes and ½", ⅝", or ¾" flat oval for larger baskets.

Various other materials are often used for this finishing step: half round reed, flat reed, braided seagrass, leather strips, or any thicker material.

Rim filler is an additional piece of round reed, seagrass, rope, or any found material that fills the gap between the inside rim piece and the outside rim. Rim filler is one continuous piece around the basket and handles. Or choose to stop and start the rim filler from handle to handle.

Trim the spokes even with the Rim Row when the last weaver is over the vertical spoke and tuck the spokes where the last weaver is under the spoke. The wine spokes are tucked while the navy spokes can be cut.

Measure around the top inside and outside rim openings. Add 2" to each measurement to allow for the needed overlap. Cut two rim pieces from flat oval reed or rim material of your choice. Shave or scarf the oval side of one end for two inches on each piece of the flat oval reed to ensure a neat overlap. Soak these along with medium chair cane, narrow flat reed, or flat oval reed for the Rim Lasher, and #6 round reed for Rim Filler. Or include seagrass as the rim filler; which does not get wet.

Apply the flat oval inside rim with the 2" overlap on one side of the basket, near a handle. The flat side of the flat oval reed touches the rim and covers the Rim Rows. The oval side of the flat oval reed faces out. Use clothespins to temporarily secure the inside rim to the basket. Then apply the outside rim with the 2" overlap on another side of the basket or handle to distribute the overlaps so they do not occur at the same place. Insert the #6 round reed or seagrass Rim Filler between the inside and outside rims. Rim filler fills in the space and is one piece around the basket and handles. Or, use two pieces for the Rim Filler; place one end up against the handle. The Filler goes from handle to handle and stops. Repeat for the other side of the basket. Adjust clothespins or clamps as needed; add cable ties to secure rim pieces.

One-Way Rim Lashing

This rim lashing is the quickest finish and was found in many Native American baskets. It serves to secure the woven basket and rim pieces together.

When basket spoke ends are trimmed and tucked to the inside of the basket, the project is ready for rimming.

Select and prepare your desired rim material as described in the Rim Preparation.

Secure the rim pieces to the inner and outer rims of the basket with clothespins or cable ties.

Tuck the end of the lasher at or near the handle, up under the inside rim, under the Rim Filler, down and under the outside rim and out to the front of the basket. Pull the lasher to tighten and then trim it close to the rim. Be sure the right, shiny side of the lasher is facing out. Wrap over and around to the front of the basket, on a diagonal to the right. Then push the end of the lasher between the next two vertical spokes, above the top row of weavers and below the Rim Row(s). Continue wrapping around to the inside and up and over the rim making sure the right side of the lasher remains facing out.

Then the lasher moves down on a diagonal before inserting it again between the next two vertical spokes. Continue all around the basket; wrap around the handles to make an X. Pull the lasher tight to keep rim pieces together and use clothespins or clamps to hold the tension. Use a lashing tool or flat screwdriver to help open the space to allow the lasher to move easily between the spokes.

Keep all materials wet while working this step; re-wet as needed.

When the lasher reaches the starting place, finish by tucking the end of the lasher under the inside basket rim.

Begin the Rim Lasher under the inside rim with the right side touching the basket and the rough side facing out. This will bring the right side facing the outside of the basket as you lash.

The Rim Lasher continues around the rim between the next two vertical spokes; above the last row of weaving and below your Rim Row(s).

To end the lasher, tuck the end up under the inside rim, under the seagrass rim filler, then under the outside rim. Pull the end down along the outside of the basket until lasher is tight, then trim close to the rim.

Double Lashing or X Rim Border

This is the most commonly used rim border found in current basketry. The Double Lashing technique, also know as an X border, continues where the One-Way Rim Border ends.

Begin as described in the One-Way Rim Lashing moving on a diagonal. Lash around the basket to the right.

At the handle, or starting place, reverse the lasher and work to the left; bring the lasher around to the front and create an X on the outside of the handle and each spoke at the rim.

Continue as before, pushing the lasher through to the inside of the basket between the next two spokes. Naturally, the X will appear near the top of the rim, above the rim filler. To adjust the lashing and to see the X along the side of the rim, move the original lasher to the left with a small tool or your finger.

When the lasher reaches the starting place, finish by tucking the end of the lasher under the inside rim, under the Rim Filler, down and under the outside rim. Pull the lasher to tighten and trim it close to the rim.

Reverse the lasher and work the opposite direction to create an X at each spoke for the X Rim Border; also know as Double Lashing.

Double X

This design reverses the Rim Lasher to create a Double X, also known as a Double Cross, at the handle or anywhere along the rim for a design accent.

When at the handle for the last time around the rim, repeat the X and alternate to be opposite the over or under in the original X. This causes the lasher to separate or divide the original X, bringing it around the handle and back to the inside of the basket.

Continue to lash to the opposite side of the basket.

Double X in the same way at this handle to complete the lashing. Trim and tuck the end under the inside rim.

Waxed Linen Lashing

This thread is the lashing material best used when there are many spoke ends and/or when spokes are very close together. Lash with a tapestry needle or curved needle and 4-ply, 7-ply, or 12-ply waxed linen. Measure a long lasher approximately five times the distance around the rim of the basket. To begin, tie the end of the waxed linen lasher around any vertical spoke below the round reed Rim Rows and above the last weaver. With a 5" tail, bring the waxed linen lasher from the inside around to the front of the basket, over the rim and across the front on a diagonal. Insert the needle to the right and between the next spokes. Lash with waxed linen in one direction around the entire rim of the basket. Pull tight to keep the rim snug and cut cable ties out of the way. At the starting place, end the waxed linen lasher by tying it to the beginning end of the lasher, trim and tuck the ends under the inside rim.

The Double X or Double Cross is found at the handle or anywhere along the rim. The second X or cross is interwoven with the first.

Cable Stitch Rim Lashing

The Cable Stitch Rim Lashing is inspired by an embroidery stitch. It can be worked with cane, narrow flat, or flexible flat oval reed.

Lash in one direction to the right as in the One-Way Rim Lashing. With a new lasher tucked under the inside rim, work in reverse. Wrap to the left over the previous lasher. The lasher stays on the outside of the rim and wraps over each previous lasher wrap, circles under it, and is then brought up near the top of the rim. Since this requires a tight, compact turn, keep the lashing material wet to avoid breaking. If it is difficult to get the lasher under the wrap, put it under at the seagrass rim filler then floss it down on the front of the rim.

Continue moving to the left of the original lasher. Circle over, around, under, and repeat; keep the lasher level in the center, or near the bottom or top of the rim, your preference.

To end, wrap the lasher around and under the first wrap and bring it down and to the inside. Finish by trimming and tucking your lasher under the inside rim.

Similar in appearance to the embroidery Cable Stitch, this rim lashing technique is a two-step process. Lash in one direction, then reverse the lasher, and work in the opposite direction. The lasher stays on the outside of the rim and wraps around each previous lasher wrap.

Fold and No-Tuck Rim Border

After the Rim Row is woven and the basket is packed tightly, re-wet the ¼" spoke ends until they are flexible. This will help to avoid reed damage in this border technique. Hold the basket with the base side up. Place the ends of spokes into a sink or container of water, your choice.

When the spokes are flexible, mark a Starting Spoke and begin working to the right. Go under 1 spoke to the right, and bring it up to the top rim of the basket.

Gently bend the spoke over 1 to the left. This is the same spoke you just wove under 1. Push down and in, through the keyhole opening, to the inside of the basket. It will tuck under and lay along the rim. Trim to 1" or so. Continue in the same way around the border: under 1 to the right, over 1 to the left, down and in.

Or, choose to gently bend under 1 spoke to the right and up for 4 or more spokes, then go back and over 1 to the left and tuck down and inside the keyhole openings.

Re-wet spoke ends as needed. Trim any fuzzy fibers for a neat finish. If reed cracks under this intense bending and folding technique, apply stain with a cotton ball or fill in with a fine line permanent marker in the same color accent

The Fold and No-Tuck Rim Border with the upright spoke ready to finish the rim.

The spoke bends down to the right and under one spoke to the right in the Fold and No-Tuck Rim Border.

The spoke continues over one spoke to the left and down to the inside of the basket.

The finished Fold and No-Tuck Rim Border is on the Ribbons to Remember Basket.

Philodendron Rim Border

When working with the natural material from the philodendron plant, soak the sheaths in warm water for several hours, until they become softer and more flexible.

Waxed linen is often used as the rim lasher.

When philodendron is ready, gently blot it with a towel to remove excess water. Apply it over the rim so the sheath covers both the inside and the outside rim. Add additional philodendron sheaths by overlapping for an inch or more.

Carefully apply clothespins or cable ties to secure the plant to the basket.

Thread the waxed linen or other lashing material through a large-eyed tapestry needle. Tie the end of the thread around one spoke below the Rim Row.

Bring it around from the inside of the basket, up and across the top of the rim. Then on a diagonal thread it down, and into the opening between the next spokes.

Continue to work this step around the rim of the basket, keeping your plant material wet and flexible. Re-wet with a spray water bottle or sponge.

At your starting point, pull the waxed linen lasher taut. Hold it with a clothespin to keep the tension and tie it to the beginning spoke as before. Trim the ends close to the inside of the basket.

Philodendron sheaths are commonly used as rim material on baskets made in Hawaii. Smaller pieces of philodendron are found as embellishments on the sides of these baskets also.

Experiment with other natural plant materials for a unique rim border.

A round basket made in Hawaii is finished with philodendron for the rim material. Other natural plant materials are woven in this unique piece from the author's collection.

More than one philodendron sheath is needed to cover this basket rim; the overlap creates an interesting rim finish.

CHAPTER SIX

HANDLES, WRAPS, WEAVING HINTS, AND FINISHING TOUCHES

Many baskets are woven with a wood handle incorporated as part of the weaving at the beginning of the project. Some have a handle added at the rim when the basket is nearly completed. Other baskets may have handles woven from reed as part of their pattern.

A variety of other items, in addition to wood and reed, can be used as handles: wire, leather, fabric, pottery, cabinet door pulls and wood knobs.

Without handles, baskets are useful for storage or are often more decorative in nature.

Handles are available in many shapes, sizes, and woods from various basketry suppliers. (See the Appendix.)

WOOD HANDLES

The handle most commonly used in basket weaving is known as the "D" handle. It resembles the letter D placed horizontally on its side and is woven in as part of the base of the basket. Sizes of "D" handles range from 2" × 3" to 14" × 20" or larger handles are available by special order.

Handles of ash, cherry, hickory, oak, or walnut are steamed and bent into shape. These are made and available in two ways: dove-tailed, glued, and pinned in corners, or overlapped and stapled. I prefer the dove-tailed, glued, and pinned handles in oak, to create a sturdy foundation on which to build the base of the basket.

Popular today is the traditional rectangular, market-style basket. It can be made using any of the "D" handles, from the smallest to the largest mentioned above.

Basket handles most commonly used today are known as "D" handles. Made of oak, walnut, ash, cherry, or hickory, these handles are steamed and then bent into the shape of the letter *D*.

Many other handle styles, including the Williamsburg, tulip, wine, sharp-top, square or flat-top, oriole, and ribbed hearth basket frame, are available.

Another stationary style handle is one that is added in at the rim and not included as part of the base. Round-top and square or flat-top handles, with notches or ears, are secured to the basket at the rim. Bushel handles are applied at the rim also. Some flat-top handles have a dip or center handle grip.

Williamsburg handles are available in several sizes. This handle style creates a basket with a smaller square base that grows into a larger round rim opening.

The tulip shape handle is pictured on the left; the sharp top handle is on the right.

The hearth basket handle and frame are the beginning to a functional ribbed basket.

A round-top add-in handle has a notch on each side, which allows a place for the rim to rest and helps secure the handle to the basket.

Flat-top add-in handles are notched on each side for the rim placement. Sometimes these handles have a center handle grip.

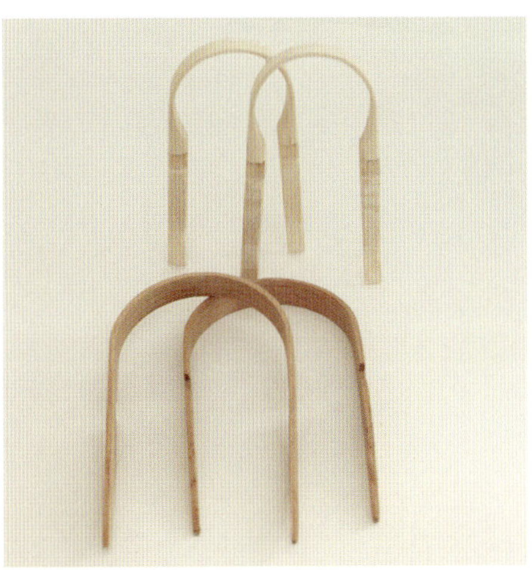

Bushel handles are available in pairs and are included on each side of a basket.

Swing or drop handles are also added in at the rim. These use pins, dowels, wooden knobs, or rivets to allow for their swing movement.

Round-top and square or flat-top handle styles provide easy access and are ideal for flower or plant baskets, or casserole or pie baskets. These handle styles will work with almost any basket style.

When the basket has been packed and spoke ends are tucked, the handle is inserted by its ears, the small wooden extensions below the swing of the handle.

Carefully insert a long, straight tool down into several rows of weaving, on the inside of the basket.

Push the ears down through this opening until the notch rests at the Rim Row.

Now, apply the flat oval reed or other rim material at the notch level. Distribute the overlaps of the rim pieces to avoid a thick rim.

Double lash to secure the handle. Also, Double X at each handle for extra support and protection.

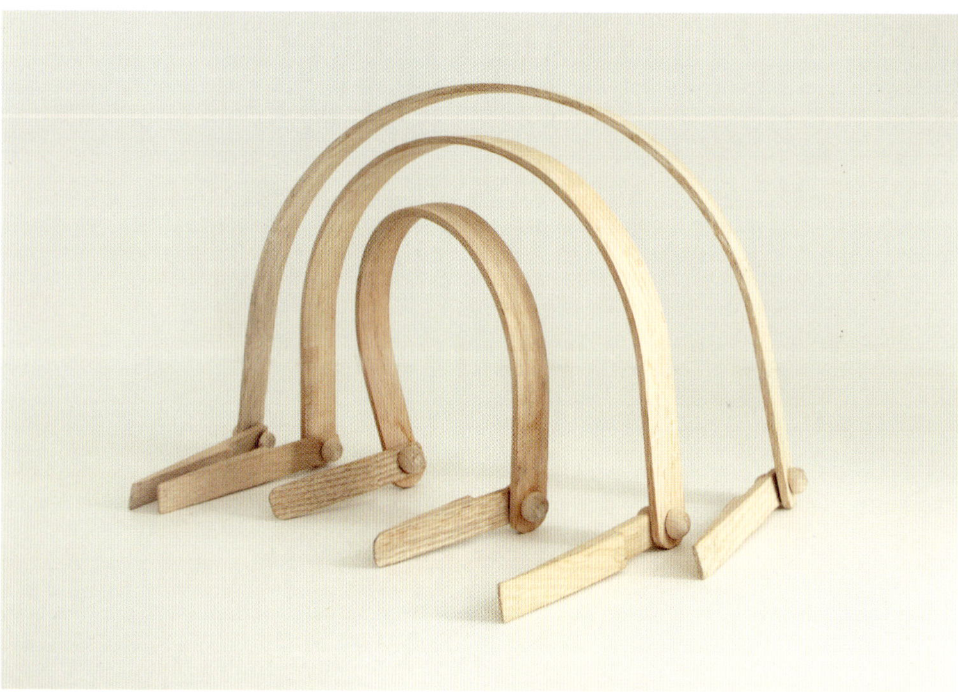

Round-top swing handles are also known as drop handles. The wood knob or rivet connects the handle to the ear, the extension below the swing. The handle movement allows easy access to the contents of the basket. This handle style is ideal for casserole baskets or flower and plant baskets, and will work with most other basket designs.

Flat-top swing handles are used in a variety of basket designs and may include a comfortable handle grip in the center.

Round and oval wood hoops, to be used in ribbed or egg baskets and on the sides of round storage baskets, are steamed, shaped, and glued.

Diameter sizes are commercially available as small as 3" and as large as 20". To create your own hoops, glue or tie round reed together with waxed linen. Use these in pairs. Begin by securing the 2 round hoops together with thread or waxed linen. The hoops are perpendicular to each other and meet at their centers.

Round wood hoops are available from the smallest 3" diameter to larger 12" to 20" sizes. These are secured together and used in pairs to create the frame for ribbed or egg baskets.

Oval wood hoops are the start to oblong-shaped ribbed or egg Baskets.

WIRE BASKET HANGERS AND HANDLES

Wire hangers or handles provide a decorative finish and are lashed at the Rim Row when spoke ends are tucked. They are often used in beanpot and jelly jar shaped baskets and can be found in the shape of hearts, stars, animals, holiday designs such as fir trees, floral designs such as tulips, and many more.

Wire handles with wood center grip are secured to the basket rim with wire ears. These are available in a variety of shapes and sizes from the jelly jar and beanpot shapes pictured here to holiday designs, animals, and many more.

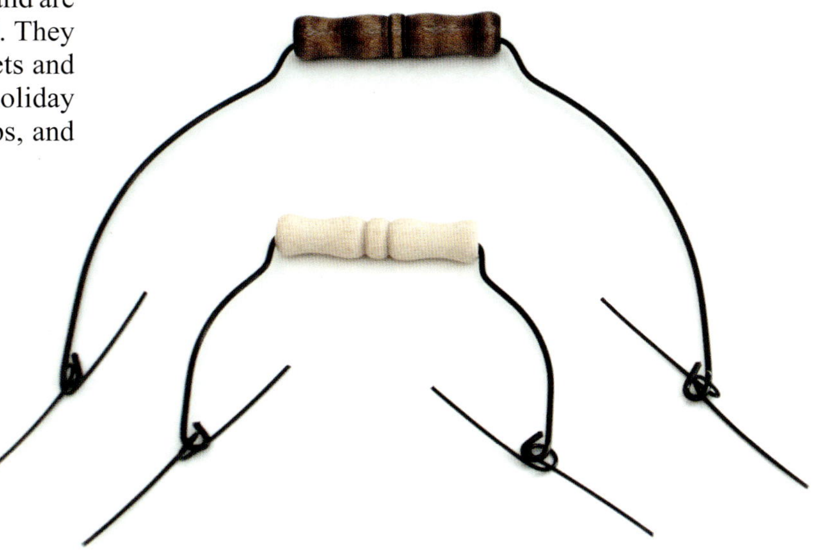

LEATHER HANDLES

Handles handcrafted from leather may be plain or braided and are available in a variety of lengths, from long, shoulder strap size to the smallest, 6" bushel handles. Leather handles are especially popular in purse and tote baskets and are available in several colors: natural, cocoa browns and blacks, navy, green, red, and other colors upon request. Some leather handles are woven from the base; others are secured to the basket with the flat oval rim reed through the leather loop.

Recycled leather belts may also be incorporated into a basket in place of commercial leather handles.

Leather shoelaces make fine handles for smaller baskets, and leather dog collars can be used to secure a bicycle basket to the handlebars.

The loop at the end of a leather handle is finished with a rivet and secured to the basket when the outer rim reed is threaded through.

Leather bushel handles are available in many colors to match the dyed accent weavers in your baskets.

A variety of leather handles, from the shortest to the longest, add a fine finish to a handwoven purse, tote basket, casserole, and other basket styles.

SHAKER TAPE FABRIC

Shaker tape, a textile found in department stores, craft shops, and fabric stores, is often woven from the base of a basket or at the basket rim to create inexpensive, strong, and flexible handles for various baskets.

This handle material is available in a variety of widths; most popular are ⅝" and 1".

Purchase this by the yard or in 75-yard rolls.

Colors such as black, navy, red, wine, hunter green, beige, brown, and blue can be cut to any length needed.

Popular for use in totes, purses, and casserole baskets, Shaker tape adds another colorful dimension to handwoven baskets.

Shaker tape is often used for handle material. It provides an inexpensive, flexible handle and can be cut to any length needed.

HANDMADE POTTERY HANDLES

Pottery handles are available from a few suppliers and usually in limited sizes or colors. If possible, find a local potter to custom make pottery handles, as these are small pieces that will help fill the kiln. These handles are fragile yet add another colorful dimension to woven baskets. Add pottery handles to casserole baskets, bread baskets, laundry baskets, or any basket design of your choice.

Colorful Pottery Handles add another medium to your handwoven baskets. Most often they are used in pairs to complement bread and casserole baskets.

HANDLE WRAPS

For a unique finish to the woven basket, a handle wrap technique can be applied in a short period of time. Wrapping a handle adds beauty and a decorative touch to any finished basket and also serves as a comfortable handle grip. Handle Wraps are completed using several different sizes of dyed and natural reed; oftentimes cane provides an added accent. Practice these techniques and experiment with your original designs.

Handle Wrap Preparation

Prior to wrapping any handle:

Wet all handle wrap materials before beginning.

Select one side of the basket handle to begin your work. All tucking and wrapping begins here. You will work from this point, up and over the handle, and down to the other side of the handle and basket.

Begin by inserting handle anchors between the outside rim of the basket and the topside of the handle.

Tuck the handle wrapper (reed or cane) under the inside basket rim, with the smooth side of the wrapper touching the handle. Wrap this around to the front with the smooth side facing out. Continue wrapping to the back of the handle. Repeat this wrapping action two to four times, until you are ready to begin the selected handle wrap pattern. Be sure the reed- or cane-wrapped rows rest tightly against the handle and lay right next to one another to create an even pattern and completely cover the handle.

Note: Keep all handle technique pieces wet and flexible so as not to compromise the material. To add a new piece for the handle wrapper when needed, tuck the old wrapper on the underside of the handle and secure the new wrapper piece by inserting it up and under several wraps on the underside of the handle with the wrong side facing out. Then wrap it around to the front of the handle with the right side of the wrapping now showing and continue your design.

Plain Wrap is the first handle wrap technique to try and will be good practice for the more intricate wrap techniques that follow.

Materials

Basket handle

3/16", 1/4", 7 mm flat reed or medium cane, 1 long piece for the handle wrapper

Optional: Flat or flat oval reed, dyed or natural, 1 piece slightly longer than the handle length, for the optional handle anchor(s)

Begin the Plain Wrap with the Handle Wrap Preparation (see above). Then continue wrapping around the handle keeping the wrapper level on the top of the handle; it will be on a diagonal under the handle. Keep wrapping tightly to the basket; be sure the smooth side of the reed is on the outside of the handle.

At the opposite side of the handle, wrap until there is no space left on the top of the handle. Bring the wrapper to the inside of the basket and tuck the end of your handle wrapper under the inside rim and trim to finish.

Option: To add texture to the handle wrap, before you begin your wrapping, tuck an optional handle anchor between the outside rim and the topside of the handle. As you begin to wrap the handle, weave your wrapper under this anchor for two or more wraps. (You choose the number of wraps, and as a result, the amount of exposure for your anchor.) Continue by wrapping over the anchor for two or more wraps. Repeat this step until arriving at about 2" above the rim on the opposite side of the handle. Trim and tuck the optional handle anchor between the outside rim and the topside of the handle at the opposite side of the basket, and wrap around all handle pieces to match the pattern you used to begin your handle wrap. Finally, tuck the end of your handle wrapper under the inside rim and trim to finish.

Begin each handle wrap technique by tucking the handle wrapper material under the inside rim at the handle.

Over and Under Checkered Handle Wrap begins the same as the Plain Wrap. However, this technique employs two dyed accent handle anchor pieces to create the colorful design. Use two contrasting colors that match the accents in your basket.

Materials

Basket handle
3/16", 1/4", 7 mm flat reed or medium cane, 1 long piece for the handle wrapper
Flat or flat oval dyed reed, 2 pieces slightly longer than the handle length, for the handle anchors

To create the Over and Under Checkered Handle Wrap pattern, begin your design the same as the Plain Wrap. Place the flexible handle wrapper under dyed accent handle anchor #1 (red in the photograph), and over the dyed accent handle anchor #2 (navy) for two or three wraps.

Now continue the design by wrapping over the red and under the navy handle anchors for two or three wraps. Be consistent with your number. Repeat this step until arriving at about 2" above the rim on the opposite side of the handle, trim and tuck two handle anchors under the outside basket rim. Continue the pattern until 1/2" above the rim on the opposite side of the handle and wrap two to four times around all the handle pieces to match the pattern you used to begin your handle wrap. Finally, tuck the end of your handle wrapper under the inside rim and trim it to finish.

The Checkered Handle Wrap technique uses two handle anchors in contrasting dyed reed. Create a colorful wrap that alternates the dyed accent reed with the handle wrapper.

Twill Wrap allows color accent to show more than most any other handle wrap technique. This creates a diagonal design that moves across the handle just as twill weaving develops diagonals in the basket weaving process.

Materials

Basket handle
3/16", 1/4", 7 mm flat reed, or medium cane, 1 long piece for the handle wrapper
3/16" or 1/4" flat or flat oval reed, dyed, 3 pieces slightly longer than handle length, for the handle anchors

Begin by inserting three pieces of dyed reed under the outside rim. These handle anchors are placed on top of the handle.

Secure handle wrapper under inside rim. With smooth side facing out, bring wrapper around to the front or top of the handle. Bring handle wrapper over the three dyed reed handle anchors and around the handle. Wrapper continues to wrap around all pieces for three or more wraps. Keep all reed damp and flexible.

Wrap Rows 1–3 over 3
Wrap Row 4 under 1, over 2
Wrap Row 5 under 2, over 1
Wrap Row 6 under 3
Wrap Row 7 over 1, under 2
Wrap Row 8 over 2, under 1
Wrap Row 9 over 3
Repeat Rows 4–9

This technique is repeated several times across the face of the handle until you are within 2" above the rim on the opposite side of the handle. Trim and tuck the dyed reed anchors under the outside rim at the handle. Continue the design until within 3/4" of the rim. Then finish as you began. Bring the handle wrapper over all pieces of dyed reed and the handle for three or more wraps.

Secure the end of the handle wrapper under the inside rim of the basket and trim as needed.

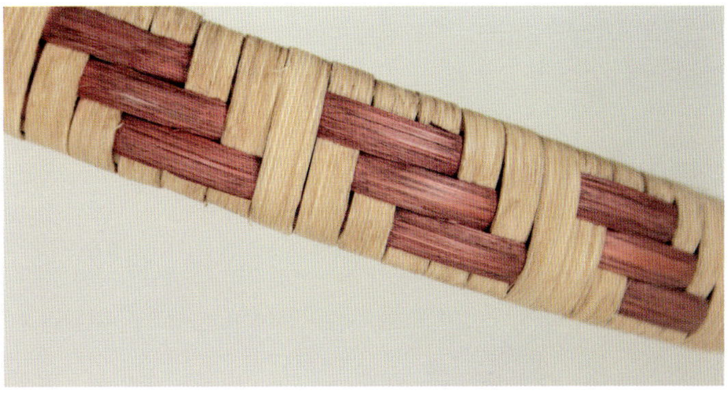

Create a diagonal design with the Twill Handle Wrap technique.

Braid Handle Wraps

The Double and Triple Braid Wrap techniques, woven with fine cane materials, are found in baskets in my collection from Thailand and the Far East. Several authors and artists in the United States have put this technique to use in many basket designs. I found Braid Wraps in Nancy Gruber's designs in *Fancy Handles for Decorative Woven Baskets.*[1]

This wrap is one of my favorites, as the end result can vary by changing the width of just one element. Change the size of the handle anchor from narrow in the Triple Braid Wrap to a wider width in the Double Braid Wrap. Doing this creates a more open and delicate design. This technique is found in two projects, the Double Handle Plaid Carryall Basket and the Cozy Wine Cradle.

Materials

- Basket handle
- Medium cane, 2 pieces for the Double Braid, 3 pieces for the Triple Braid
- 3⁄16", ¼", 7 mm flat reed, or medium cane, 1 long piece for the handle wrapper
- ¼", ⅜", ½" or wider flat reed, natural or dyed, 1 piece slightly longer than the handle length for the handle anchor

Select the Double or Triple Braid Wrap to determine the number of pieces of cane needed for the design.

Insert two or three pieces of medium cane, one at a time.

Place the wrong side of cane #1 up; the right side of the cane touches the handle. Secure cane under the handle anchor accent piece only; pull the cane until the center of the piece is resting under the anchor. This leaves an equal length of cane on each side of the handle.

Then wrap around all layers of the handle with the handle wrapper and secure with a clothespin. Repeat with cane #2, and then again, wrap one time all the way around the handle as above.

Add one additional piece of cane in the same way for the Triple Braid.

Proceed with the Double or Triple Braid technique by working with the bottom piece of cane. Take the left side of the Braid cane place it over, on a diagonal, to the right side of the handle. Bend a miter turn and tuck it to the left, under the handle anchor with the wrong side of the cane up. Now let this piece hang down to the left side of the handle as it started.

Work now with the right half of this bottom piece. Place it over, on a diagonal, to the left side of the handle. Bend a miter turn and tuck it to the right under the handle anchor with the wrong side of the cane up. Allow it to hang down to the right side of the handle.

Wrap with the handle wrapper one time above this X and do so each time another X is created with the cane.

Continue with the Braid technique, always working with the bottom piece of cane.

When the opposite side of the handle is reached, allow ample space to complete the same number of plain wraps as you made at the start.

End all pieces of the Braid cane under the handle anchor.

Trim and tuck the dyed reed anchor under the outside rim at the handle.

Bring the handle wrapper to the inside of the basket, tuck it under the inside rim, and trim it to end.

The cane ends of the braid are trimmed with side cutters or small scissors as close to the end of the handle as possible. These will not come loose as the handle anchor and the handle wrapper secure the cane.

Handle Anchor(s) of flat or flat oval reed, used to secure the various design elements, are found in most handle wrap techniques.

Start handle wrap techniques with several plain wraps over the handle anchor before beginning any design.

The Double Braid Handle Wrap technique uses two pieces of cane, each secured under the handle anchor and separated with a plain wrap.

Begin the Braid Handle Wrap technique with cane #1 under the handle anchor.

Secure each piece of cane with one plain wrap above it.

Three pieces of cane are needed for the Triple Braid Handle Wrap technique.

Begin the braid with the bottom left cane moving on a diagonal to the right across the handle, miter turn to the left under the anchor, and out to the left side of the handle.

One complete X or cross has the left cane moving from left to right and under the anchor; then the right cane moves right to left under the anchor and out to the right.

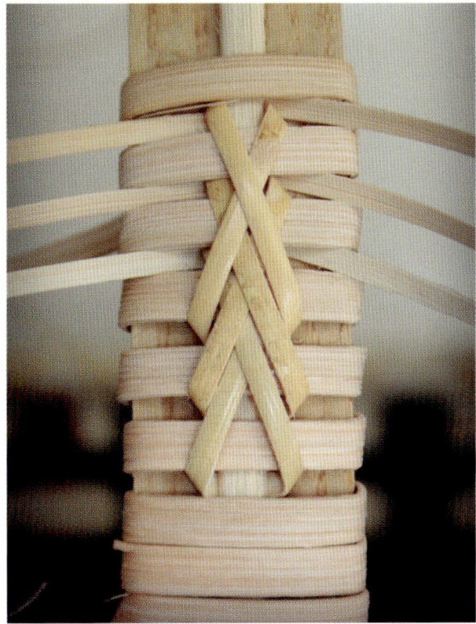

The Triple Braid Handle Wrap technique is in progress with all three cane pieces creating this tight wrap design.

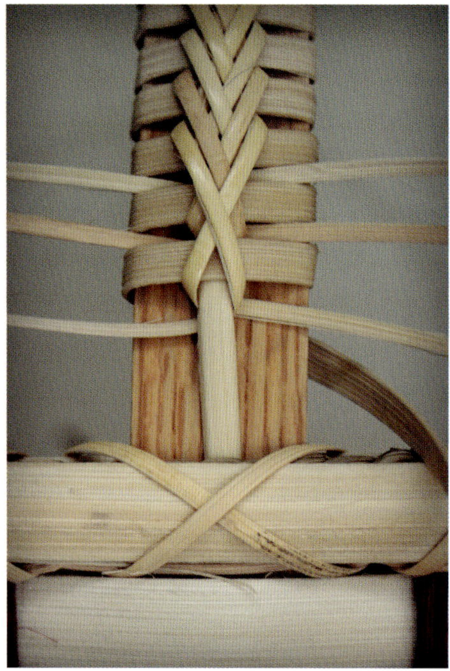

At the opposite side of the handle, end the cane braid under the handle anchor.

In Triple Braid Wrap, all cane ends under the handle anchor at the same location on the opposite side of the handle.

To secure the ends of the braid, wrap around the handle and all cane pieces.

Plain wrap around the handle; match the number of wraps on the opposite side of the handle.

The Double Braid Wrap technique with a ⅝" or ¾" wide, dyed handle anchor will have a delicate, lacy appearance with your color showing through the design.

The Triple Braid Wrap technique with a ¼" handle anchor creates a tight, compact design, which resembles a Native American arrow technique.

Arrow Wrap, Also Known as Flying Geese or V Handle Wrap

This handle wrap design dates back to our ancestors in the early Middle Ages. The arrow is an upside down V-shaped symbol. Found in early rock carving art, the geometric figure resembles the peak on a roof and is a sign of protection. Our Native American ancestors used this arrowhead design in many baskets as an accent. Chasing Diamonds, a twill weave project in this book, uses the arrow in a continuous design.

The Arrow Handle Wrap design dates back to our early ancestors. This technique is also known as Flying Geese and the V-Handle Wrap.

Materials

Basket handle
3⁄16", 1⁄4", 7 mm flat reed, or medium cane, 1 long piece for the handle wrapper
Medium cane, 1 long piece for the arrow design
3⁄16" or 1⁄4" dyed reed, 2 pieces slightly longer than the handle length, for the handle anchors

Place the two dyed accent reed handle anchors on the outside of the handle and tuck them under the outside rim.

Tuck the handle wrapper around and over the front of the handle and the dyed reed anchors; continue wrapping to the back of the handle. Repeat this wrapping action for two or more rows.

Begin the Arrow Handle Wrap design with two long pieces of cane. Slide cane #1 under the dyed reed anchor on the left. Make sure the right side of the cane touches the handle; the wrong side faces out and the long end protrudes from the center of the handle and between the two anchor pieces. Secure cane #2 under the right handle anchor in the same manner.

Now with the Arrow cane secured, wrap above the cane with the handle wrapper, passing over the dyed reed anchors for two rows.

Take the two ends of the arrow cane and weave on a diagonal, over the two handle-wrapped rows, and to the outside edge of the handle to create the arrow.

The arrow cane ends are then taken under the dyed anchor pieces, in a miter turn, to the inside of the handle, with the wrong sides of the arrow cane facing up. Let these cane ends hang loosely as you continue to wrap 2 rows with the handle wrapper. You are now ready for the next arrow.

Continue wrapping up and over the handle in this manner until one to two inches remain on the handle.

To end the wrapper, secure the arrow cane pieces under the two dyed reed anchors. Trim and tuck the dyed reed anchors under the outside rim at the handle. Finally, wrap the handle wrapper for two or more rows, around all. Trim the wrapper as needed and tuck it under the inside basket rim.

WEAVING HINTS

1. Weave with the smooth, shiny side of reed facing out, while the rough, or wrong, side touches the basket. To determine the right and wrong side of basket reed, wet it briefly, then bend gently. Look for the hairy fibers that pop up on the rough or wrong side of the reed.
2. Wet reed briefly; you do not need to soak it a long time. Depending on the size of the reed, soak for one to five minutes until it is flexible. Thick flat oval or half round reeds and some natural gathered materials, for example philodendron, may need a much longer time to soak. Avoid soaking materials overnight. Wet dyed reed in a separate container from natural reed.
3. To measure the center of base spokes, bend the two ends to touch each other. Slide your thumb to indicate the center of the spoke; make a light pencil mark on the rough side. Or place spokes on the table, line up the ends, measure one spoke, then place your ruler perpendicular and make a mark on each spoke in the center.
4. Use a sponge or small spray bottle to re-wet base spokes before upsetting to weave the sides of the basket. When weaving with wider spokes, crimp the spokes at the base. Slowly upsett, gently bending the spokes upright to avoid cracking the reed. I use this technique with ⅝" and ¾" spokes.
5. With #1 or #2 round reed, twine one row around the base of your basket. This secures your base measurements and eliminates any movement or shifting. (Refer to chapter 4, Weaving Techniques.)

   Wet the round reed, fold and crimp near the center of the reed, and hairpin or loop this folded end around the second or third spoke from the corner.

   To end the twining, complete the last twist or X before the Starting Spoke, insert both ends under the original loop from the outside of the base, pointing in. Repeat this by tucking the ends under the twine on the next spoke. Trim to ½" long. Ending in this way keeps the round reed in the same horizontal line as the twining.
6. Start each weaver on the outside of the basket, in the over position. To finish the weaver, you will weave on top of/over this original weaver, under the next spoke, over the next, trim and tuck the end under the fourth spoke. This keeps the cut end from being visible.
7. To establish crisp corners in a square or rectangle basket, start weaving the first row; then at the second side of the basket, begin the second weaver to chase the first. Working with two weavers helps create the corners. Be sure to use clothespins to keep weavers secured and packed close together.
8. Use ample clothespins to help shape your baskets. I keep a clothespin in each corner to hold the weaver in place and as a reminder not to weave too tightly or too loosely.

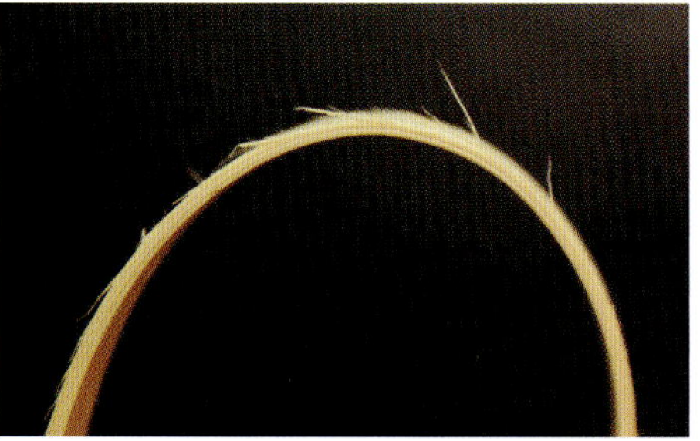

To determine the right and wrong side of basket reed, wet it briefly, then bend gently. Look for the hairy fibers that pop up on the rough or wrong side of the reed. The smooth, shiny side is the right side that faces outside the basket.

   Remove the clothespin, weave past the corner, replace the clothespin at the corner, then continue to weave.
9. In shaping your basket, remember the reed needs to be damp. When you attempt to shape dry reed, it will return to its same shape. When reed is damp, you can pinch the corners and shape other parts of the basket more easily.
10. It is helpful to rinse dyed reed in a mixture of one cup distilled white vinegar and one gallon of water. Sometimes two or three rinses are needed for the rinse water to run clear. If you do not mind the odor, add a tablespoon or more of vinegar to the water in your spray bottle.
11. When weaving with dyed reed that has been previously rinsed, re-wet it, and wipe the dyed reed gently several times with an old towel to remove excess dye.
12. Weaving with dyed round reed or any dyed reed, I trim the ends using a **back cut**. Hold your scissors on an angle, trim the reed on this angle or a diagonal with the widest part of the cut on the under side of the reed. The end will show the dyed color while the natural reed that shows through in the center of the reed will be hidden. If you find natural color showing through the dyed reed color, use a fine line permanent marker in a matching shade and color in the place to blend into the reed.

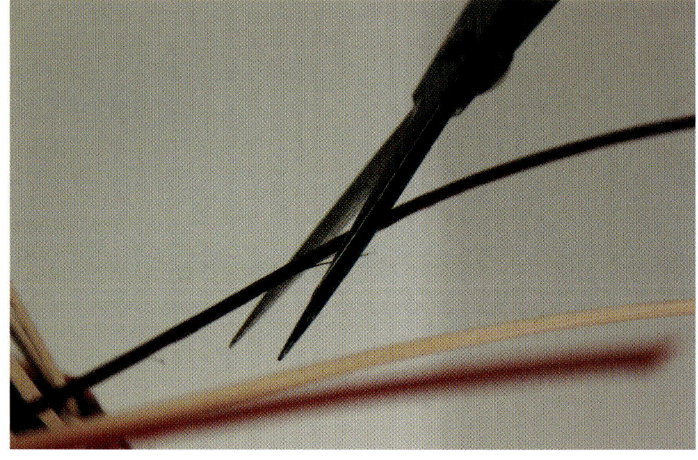

Hold your scissors at such an angle to make a back cut allowing the dyed reed cut end to be under or on the lower side of your basket.

Since dye does not completely penetrate reed, the center remains natural in color and is noticed when dyed reed is cut. Practice the back-cut scissors angle and place this natural cut end down into your basket to avoid seeing it later.

13. When your weaver needs to be tapered to a thinner width, as in a continuous weave technique, trim the side that will be facing in the downward position, towards the base. You will not see the raw edge in your finished basket.
14. To prepare the rim of your basket, re-wet the ends of the spokes until they are flexible. Trim every other spoke even with the top of your Rim Rows. Then cut the remaining spokes at an angle or to a blunt point. Use a weaving tool or flat screwdriver to open the space and tuck the spoke ends into the inside of the basket under the third weaver from the rim.
15. The rim of the basket is usually flat oval reed. This is stiffer than most other reeds and needs to be soaked a few minutes longer. Cut the flat oval reed two inches longer than the circumference of the basket rim. Shave or scarf the oval end of the rim reed then apply to the inside and outside of the basket rim. Distribute the 2" overlap of the flat oval reed to avoid a thick buildup on one side of your basket. Choose to place the overlap on opposite sides of the basket or either side of the handle. Use plenty of clothespins and/or cable ties to secure the rim.
16. Lash the flat oval rim and rim filler to the basket with medium chair cane or other narrow flat reeds: 11/64", 3/16" or 1/4" in size.
17. To store, sort reed by kind: flat, flat oval, round, and by the size of reed. Place dry reed in totes, paper bags, or other storage boxes. Allow some air circulation and avoid exposure to moisture and heat sources. If you have ample space, hang the coils of reed by size on pegboard or stack on open shelving.
18. Allow damp or wet materials to dry thoroughly before storing to avoid any mildew or mold growth.

FINISHING TOUCHES

Personalize. When the basket is dry, personalize the base to indicate basic information about the basket and the weaver for future reference. Use a wood burning pen or permanent fine-line marker. Sign your name or initials, the date or year the basket was made, and the number assigned from your list of completed baskets.

Keep a current list of all the baskets you have created. Assign a number to each basket as it is finished. I created and numbered more than 2,600 baskets during my weaving career to this point. Without my list started back in 1987, I would not know how many baskets are in my personal weaving collection. Many have been given away as gifts, donated, or sold at various craft shows, gift shops, and artisan centers.

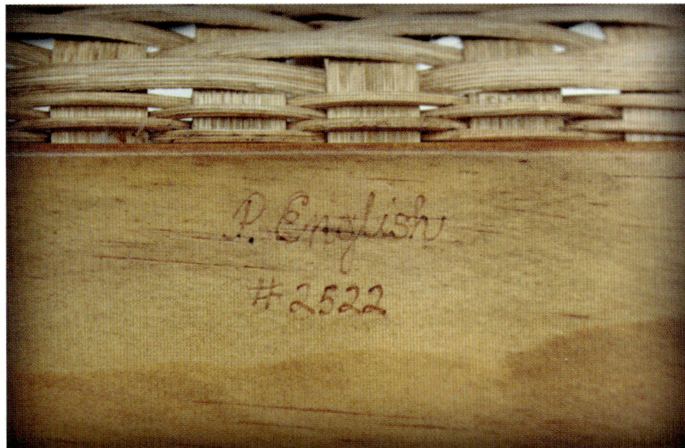

Personalize your finished basket on the base by signing your name or initials and the number assigned to it in your personal collection. Use a wood burning pen or a fine line permanent marker.

Stain. Choose to keep the basket natural, or finish the basket with a natural walnut hull stain or dye. (Refer to the recipe in chapter 2.) This process gives the basket an aged appearance and enhances its beauty. Or, spray the finished basket with a commercially available stain in the color of your choice. I prefer the natural stain since it has very little odor and dries evenly. Some weavers apply a mixture of linseed oil and turpentine, while others use mineral oil, baby oil, or tung oil to enhance their baskets.

Trim any hairy ends for a neat finish. Use small scissors or carefully singe or burn the fibers while the basket is still damp.

CHAPTER SEVEN

AWARD-WINNING BASKET PROJECTS

Basket Pattern Skill Levels

The following skill level descriptions are guidelines for selecting patterns that best fit the weaver's skill level.

Beginner patterns are for those who have very little or no weaving experience.

Beginner/Intermediate patterns are for beginner weavers with the confidence to attempt techniques geared for the next level.

Intermediate patterns are for weavers with knowledge of basic basketry skills and techniques.

Intermediate/Advanced patterns are for Intermediate weavers who are ready to undertake new, more difficult techniques.

Advanced patterns are for the more experienced weavers looking to increase their skills and experiment with new techniques and materials.

SHAKER CATHEAD

This design earned a Museum Purchase Award in 1999 at the Pickens Museum of Art and History, Pickens, South Carolina. The museum purchased this basket and it is currently displayed in their permanent collection.

The Shaker Cathead Basket was juried in the South Carolina State Museum 2004 Triennial Exhibit in Columbia, South Carolina.

The Shaker Cathead Basket, when turned upside down, resembles the shape of a cat's head with ears as the points where the basket rests. Historically, the Shakers wove baskets over wooden molds to create consistent shapes. This design is woven without a mold and shaped by the weaver's hands.

Beginner/Intermediate.

Approximate size: 6" (w) × 6" (l) × 7½" (h); 12" with handle

Materials

- 6" round-top swing handle with wood knobs
- ½" flat reed cut as follows for base spokes: 14 spokes at 26" long
- #2 round reed, Twine, 20'
- ¼" flat oval reed, natural, 80', and dyed, 10', Weavers
- ⅜" flat reed, Rim Row/False Weaver, 3'
- ½" flat oval reed, Rim, 6'
- #3 seagrass or #6 round reed, Rim Filler, 3'
- Medium cane or ¼" flat reed, Lasher, 15'

The Shaker Cathead Basket is a Start and Stop Weave in ¼" flat and flat oval reed. Weave three rows of dyed accent reed and create the Chain or Belt Buckle design. Add a swing handle with wooden knobs for a functional finish to this traditional basket.

Instructions

1. **Base**. With ½" flat reed, cut 14 spokes at 26" long. Wet the spokes briefly along with #2 round reed for twining and ¼" flat oval reed for weavers.
2. To begin weaving a cathead base, mark the center on the smooth, right side of 7 of the ½" flat reed spokes. On your work surface, place one marked spoke as the center horizontal spoke and three spokes on each side above and below the center spoke, approximately ½" apart. Anchor these original seven spokes with spoke weights to keep them flat, and line up your center marks.
3. Weave the remaining seven spokes, with smooth side facing up and marked in the centers. Begin at the center marks and weave the center, vertical spoke, over first, then under, over then under, through the horizontal spokes until reaching the opposite side. Pull this spoke past the horizontal spokes until you can line up the center marks. The spoke end is approximately 10" beyond the base. Next weave one spoke to the right of this center spoke. Start under, then weave over and under, matching center marks. Continue the next vertical spoke to the left of the center spoke. Start under, then weave over, under then over as before. Alternate over and under as you weave the remaining vertical spokes to the right and left of the center spoke, for a total of three spokes on each side of the center spoke, all spaced ½" apart. Adjust for equal spacing between each spoke with all center marks lined up.
4. The woven base measures 6 inches by 6 inches square; adjust spokes as needed. Place a clothespin at each corner to keep the spokes from shifting and your measurements accurate.
5. With #2 round reed, twine one row around the base. Crimp this round reed in half and loop around the second spoke from the corner. Work the ends to the right. (Refer to chapter 4, Weaving Techniques.) Twist this round reed weaver with one piece over then under and out to the front of the base spoke. Next, work with the opposite piece and weave over, under, and out to the front of the base spoke. Continue to twine as close to the base as possible; this secures each spoke. At each corner, be sure the weaver makes a sharp turn and does not slide under the corner spoke. Turn the woven base over and tuck round reed ends at the starting loop to end this twining on the wrong, rough side of the base. Trim so the ends are ½" long.
6. Re-wet the woven base and place it so your smooth side faces up and your rough, wrong side touches the work surface. Clothespin close to the base, the four corner spokes at each corner, take two corner spokes from each side and pull these together; the base will uplift to shape the cathead ears from the start.

6

The 6" square open weave base is transformed into a cathead with four clothespins each securing four corner spokes, two from each side. This causes an uplifting and the ears are created.

7. The **Over and Under, Start and Stop Weaving technique** is started with weavers of ¼" natural flat oval reed, the right side (oval side) faces out. With the base flat on the table work surface, place the **Row 1** weaver near the left side of the base, on the outside of the second or third spoke, and over a spoke that is opposite that of the base weaving. Then begin weaving under one spoke, over one spoke, under, over continuing around the basket, adjusting clothespins at corners as needed. At each corner, begin the shaping process by pulling up and back on the corner to form an arch in the base. When you remove the clothespin at the corner, your left hand can hold the corner up and in place while you weave around the four corner spokes. Keep clothespins or small clips at each of the four corner spokes and continue to clothespin these together to enhance the cathead ears. Overlap each row for four to six spokes, trim the flat oval weaver, and tuck the end under. Shave the oval side for one inch on the end of the weaver to eliminate build-up at the overlap.
8. **Shaping**. Move to the next side of the basket as you begin to weave each new row to distribute placement of reed overlaps. Continue to weave **Rows 2 to 6** with ¼" natural flat oval reed, alternating under and over with each new row. To enhance shaping, re-wet the woven base using a small sponge or a spray bottle. Check for equal distance between each spoke and use mini clips or clothespins as needed. After the first three rows are complete, evaluate the shape of the basket and make any needed adjustments. Continue to hand shape; pull up and back on each corner with your thumb or two fingertips and bend the base to form an arch. Over-exaggerate this step to achieve the cathead while still weaving flat on the table. For an enhanced cathead shape, weave these first six rows flat on the table; the longer you weave on the work surface, the wider, more defined the shape will become. Pack each row to avoid gaps between weavers. To aid in packing, shave the oval side of the beginning or at the end of the weaver.
9. Now turn the basket upright and begin a gentle upsett with the next six rows of weaving. This is a gradual flare, not a sharp, upright bend. With this transition, you may need to make adjustments, to tighten or loosen the previous row(s). Spokes are relaxed on a diagonal outward. Spray a small amount of water on the spokes to keep them flexible and to assist in hand shaping. When reed is dry, it is difficult to adjust the shape.
10. At this point, the cathead is well established. Pack each row of weaving using a packing tool or a flat screwdriver. Push down and pack all weavers so they touch. Tighten any gaps and adjust corners; use clothespins or mini-clips to keep tension on the weavers.

After weaving 6 rows with the base flat on the table and the right side up, turn the basket to an upright position. This gentle upsett has spokes flared out and relaxed, with the cathead base apparent in the center arch.

Hand shaping is important throughout a cathead basket. From the base spokes secured with clothespins to this technique where one hand holds the base in the corners and the other hand pulls up on the three center spokes one at a time. Repeat this on each side of the basket many times throughout the weaving process and you will be rewarded with a graceful cathead shape.

Insert the round-top swing handle with wooden knobs alongside the center spokes in the Cathead Basket. The notch helps to keep the rim row and flat oval rim in place.

Three consecutive rows of dyed weavers create this Chain Weave also known as a Belt Buckle design.

Hint: Re-wet the woven base. To assist in shaping, place your index finger in one corner and your thumb in the opposite corner, holding the base on the table. With your other hand, pull up on the center spoke on each side of the basket. Repeat this adjustment with each of the three center spokes to emphasize the cathead. The cathead arch is accentuated and uplifted. Check for equal distance between each vertical spoke, especially at the corners.

11. Continue to weave with ¼" flat oval reed for a total of 15 rows. At this point you will have reached the widest diameter of the basket. **Rows 7 to 15** are woven in an outward flare, with left-hand pressure pushing from the inside **outward** to a 9" to 10" diameter. This is consistent with right-handed weavers. If you are left-handed, then you will use right-hand pressure while weaving. Now re-wet the spoke ends and transition to straight upright spokes. Then use left-hand pressure to push **inward** on the vertical spokes while weaving **Rows 16 to 20**, five rows of natural ¼" flat oval reed, to a rim diameter of 7" to 9".
12. **Insert Handle**. Sand and round off the ends of the handle ears that extend below the wooden knobs. These allow the handle to swing. Without sanding, a thick piece of wood, or ear, extended into the basket can create an unwanted change in the basket shape. Use a long, straight weaving tool or flat screwdriver to open the weavers at the center spoke, to allow the end of the handle ear to tuck down, approximately seven rows on the inside or outside of the basket. Repeat on the opposite side of the basket and insert the ear at the center spoke as before. Pack the natural flat oval weavers before adding dyed accent weavers in the next step.
13. In Rows 21 to 23, a **Chain Weave technique** continues the Over and Under, Start and Stop Weave with ¼" dyed accent weavers in the color of your choice. Briefly wet, then wipe dyed reed gently through an old towel, and weave three consecutive rows of color accent, alternating over and under to create the Chain Weave design that also resembles a belt buckle.
14. Return to weaving with ¼" natural flat oval reed for the remaining three or more rows. In **Rows 24 to 26**, again use left-hand pressure to push inward on the vertical spokes to decrease the diameter of the rim opening. The basket is now approximately 7" tall. If the rim opening does not decrease, gently tug on the weaver and clothespin it to hold the tension; then continue weaving. Tug after each corner to notice some movement, keeping watch that spokes do not slant. Adjust spokes as necessary.

15. **Rim Preparation**. Twine three Rim Rows with #2 round reed to aid in shaping the rim opening; or weave one Rim Row with ⅜" flat reed. Pack all rows of weavers for the final time. Re-wet spoke ends. When flexible, carefully bend spokes to the inside of the basket. Cut the spoke ends on a diagonal or to a blunt point. Then tuck each spoke, or every other spoke, under the top row(s) of weavers.
16. **Rim**. Measure and cut two rim pieces from flat oval reed. Soak these along with the Rim Lasher and round reed Rim Filler. Or include seagrass as the Rim Filler, which does not get wet. Use clothespins to temporarily secure the flat oval rims to the basket. Distribute the overlaps, insert the Rim Filler and adjust clothespins or clamps as needed. Add cable ties to secure all rim pieces.
17. Lash with medium chair cane or narrow flat reed. Tuck the end of the lasher up under the inside rim at or near the handle. Be sure the right, shiny side of the lasher is facing out. Lash around the basket on a diagonal to the right. Pull the lasher tight to keep rim pieces together and use clothespins or clamps to hold the tension.

    When the lasher reaches the starting place, finish by tucking the end of the lasher under the inside basket rim at your starting place.
18. Choose to reverse the lasher and Double Lash to the left to create an X as the rim border. End the lasher at the starting place. (Refer to chapter 5, Rim Borders, for additional instruction.)
19. Check the overall shape of your basket and adjust where necessary. Allow your finished basket to completely air dry; turn the basket upside down with the base side up.
20. **Stain**. Finish the basket with a natural walnut hull stain or dye. (Refer to the recipe in chapter 2.) Or, spray the finished basket with a commercially available stain. This process gives the basket an aged appearance and enhances its beauty.
21. Personalize the woven base with a wood burning pen or a permanent fine line marker for future reference. Sign your name or initials, the date or the year the basket was made, and the number assigned from your list of completed baskets. (Refer to chapter 6, Finishing Touches.)

The Shaker Cathead Basket is finished with a Double X Lashing in cane.

DOUBLE HANDLE PLAID CARRYALL

This is a Fine Craft Award Winning Design from the 20th Annual Anderson County Arts Center Juried Art Show, Anderson, South Carolina. The Double Handle Carryall Basket was displayed for one year at The Wren House, a *Southern Living Magazine* Showcase Home at the South Carolina Botanical Garden at Clemson University. It was also photographed and appeared in the September 1998 edition of *Southern Living Magazine* and is currently in the permanent collection of The Fran Hanson Discovery Center at Clemson University, Clemson, South Carolina.

Beginner/Intermediate.

Approximate Size: 12" × 12" square (w) × 8" (h); 14" with handles

Materials

- Two 12" × 14" D handles, notched in the center
- ¾" flat reed, dyed and cut as follows for the base: 16 spokes at 36" long; 8 spokes dyed navy, 8 spokes dyed wine
- #2 round reed, Twining, 45'
- ¼" flat reed center weaver overlay, handle wrap, God's Eye; cut 16 overlays at 9"
- ¼" flat oval reed, natural or dyed, handle wrap anchor, 4'
- ½" flat reed dyed navy, Weavers, 5 rows
- ½" flat reed dyed wine, Weavers, 2 rows
- ⅝" flat reed, natural, Weavers, 5 rows
- ⅝" flat oval reed, natural, Rim pieces, 9'
- Seagrass, Rim Filler, 4½'
- Medium cane, Rim Lasher, 20' and 6 long pieces for the braid handle wrap

A Fine Craft Award Winning Basket, the Double Handle Plaid Carryall Basket also appeared in *Southern Living Magazine* and is currently in the permanent collection of the Fran Hanson Discovery Center at Clemson University, Clemson, SC.

Two handles are notched out for 1" to accommodate the intersection of the two. *Photography by Glenn English.*

Place one notched handle inside the other in the Double Handle Plaid Carryall Basket. *Photography by Glenn English.*

Instructions

1. **Base**. Cut 16 spokes at 36" long for the base, as noted in the Materials list, with ¾" dyed flat reed in your choice of 2 contrasting colors. For example: 8 navy spokes and 8 wine spokes. With ¼" natural flat reed, cut 16 overlays at 9" long to be inserted after the basket has 3 rows of weavers.
2. Briefly soak all spokes in warm water; I add white distilled vinegar to my water when using these dark colors. Briefly wet a long weaver of #2 round reed for twining around the base. Remove dyed reed spokes from the water and wipe these through an old towel to remove excess dye. Mark these ¾" spokes in the center with a pencil on their wrong, or rough side. Use a white colored pencil on dark spokes.
3. Place 4 wine spokes horizontally on the table with center marks facing up and spaced approximately 2" apart. Secure the ends of spokes with spoke weights.
4. Place the two notched handles on top of center marks of the original wine spokes. Handles are notched to allow both handles to rest flat. Use a chisel or dremel on the inside of each handle in the center for the same width as the handle, about 1", and notch each approximately ⅛" deep. The ¾" navy spokes are placed on top of the handle horizontally, alternating between the original wine spokes and spaced approximately ⅝" apart. Weave the remaining 8 spokes vertically, four on each side of the handle, alternating navy and wine spokes. Begin with a navy spoke to the right of the handle. Weave over the navy spokes and the handle, and under the wine spokes.

The plaid pattern is evident in this basket base with contrasting wine and navy spokes.

Two "D" handles are notched with a chisel or dremel to allow both handles in the Plaid Carryall Basket to rest flat.

5. On either side of a handle, the closest spokes will be of the same color while the second handle will have the contrasting color.
6. Adjust the base to measure approximately 12" × 12". Be sure to measure spokes that extend beyond the base so all are about 11" to 12" long. Adjust where needed and then place a clothespin at each corner.
7. Begin twining with #2 round reed on the second or third spoke near the corner on the left side of the base. (See chapter 4, Weaving Techniques.) Twine around the base for one row, squaring off at each corner. To secure the ends of round reed, tuck them under the original loop and to the next spoke before trimming to ½" long.
8. **Over and Under Start and Stop Weaving technique.** Re-wet the base from the inside of the basket using a sponge or spray bottle to avoid bleeding of dyed color accent reed. When the spokes are flexible, upsett (bend each spoke upright), and then clothespin the corners together at the ends to help shape the sides of the basket. When spokes are stiffer or thicker, crimp them at the edge of the woven base with needle nose pliers.
9. Rows 1 to 2. Push the spokes up and away from you as you weave with ⅝" flat natural reed for 2 rows. Start Row 1 on the left side of the basket, over or on the outside of the basket opposite the base weave. Place the basket on its side and weave over the wine spokes and under the navy spokes. Place a clothespin at the starting place to hold the weaver in place. Continue alternating over and under each spoke as you weave around the basket. Use additional clothespins to keep the weaver packed close to the base, especially at handles and corners.
10. To end each row, weave past the starting place and create an overlap using the first four spokes. Trim the weaver and tuck it under the fourth spoke to hide the end. Place a clothespin at the overlap, corners and handles, as needed. Pack each row tightly to avoid gaps.

Plaid Pattern

To create the plaid pattern, ½" dyed navy weavers are woven under the vertical spokes of this same color, and over the contrasting wine spokes; while ½" dyed wine weavers are woven over the navy vertical spokes and under the wine vertical spokes. Check the overall shape of the basket after Rows 1 to 3 and adjust as necessary to keep it square. After Row 3, insert short overlays at the navy spokes. Periodically check the corners and handles while weaving the sides of the basket following this plaid pattern.

Weaving Summary

Rows 1–2:--------	⅝" flat reed, natural, 2 rows
Row 3:------------	½" flat reed, dyed navy or color accent #1; insert short overlays
Row 4:------------	⅝" flat reed, natural
Row 5:------------	½" flat reed, dyed navy or color accent #1
Row 6:------------	½" flat reed, dyed wine or color accent #2
Row 7:------------	½" flat reed, dyed navy with ¼" overlay woven together as one
Row 8:------------	½" flat reed, dyed wine or color accent #2
Row 9:------------	½" flat reed, dyed navy or color accent #1
Row 10: ----------	⅝" flat reed, natural
Row 11: ----------	½" flat reed, dyed navy or color accent #1
Row 12: ----------	⅝" flat reed, natural
Rim Row(s)------	#2 round reed, natural, 3 rows, or ⅜" flat reed, 1 row

11. **Rim Preparation**. Twine three Rim Rows with #2 round reed to aid in shaping the rim opening; or weave one Rim Row with ⅜" flat reed. Pack all rows of weavers for the final time. Re-wet the ends of the spokes. When flexible, carefully bend spokes to the inside of the basket. Cut the spoke ends on a diagonal or to a blunt point. Then tuck each spoke, or every other spoke, under the top row(s) of weavers. Trim the ¼" overlay spokes also.
12. **Rim**. Measure and cut two rim pieces from ⅝" flat oval reed. Soak these along with the Rim Lasher. Use clothespins to temporarily secure the flat oval rims to the basket. Distribute the overlaps, insert the seagrass Rim Filler and adjust clothespins or clamps as needed. Add cable ties to secure all rim pieces.
13. Lash with medium chair cane or narrow flat reed. Tuck the end of the lasher up under the inside rim at or near the handle. Be sure the right, shiny side of the lasher is facing out. Lash around the basket on a diagonal to the right. Pull the lasher tight to keep rim pieces together and use clothespins or clamps to hold the tension.
    When the lasher reaches the starting place, finish by tucking the end of the lasher under the inside basket rim at your starting place.

Flat oval reed, shaved on the oval side, allows a neat overlap at the outer rim of the Double Handle Plaid Carryall Basket.

14. Choose to reverse the lasher and Double Lash to the left to create an X as the rim border. End the lasher at the starting place. (Refer to chapter 5, Rim Borders, for additional instruction.)
15. Check the overall shape of your basket and adjust where necessary.
16. Allow your finished basket to completely air dry; turn the basket upside down with the base side up.
17. **Stain**. Finish the basket with a natural walnut hull stain or dye. (Refer to the recipe in chapter 2.) Or, spray the finished basket with a commercially available stain. This process gives the basket an aged appearance and enhances its beauty.
18. **Personalize** the woven base with a wood burning pen or a permanent fine line marker for future reference. Sign your name or initials, the date or the year the basket was made, and the number assigned from your list of completed baskets. (Refer to chapter 6, Finishing Touches.)

Triple Braid Handle Wrap

Double Handles are wrapped with medium cane in the Triple Braid Wrap technique described in chapter 6, Handle Wrap techniques.

Start the Triple Braid Handle Wrap technique with 3 lengths of cane. Create an X with each cane then wrap above it with the handle wrapper to secure it to the handle.

The Triple Braid Handle Wrap adds a finishing touch to this Double Handle Plaid Carryall Basket.

God's Eye

For a decorative finish, a long piece of ¼" flat reed is woven into a God's Eye, added on top of the intersection of the two handles.

Briefly wet the long ¼" flat reed. Place the wrong side of the reed under the handles on a diagonal. Wrap the smooth side over on top of the handle at the left of the handle intersection. Come down over the top of the intersection of the two handles on a diagonal to the right below. Then bring the reed under the handle from the right side of the handle under to the left side. Finish the X by bringing the ¼" reed on top of the handles over the intersection on a diagonal, to the right and back down to the starting point.

Continue wrapping in this way, moving the handles clockwise ¼ turn after each wrap, over and under the handle. Keep the wrong side of the ¼" flat reed touching the under side of the handle, while the smooth side of the ¼" reed overlaps the edges of the previous row slightly. Each wrap lays on top of the preceding one on the top or right side of the basket handles. Work 6 wraps toward the outside of the God's Eye to reach the desired size. Count the number of wraps under the handle. To end the God's Eye, tuck the reed under the last wrap at the starting place, under the handles, and trim it to ½" long.

This God's Eye at the intersection of two handles was inspired by a Nancy Gruber round basket design with long handle spokes generating from the base at the start of the basket[1] rather than the "D" handles found in this basket design.

Double handles are joined with a woven God's Eye. Tuck the ¼" flat reed under the handle wrap at the intersection of the two handles.

The God's Eye is a decorative finish that must be completed with a sequence of steps. The ¼" reed comes from under the handle, wrap from the top left down on a diagonal to the bottom right of the intersection.

The ¼" reed moves from the bottom right corner under the handle to the bottom left corner and wraps on a diagonal to the right to complete an X on the top of the handle.

Continue the ¼" reed from the top right corner down under the handle to the bottom right corner.

The beginning of the second X of the God's Eye.

The God's Eye continues to build from the inside, wrapping around to the outer edge.

There are two complete wraps on the God's Eye. You can also count the number of wraps on the inside of the design.

The ¼" reed is back at its starting place. Repeat for a total of 6 or 8 wraps to complete the God's Eye.

The God's Eye design joins the two handles for a decorative handle grip.

COZY WINE CRADLE

Inspired by an antique basket, the Cozy Wine Cradle earned a 3rd Place ribbon at the North Carolina Basket Association Convention, NCBA, 2013 Exhibit in the Professional Flat Reed Category.

Intermediate Twill Weave design.

Approximate Size: 4" to 6" (w) × 11" to 12"(l) × 4½" to 6" (h), 11" with handle

Materials

- 3" × 10" slotted racetrack wood base, pre-finished with stain and urethane
- 6" round notched add-in handle, ears tapered and sanded
- ½" flat reed, cut 32 base spokes 10" long
- #1 or #2 round reed, Chase weave base, Rim Rows
- ¼" flat oval reed, Weavers
- #2, #2.5, or #3 round reed, dyed & natural, 3-Rod Wale Spiral, 8 rows; and Triple 3-Rod Wale before the rim
- ⅜" flat reed, Rim Row option
- ½" flat oval reed, Rim
- Seagrass, Rim Filler
- Medium cane, Rim Lasher and handle braid wrap
- 3⁄16", ¼", or 7 mm flat reed, natural, handle wrapper
- ½" flat reed, natural or dyed, handle anchor

With a racetrack wood base, the Cozy Wine Cradle displays your favorite bottle. With its unique shape, it also serves as a fruit basket or baby doll cradle. The Twill Weave technique, Outside Spiral, and Triple Three Rod Wale add texture and color to the basket.

Instructions

1. **Base**. Pre-finish the racetrack wood base; sand and stain the wood then allow it to dry. Apply three coats of urethane allowing each to dry completely between coats. See chapter 3.
2. With ½" natural flat reed, cut base spokes as indicated in the Materials list: 32 spokes at 10" long. The number of spokes is divisible by 3 minus 1 for the outside spiral design. So, in this case, the number 33 is divisible by 3; 3 minus 1 equals 32.
3. Divide the wood base into four quadrants or quarters. With a pencil, mark the quadrants' centers near the edge of the base to assist inserting spokes with equal distance between each spoke within each quadrant. From paper, cut a template the same size as the wood base. Fold the template in half, then fold it in half once again. Next place the open template on the wood base and mark the four quadrants. You may also do this by approximating if you choose.
   Check the slotted grooved opening before inserting spokes into the base. If the groove is narrow and the spokes fit tight, do not wet them. If the groove is wider and your spokes move about and are loose, wet the spokes briefly. When water is absorbed, it will temporarily enlarge the spokes, helping them to stay in place. If these steps do not solve the movement issue, apply a small amount of fast-drying gel glue before inserting the end of the spoke into the groove.
   Insert base spokes rough side facing up. Check the spacing, creating an equal distance between each spoke, approximately ¼". Push all spokes firmly into the slot or groove. When finished, count the total number of spokes to be sure the accurate number are in place. (Refer to chapter 3 for additional instructions.)
4. **Chase Weave.** Begin with the first weaver in #1 or #2 round reed on the long side of the base and as close to the side of the wood base as possible. Wet, crimp and bend the end of the round reed **Weaver #1** and insert into the slotted groove in the base between 2 spokes. This eliminates seeing the end. Weave over, then under, and continue weaving until reaching the next mark. Add remaining base spokes if you have not done so; check spacing between spokes. Push spokes into the base and use a small tool to push the weaver in close to the wood base. Chase Weave with **Weaver #2**. Insert the end into the slotted wood base in the space before, to the left of, round reed Weaver #1. Weave over and under, opposite Weaver #1, around the base until you are 2 spokes away from the first weaver. Alternate to round reed Weaver #1 and continue

This 3" × 10" racetrack wood base has a template folded in half and in half again to mark the centers for spoke placement.

Chase Weave with round reed to secure base spokes. Crimp and tuck the end of the round reed Weaver #1 into the slot/groove on the side of the base. Weave over 1 spoke, under 1 spoke around the base. Insert round reed Weaver #2 in front of/to the left of Weaver #1.

Weaver #2 chases Weaver #1 opposite the over and under sequence.

Continuous Twill Weave, over 2 spokes, under 1 spoke, beginning with a tapered weaver.

to weave over and under around the base to just before Weaver #2. **Chase Weave** for a total of **2 or more rows**. Tuck the ends of the round reed weavers under the previous row of Chase Weave at the starting place, and trim them to end.

5. Spray the spokes and avoid getting the wood base wet. Wipe wood dry if it becomes wet. Gently bend the spokes to upsett. Clothespin the ends of 4 or more spokes in several places to help shape the sidewalls of the basket.
6. **Continuous Twill Weave** in an Over 2, Under 1 Twill Weave for **6 Rows.**

   Rows 1 to 6. Wet ¼" flat oval natural reed. Begin by tapering the weaver for 4" to 6" before weaving Row #1 of the basket. Start with the tapered end under the 3rd spoke from the left on the long side of the base. Weave over 2 spokes and under 1 spoke around the basket. Keep the weaver packed and use clothespins to assist in the Continuous Weave technique. This Twill Weave will move up and over one spoke to the right (or left) with each row. Check the weaver as it splits the pair of over 2 spokes on the previous row; continue weaving over 2, under 1. Add in a new weaver as needed with a 3 or 4 spoke overlap, shave one oval end for 2" for ease in packing weavers. Look for the diagonal design as you weave a total of **6 Rows** with ¼" flat oval reed; adjust spokes so they are upright and vertical. Avoid pulling in too tightly at rounded corners. Pack rows of Continuous Twill Weave before the next step and use clothespins to control the tension. Check the handle fit periodically for an accurate rim opening later. Re-wet spoke ends and determine the front of the basket to be on a short side of the base. Begin to push down and out to flare the spokes on this one end of the basket to hold the wine bottle or other contents.
7. **Rows 7 to 14: Three Rod Wale Outside Spiral.** Briefly wet #2, #2.5, or #3 round reed; begin near the left side of the basket with 3 pieces of round reed, two dyed accent colors and 1 natural. Where the flat oval tapered weaver ends, mark the Starting Spoke with a pencil, snip the end to a point, add a wire twist tie, or cable tie to note for future reference. Wipe dyed reed weavers 3 times through an old towel or paper towel to remove excess dye.

   Weaver #1, natural, on the far left side begins under the Starting Spoke, vertical spoke #1. Weave over 2 spokes to the right, spokes #2 and #3, then under 1 spoke, the 4th spoke, and continue out to the front of the basket.

   Weaver #2, navy is now the left-most weaver, weave over 2 spokes, under 1 spoke, and bring the weaver out to the front.

Weaver #3, wine is on the left. Weave over 2, under 1, and out to the front. Continue alternating weavers in this way around the basket. As a Continuous Weave, pack each row while it is woven, and adjust the shape as needed. Count the number of rows on the natural weaver diagonal. Continue to push down on spokes to flare out one end of the Cozy Wine Cradle. Weave with your left hand on the inside of the basket to help flare. After weaving **8 rows** of this Outside Spiral, upon reaching the 6th spoke past the Starting Spoke, step-up to end these weavers and complete the pattern. To step-up, stop the Three Rod Wale at the spoke to the left of the 6th spoke. Weave with the right-most round reed weaver, which will be woven over 2, under 1, then trim and place the weaver inside the basket. Continue with the next weaver on the right, over 2, under 1 and bring to the inside of the basket. Finish with the remaining round reed weaver. Trim and bring ends to the inside. Crimp each end and tuck under Three Rod Wale. Or tuck under the previous rows. A third way to end the round reed weavers is to trim behind the next spoke to end.

8. Return to **Continuous Over 2, Under 1 Twill Weave** with ¼" natural flat oval reed for **5 Rows**. See Step 6 for details.
9. **Handle.** Pre-sand, thin down, and round the ends/ears before you insert the 6" round-top notched handle. At the center spokes on opposite sides of the long sides of the basket, carefully push a long, flat weaving tool or an awl to open a space for the handle. Next, insert both handle ends down along the center spoke under several rows of weaving on the inside of the basket.
10. **Increasing and Decreasing Twill Weave** in the Start and Stop technique. On one of the rounded curved short sides of the basket, fold, crimp, and hairpin the flat oval **Weaver #1** around the spoke **to the left of the center spoke** on this short, flared side of the basket. Weave over 2, under 1, and continue until nearly reaching the center spoke on the opposite side of the basket. Trim and taper the weaver, then place the end inside behind the last spoke before the curve of the base begins on this opposite side.
11. Repeat on the opposite side of the center spoke to increase the second side of the basket. Continue to weave Start and Stop rows of the Increasing and Decreasing Twill. Begin **Weaver #2 on** the same spoke as Weaver #1. Fold, hairpin or loop around as before. You may need to adjust the weaver to go over 3 spokes at this hairpin, or over 1 under 1 then over 2 under 1, to keep the remainder of the twill weave accurate.

The Outside Spiral technique in this Cozy Wine Cradle is a Continuous Three Rod Wale with a Step-up at the end of the last row.

A round-top notched add-in handle is pre-sanded then inserted at the center spokes of the Cozy Wine Cradle. Use a long handle flat tool to make room for the handle ears.

The Increasing/Decreasing technique is a Start and Stop weave with short pieces of flat oval reed, tapered at one end. Crimp and turnback to weave over 2 spokes, under 1 spoke twill pattern.

There are four rows of the Increasing/Decreasing Twill technique; one more row is needed to complete the pattern.

Start Triple Three Rod Wale with three triple weavers. Weave over two spokes and under one spoke.

Triple Three Rod Wale adds a decorative three-dimensional accent near the rim of the Cozy Wine Cradle.

12. **Rows 3 to 5.** begin the weaver one spoke away each time and taper the weaver to end behind one spoke sooner each row. Pack each of these Start and Stop rows. By Row 5 of this technique, the Wine Cradle has an up and down uneven rim opening as well as the outward flare. This allows the bottle of wine to be stored in a horizontal position on its side. The rim opening is suitable for flower gathering, fruit storage, as well as cradle a baby doll.
13. **Triple Three Rod Wale** for **1 row**. (See chapter 4, Weaving Techniques.) This technique uses three weavers of round reed, one weaver of each color and one natural, together as one triple weaver, thus Triple Three Rod Wale. Three weavers are needed, for a total of nine short pieces. Begin on the left side of the basket at the Starting Spoke with the left-most weaver, over 2 spokes, under 1 spoke. Continue alternating round reed weavers in this way around the basket, following the up and down of the rim opening. Stop one spoke before reaching the Starting Spoke and end with a Step-up.

Weaving Summary

Rows 1–6:-------- Over 2, Under 1 Continuous Twill Weave, 6 Rows
Rows 7–14: ------ Three Rod Wale Outside Spiral, 8 Rows
Rows 15–19:----- Over 2, Under 1, Continuous Twill Weave, 5 Rows
Rows 20–24:----- Over 2, Under 1 Twill Increasing and Decreasing, 5 Rows
Row 25: ---------- Triple Three Rod Wale, 1 Row before the rim row
Rim Row(s)

14. **Rim Preparation**. Twine three Rim Rows with #2 round reed to aid in shaping the rim opening. Pack all rows of weavers for the final time. Re-wet the spoke ends. When flexible, carefully bend spokes to the inside of the basket. Cut the spoke ends on a diagonal or to a blunt point. Then tuck each spoke, or every other spoke, under the top row(s) of weavers. (Refer to chapter 5 as needed.)
15. **Rim**. Measure and cut two rim pieces from ½" flat oval reed. Soak these along with the Rim Lasher and round reed Rim Filler. Or include seagrass as the Rim Filler, which does not get wet. Use clothespins to temporarily secure the flat oval rims to the basket. Distribute the overlaps, insert the Rim Filler and adjust clothespins or clamps as needed. Add cable ties to secure rim pieces.
16. **Lash** with medium chair cane or narrow flat reed. Tuck the end of the lasher up under the inside rim at or near the handle. Be sure the right, shiny side of the lasher is facing out. Lash around the basket on a diagonal to the right. Pull the lasher tight to keep rim pieces together and use clothespins or clamps to hold the tension.
    When the lasher reaches the starting place, finish by tucking the end of the lasher under the inside basket rim at your starting place. (Refer to chapter 5, Rim Borders.)
17. Choose to reverse the lasher and Double Lash to the left to create an X as the rim border. Create a Double X, at each handle; weave over or under and alternate the cane from the first X. Where the cane is under in the beginning X, create the second X by weaving over the original cane. End the lasher at the starting place.
18. Check the overall shape of your basket and adjust where necessary.
19. The **Handle Wrap** on this basket is a Double Braid technique. This wrap adds a decorative finish that fits comfortably in your hand. See chapter 6, Handles and Wraps, for instructions.
20. Allow your finished basket to completely air dry; turn the basket upside down with the base side up.
21. **Stain**. Finish the basket with a natural walnut hull stain or dye. (Refer to the recipe in chapter 2.) Or, spray the finished basket with a commercially available stain. This process gives the basket an aged appearance and enhances its beauty.
22. **Personalize** the wood base with a wood burning pen or a permanent fine line marker for future reference. Sign your name or initials, the date or the year the basket was made, and the number assigned from your list of completed baskets. (Refer to chapter 6, Finishing Touches.)

When lashing the rim, weave a second X at the handle in the opposite over/under sequence for a Double X also known as a Double Cross.

CHASING DIAMONDS

An Award Winning Pattern, this basket earned a 1st Place Ribbon at the North Carolina Basket Association, NCBA, 2003 Exhibit in the Professional Flat Reed Category.

The Chasing Diamonds Basket was inspired by a Native American diamond design. The diamond is also prevalent in baskets woven by women of the Zulu tribe in Africa.

Woven in two contrasting colors of your choice, with a twill base in paired spokes, the twill zigzags around the basket without a pattern break; the twill continues uninterrupted and the zigzags match up. Waxed linen lasher finishes the border.

Intermediate Twill design.

Approximate Size: 10" Square Base × 10" (h), 12" including wooden feet, with a rim opening of 16"

Materials

- Wooden feet, dyed or painted black
- ¼" or 7 mm flat reed, dyed black, 2 Weavers, and cut as follows for the base: 72 spokes at 36" long
- Black waxed linen for Base Twine, 10', and Rim Lasher, approximately 18'
- ¼" flat reed, dyed wine, Weavers, 250'
- ⅜" flat oval reed, dyed black, Rim, 10'
- Optional: ⅜" half round reed, dyed black, Outside Rim, 5'
  #6 round reed, dyed black, Rim Filler, 5'

Chasing Diamonds has a different design on each side of the basket. Double diamonds are woven in a continuous twill pattern.

The Chasing Diamonds Basket has 72 base spokes.

Start the twill base at the bottom left corner with a four-spoke repeat pattern at the beginning of the vertical spokes: Row 1 is over 4 spokes to start. Row 2 is over 2 spokes to start. Row 3 is under 4 spokes and Row 4 is under 2 spokes. Repeat until all 36 spokes are in place.

Instructions

1. **Base**. With ¼" or 7 mm flat reed, cut 72 base spokes at 36" long, in black dyed accent color or the color of your choice. Wet these spokes briefly or spray them to dampen and wipe them gently with a paper towel or an old terrycloth towel to remove any excess dye.
2. Place 36 spokes horizontally on the table, rough sides facing up, and anchor them with spoke weight(s). Put a pencil mark at 13 inches from each end of the spokes to mark where the twill base will begin and end. A white pencil will better show the center marks on darker dyed reed.
3. The **Over 4 Under 4 Twill Base Weaving technique**, also known as an Over 2, Under 2 Twill with paired spokes, will be used. Paired spokes are two spokes put together and treated as one. Beginning at the left pencil mark, weave vertical spokes as paired spokes;

   Begin **Spoke #1** (pair of spokes 1 and 2) by weaving over 4 spokes, or over 2 pair, and under 4 spokes, or under 2 pair, continuing to the opposite side of the horizontal spokes. Pull the paired spoke beyond the base to match up the center marks.

   Spoke #2 (spokes 3 and 4) are woven over 2 spokes or 1 pair, then under 4 spokes, or 2 pair, over and under 4, ending under 2 spokes or 1 pair. This is the first indication of the twill design.

   Spoke #3 (spokes 5 and 6) will begin under 4 spokes or 2 pair, over 4, under 4, through the base and end on the opposite side under 4 spokes or 2 pairs.

   Spoke #4 (spokes 7 and 8) is woven under 2 spokes or 1 pair, over 4 spokes or 2 pair, under and over; to the opposite side. End over 2 spokes or 1 pair.

   Follow this pattern of weaving paired spokes carefully. Repeat the pattern as above until all 18 pairs or 36 vertical spokes are woven. Count the number of spokes to avoid spokes overlapping and hiding under the adjacent reed.
4. Pack each row, horizontally and vertically, as you weave, it is difficult to pack later.
5. The finished base measures approximately 9 ½" × 9 ½" square, depending on the size reed used for base spokes. Make any necessary adjustments and place a clothespin at each corner to hold the measurements accurate.
6. Fold a long piece of black waxed linen or a matching color in half. Use this as your twine material instead of round reed due to the tightly woven base. Twine over 2 spokes or 1 pair, under 2 spokes or 1 pair and continue weaving around the base. At the starting place, tuck the ends under the original loop and trim to end.

Side #1 of the Chasing Diamonds design has one center diamond in the pattern.

Side #4 of Chasing Diamonds has continuous lightning bolts or zigzag lines in an over 3, under 3 twill pattern.

7. Re-wet all spokes until they are flexible. Upsett the spokes to create the sides and clothespin four to six spokes together at each corner to assist in shaping the sidewalls of the basket.
8. Briefly wet or spray to dampen several long weavers of ¼" flat reed, dyed wine, or the color of your choice. Wipe each piece of reed gently with a towel to remove any excess dye. Wrap these weavers in a towel until you are ready to use them. This will keep the reed damp and colors from bleeding when weaving.
9. **Over 3 Under 3 Twill Weave technique.** Begin this weaving pattern at the left side of the base. Chasing Diamonds uses an over 3 spokes, under 3 spokes Twill Weave except for the diamond design. The twill zigzags around the square basket without a pattern break. You will follow the graphs on pages 91 to 94. **In the graphs, the darker color squares are weavers that are woven over the spokes while the white squares are weavers that are woven under the spokes** to create the design.

   Use a ruler to indicate your place on the graph and move it up the graph, one row at a time, as you weave around the basket.
10. At **Row 1**, mark the 5 center spokes on 2 opposite sides of the basket. There is an even number of spokes, 36, on each side. To find the 5 center spokes, count from the left corner to the right; choose spokes #17 to #21, with spoke #19 as the center spoke. This is the location of the Diamond design. With a dyed weaver, **begin Row 1 under the center spoke on any side of the basket.** This becomes Side #1 with one woven Diamond in the design. Weave under 1 spoke, the center spoke, over 3 spokes, under 3 spokes, over 3 spokes, under 3, over 3, under 2 spokes and turn the corner including the first spoke on this second side of the basket, in this group to be under 3. This is Side #2 with lightning bolts or zigzag lines. Continue over 3, under 3 to the corner. Weave under 2 spokes, turn the corner and include the first spoke to make this a group of 3 spokes. Weaving on the third side of the basket, Side #3, continues over 3, under 3, over 3, until reaching the 5 center spokes. At this point, you will weave under the 5 center spokes. Then continue weaving over 3, under 3, to the corner. To complete Row 1, weave over 3, under 3, over 3 on Side #4 and continue around to the center spoke on Side #1. Overlap seven spokes, then trim to end.

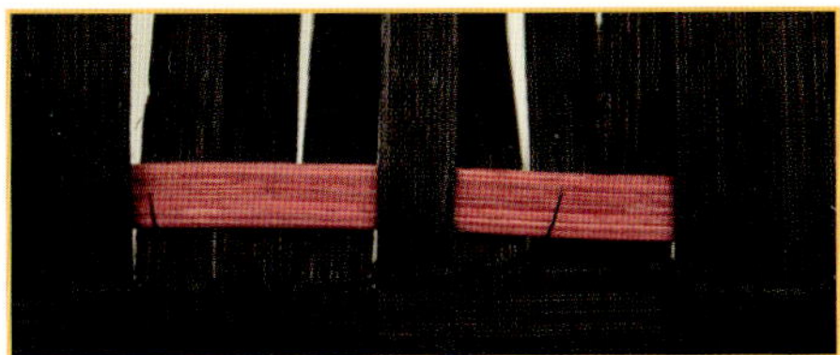

Row 1, Side #1, Chasing Diamonds. Determine the center spoke; this weaver is over 3, under 3 except at the center spoke. To begin the design, weave under one center spoke and continue over 3, under 3 around the basket.

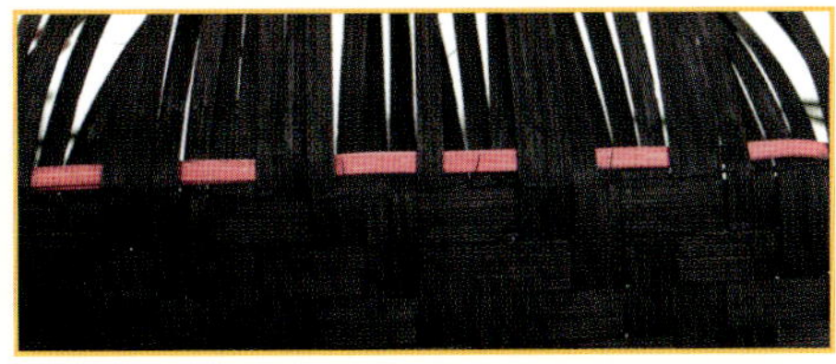

Row 1, Side #1, Chasing Diamonds is an over 3 spokes, under 3 spokes twill pattern with a change at the center spoke.

Row 2, Side #1, Chasing Diamonds is over 5, under 3 spokes, and continues over 3 to the opposite side of the basket.

Row 2, Side #1, Chasing Diamonds is over 3, under 3 until you reach the center spokes.

Row 2, Side #1, Chasing Diamonds is over 3, under 3 before and after the center spokes.

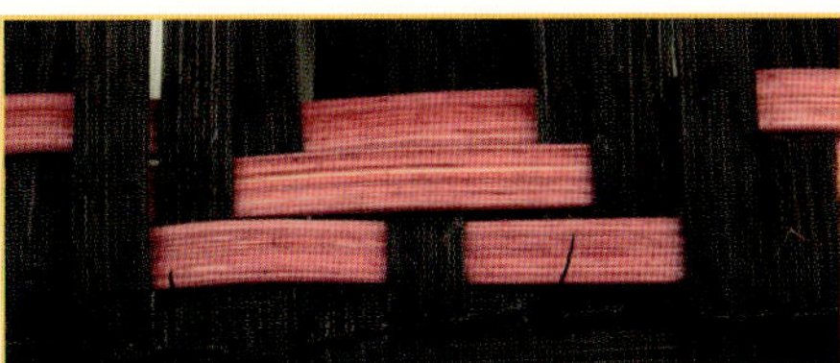

Row 3, Side #1, Chasing Diamonds is over the three center spokes.

Row 3, Side #1, Chasing Diamonds is over 3, under 3, over the 3 center spokes and continues around to the opposite side.

Row 4, Side #1, Chasing Diamonds is over 3, under 3, over 1 center spoke, and continues, over 3, under 3.

Row 4, Side #1, the Chasing Diamonds pattern is beginning to emerge.

Row 5, Side #1, Chasing Diamonds.

Row 7, Side #1, Chasing Diamonds is under 1 center spoke, the same as Row 1.

Side #2, Chasing Diamonds is always over 3 spokes and under 3 spokes on this side.

On Side #3, Chasing Diamonds, the beginning of the Double Diamond design, is evident in the first six rows.

Side #4, Chasing Diamonds is always over 3 spokes, under 3 spokes, as is Side #2. These two opposite sides are opposite in direction, moving to the left or to the right.

On the corners of the Chasing Diamonds Basket, you can see there is no pattern break. The lightning bolt zigzag lines continue in their pattern with no interruption or change.

11. After completing **Rows 5 to 7**, check the overall shape of the basket.
12. **Wooden Feet**. Insert the four wooden feet, one at each corner spoke. Follow the woven pattern and use a long weaving tool or a flat screwdriver to open the space. Insert the foot. The corner spoke and the wooden foot become one spoke; clothespin these together or use a cable or twist tie wire to secure them.
13. Check for a square shape and continually pack each row while weaving. Use clothespins to keep your rows packed. Follow the graphs and as the pattern develops, you will anticipate the next row in this twill basket.
14. At **Row 24**, re-wet the ends of the spokes and push all of the spokes outward to flare. Turn the basket, base side up, with spoke ends resting on the table. Gently push down on the base to accentuate the flared shape at the top third of this basket to achieve this traditional Native American inspired design.
15. Follow the graphs to complete a total of 35 rows with wine weavers.
16. Finish with the final 3 rows of weavers in black reed, weaving over 3 spokes and under 3 spokes. The third black weaver is the Rim Row and will be covered with the rim in the next step.
17. **Rim.** After completing the Rim Row in black reed in the over 3, under 3 twill weave, re-wet the ends of all the spokes until they are flexible. Tuck spokes to the inside of the basket following the woven pattern. Tuck one or more of each set of three spokes when possible. Trim the remaining spokes even with the top rim of the basket.
18. Measure the inside and the outside rim openings, adding 2" to each measurement for the overlap in the rim. With ⅜" flat oval reed dyed black, cut the inside rim. With ⅜" flat oval or half round reed dyed black, cut the outside rim. Then soak these briefly, along with #6 round reed dyed black rim filler, in warm water until they are flexible. Wipe the dyed reed rim pieces gently with a towel to remove any excess dye.
19. Clothespin the ⅜" flat oval inner rim to the rim of the basket. Apply the outer rim and adjust the clothespins.
20. Add #6 round reed rim filler, dyed black, between the two rims ending with a 1" overlap. Scarf the round reed rim filler ends to meet at an angle. Adjust clothespins once again or use cable ties to hold rim pieces snug.
21. **Waxed Linen Lashing.** This thread is the lashing material best used when there are many spoke ends and spokes are very close together. Lash with a tapestry needle or curved needle and 4-ply or 7-ply waxed linen. Measure a long lasher approximately five times the distance around the rim of the basket. To begin, tie one end of the waxed linen around a vertical spoke below the Rim Row, the last black weaver. Leave a 5" tail, bring the waxed linen lasher from the inside around to the front of the basket, moving to the right 2 spokes or 1 pair each time.

    Lash with waxed linen in one direction around the entire rim of the basket. Pull tight to keep the rim snug and cut cable ties out of the way. At the starting place, end the waxed linen lasher by tying it to the beginning end of the lasher, trim and tuck the ends under the inside rim.
22. While Chasing Diamonds is still damp, check the finished square-to-round shape of this basket. Make adjustments as needed to be sure the basket rests level on the four wooden feet.
23. Trim any hairy ends for a neat finish. Do not pull on a stray fiber as the black or other dark dye colors do not penetrate completely through the reed. If so, you will have a white or natural line on your reed. When this occurs, use a permanent marker to match the dye and color in the affected reed.

    This finished basket does not need any additional stain as the basket is woven completely in dyed reed with good contrast. Allow the basket to air dry.
24. **Personalize** the woven base with a wood burning pen or a permanent fine line marker for future reference. Sign your name or initials, the date or the year the basket was made, and the number assigned from your list of completed baskets. (Refer to chapter 6, Finishing Touches.)

Chasing Diamonds Pattern
Side 1

Chasing Diamonds Pattern
Side 2

Chasing Diamonds Pattern
Side 3

Chasing Diamonds Pattern
Side 4

DIAMONDS ALL AROUND

Diamonds All Around earned an Honorable Mention and $250 Award in the 2009 North Charleston Cultural Arts Exhibition, as well as 3rd Place at the North Carolina Basket Association Convention, NCBA, 2008 Exhibit in the Professional Flat Oval Reed Category.

It was also on loan for the year 2009 to the South Carolina State Museum Palmetto Hands Traveling Art Exhibit.

The Cherokee diamond design is a continuous diamond pattern resting between mountain peaks or arrows. There is no pattern break, the design is uninterrupted; it continues around the basket matching all lines. This is a shape often used in Cherokee basketry patterns.

Intermediate/Advanced Twill design.

Approximate Size: 8½" Square Base × 10" (h)

Materials

- $\frac{3}{16}$" flat reed, dyed red and cut as follows for the base spokes: 75 spokes at 34" long
- $\frac{11}{64}$" flat reed, natural or walnut, 110', dyed red, Weavers, 150'
- 7 mm flat oval reed, dyed red, Rim,10'
- #4 round reed, dyed red, Rim Filler, 5'
- Red waxed linen, Base Twining, 12', and Rim Lasher, approximately 21'
- Tapestry needle

Diamonds All Around begins with a 75-spoke twill base that continues up the sides of the basket creating the diamond pattern with a Start and Stop weave.

Begin the twill base in Diamonds All Around at the bottom left corner. Weave over 3 spokes and under 3 spokes.

There are 75 base spokes in the Diamonds All Around pattern.

Instructions

1. **Base**. With 3⁄16" flat reed, cut 75 spokes at 34" long in dyed accent red reed or the color of your choice. If you are weaving with natural spokes, soak them briefly before you begin. With dyed spokes as pictured here, wet briefly, just in and out of the water, or spray the dyed spokes to dampen. They should not be soaked long. Wipe all dyed reed gently with a towel or paper towel.
2. With spoke weights, anchor 37 spokes horizontally on the work surface with the rough (wrong) side of the reed facing up. Make a small pencil mark at 13" from the end of each spoke to indicate the perimeter of the twill base. Use a white pencil when weaving with darker dyed reed.
3. The **Over 3 Under 3 Twill Base technique** has a six-spoke repeat in the vertical spokes pattern; after weaving the first six vertical spokes, you will go back to Spoke #1 and repeat the same sequence through to Spoke #6.

   Spoke #1: At the left pencil mark, on the first vertical spoke, weave over 3 spokes, under 3 spokes, over 3, and under 3 through all horizontal spokes. End under the last horizontal spoke. Now, at this opposite side of the horizontal spokes, pull the first vertical spoke until the center marks line up with approximately 12" to 13" beyond the base.

   Spoke #2: weave over 2 spokes, under 3 spokes, over 3, and under 3. Continue this weave and end with over 2 spokes.

   Spoke #3: weave over 1 spoke, under 3 spokes, over 3, and under 3. Continue in this way, then end with over 3 spokes.

   Spoke #4: weave under 3 spokes, over 3 spokes, under 3, and over 3. Continue and end under 1 spoke.

   Spoke #5: weave under 2 spokes, over 3 spokes, under 3, and over 3. Continue and end under 2 spokes.

   Spoke #6: weave under 1 spoke, over 3 spokes, under 3, and over 3. Continue and end under 3 spokes.

   Spokes #7 to #38: Repeat the pattern described in Spokes #1 to #6. When you begin a new vertical spoke, the weave changes to create the diagonal: Spoke #1 starts over 3, then Spoke #2 starts over 2, next, Spoke #3 is over 1. Continue with Spoke #4 start under 3, Spoke #5 starts under 2, Spoke #6 starts under 1, and repeat.
4. Keep the horizontal spokes close together while weaving the vertical spokes. Continue to pack each spoke as it is woven in place to avoid shifting later. Pack horizontally and vertically.
5. Adjust the twill base to measure 10" × 10" square. Adjust spokes as needed; then place a small clip or clothespin at each corner to keep the base measurements accurate.

6. With approximately three yards of red waxed linen, or thread color of your choice, you are ready to begin twining around the base spokes. Rather than twining over 1 spoke, under 1 spoke as is customary, twine over 2 spokes, and then under 2 spokes around the base. This keeps spokes close to touching while securing the many base spokes. At the starting loop, tuck the ends of the waxed linen or tie it off to end.
7. Spray to re-wet the spokes 2" beyond the woven base. Crimp all spokes at the waxed linen twining and bend them up into an upright position. Flexible spokes will bend over your thumb easily for the upsett of the sidewalls.
8. With dyed 11/64" flat reed in the same color as the base spokes, begin weaving at the left corner of the basket. Look at the base weaving on the left side and begin where the last horizontal spoke is in an over 2, spoke position. This allows you to continue the Twill Weave pattern correctly. Begin weaving with over 3 spokes.

The twill weave continues from the base weave pattern and transitions up the sides of the Diamonds All Around Basket.

Diamonds All Around Weaving Pattern

9. **Over and Under Start and Stop Twill Weaving technique:**

Row 1: *weave over 3 spokes, under 3 spokes the entire row; end with a six spoke overlap. In this Start and Stop technique, avoid a thick build-up where the spokes overlap by giving the basket a one quarter turn clockwise before the start of each new row.*

Rows 2 through 5: *weave over 3 spokes, under 3 spokes.* **Be sure to begin each new weaver by moving one spoke to the right to create the diagonal twill weave** *that resembles stair steps.*

Rows 6 to 38: *These rows create the diamond shapes that connect and continually chase around the four sides of the basket, and the Twill Weave will vary from the over 3 spokes, under 3 spokes to keep the twill continuous and without a pattern break. To achieve this, at each corner beginning at Row 6, include one extra spoke in the over 3, making it over 4 spokes. From this row on, the last 2 spokes of the over 4 pattern will be counted as one spoke and will be treated this way to keep the pattern going as an over 3.*

Row 6: *Begin on the 38 spoke side of the base and be sure the weaver passes under 1 spoke at the* center *spoke to begin the first diamond shape. Then weave over 3, under 5, over 3, and begin the repeat with under 1. Just before the first corner, the pattern changes as described above. Weave over 4 spokes (where the last 2 spokes of this over 4 are treated as one spoke for future rows). The 11/64" weaver continues around the corner with an under 6 making the last 2 spokes of this under 6 become 1 spoke. It will be treated as 1 from this point on. This* **pattern change at the first corner and third corner** *keeps the pattern going. Be sure to keep these 2 spokes as 1 before and after the corner. Just before the opposite two corners, weave over 4 spokes (where the last 2 spokes of this over 4 are treated as one spoke for future rows). This pattern change only occurs before the corner. Attach a twist tie wire as a reminder for future rows. At the remaining two opposite corners, the pattern change only occurs on one side of the corner, include two spokes as one before turning the corner, however after the corner, do not include two spokes as one. This changes the number of spoke ends for the pattern to continue the rest of the basket.*

Row 7: *The weaver moves one spoke to the right and continues the pattern with over 3 spokes and under 3 spokes for one row.*

Use a ruler below to mark the row you are weaving. Move the ruler as you progress. The weaving pattern for Rows 8 through 38 is as follows:

Row 8: *over 3, under 1, over 3, under 5, and repeat.*

Row 9: *over 5, under 3, over 1, under 3, and repeat over 5…*

Row 10: *over 3, under 3, over 3, under 3…*

Row 11: *under 3, over 5, under 3, over 1, and repeat under 3…*

Row 12: *over 3, under 1, over 3, under 5, and repeat over 3…*

Row 13: *under 3, over 3, under 3, over 3…*

Row 14: *over 3, under 1, over 3, under 5, and repeat over 3…*

Row 15: *under 3, over 5, under 3, over 1, and repeat under 3…*

Row 16: *over 3, under 3, over 3, under 3…*

Row 17: *under 3, over 1, under 3, over 5, and repeat under 3…same as Row 15*

Row 18: *over 3, under 1, over 3, under 5, and repeat over 3…same as Row 14*

Row 19: *under 3, over 3, under 3, over 3…same as Row 13*

Row 20: *over 3, under 1 center spoke, over 3, under 5, repeat, same as Row 12*

Row 21: *under 3, over 5, under 3, over 1, repeat under 3…same as row 11*

Row 22: *over 3, under 3, over 3, under 3…same as Row 10*

Row 23: *under 3, over 1, under 3, over 5, repeat, same as Row 17*

Row 24: *over 3, under 1, over 3, under 5, repeat, same as Row 20*

Row 25: *under 3, over 3, under 3, over 3, same as Row 12*

Row 26: *over 3, under 1, over 3, under 5, same as Row 14, diamonds alternate*

Row 27: *under 3, over 5, under 3, over 1, repeat under 3, same as Row 21*

Row 28: *over 3, under 3, over 3, under 3…same as Row 16*

Row 29: *under 3, over 5, under 3, over 1, repeat over 3, same as Rows 27 and 21*

Row 30: *over 3, under 1, over 3, under 5, repeat, same as Row 26*

Row 31: *under 3, over 3, under 3, over 3…same as Row 25*

Row 32: *over 3, under 1, over 3, under 5, same as Row 8*

Row 33: *over 5, under 3, over 1, under 3, same as Row 9*

Row 34: *over 3, under 3, over 3, under 3…same as Row 10*

Row 35: *under 3, over 5, under 3, over 1, repeat under 3, same as Row 11*

Row 36: *over 3, under 1, over 3, under 5, repeat over 3, same as Row 12*

Row 37: *under 3, over 3, under 3, over 3…same as Row 13*

Row 38: *over 3, under 1, over 3, under 5, repeat over 3, same as Row 14*

This ends your weaving with natural reed, and you will now return to weaving with red dyed reed or a color of your choice.

Rows 39 to 58: *Weave over 3 spokes, under 3, over 3, under 3. Remember to move one vertical spoke to the right with each new weaver in order to keep the twill diagonal accurate.*

The dyed weavers above the diamond design stairstep over 3 spokes, under 3 spokes to continue the weaving pattern from Row 38, the final row of natural weavers.

Rows 39 through 50: *To decrease the size of the rim opening, use more left-hand pressure; push in while weaving. Continue to weave and place a clothespin or clamp as needed to maintain tension. Pull gently on the weaver to see more movement; at the same time, keep spokes upright and not slanted.*

Row 50: *Re-wet the ends of the spokes and place the basket base side facing up with spoke ends touching the work surface. Push down on the base. This will make the spokes flare out at the ends and create the traditional Cherokee shape.*

Rows 51 through 58: *Weave with left hand pressure from the inside of the basket, pushing out to increase the outward flare of the spoke ends and increase the rim opening. Or, keep the basket base side up with spoke ends flared and weave the remaining rows in this position. Pack each row by pushing it up to meet the previous weaver. Use a bent tip or packing tool to assist in this step.*

Rows 59 to 60: *Twine with #1 round reed dyed red, or the color of your choice, as the Rim Rows in preparation for the basket rim. Round reed is used to fit in the small spaces between the spoke ends. In Twining, repeat the same over 2 spokes, under 2 spokes you used in weaving around the base spokes.*

The Diamonds All Around twill design has two distinct rows of diamonds.

Near the rim opening of the Diamonds All Around Basket, transition from natural walnut weavers to dyed red weavers and continue the over 3, under 3 twill.

The Diamonds All Around rim decreases in diameter to create the neck of the basket in all red dyed weavers.

Diamonds All Around twill design continues in Rows 21 to 60.

10. **Rim.** In preparation for the rim, turn the basket, base side up, and wet the spoke ends until flexible.
11. For a neat finish on the inside of the flared basket rim, choose to tuck the spokes to the inside of the basket following the woven pattern. For example: over 3 weavers; trim and tuck spoke ends down and under the top 2 or 3 weavers. When possible, tuck one or more spokes in each set of three. Trim the remaining spokes even with the top rim of the basket.
12. Prepare the 7 mm flat oval reed dyed red for the rim. Shave or scarf the oval side on one end of the rim reed for a level overlap. Soak 7 mm flat oval reed along with #4 dyed round reed rim filler. When the reed is flexible, remove it from the water and wipe the dyed reed gently with a towel several times to remove excess dye.
13. Measure around the inside and outside rim openings. Add 2" to each measurement for needed overlap; then cut each rim and the round reed rim filler. (Refer to chapter 5, Rim Borders, as needed.) Attach 7 mm flat oval rim reed, add the rim filler between the inner and outer rims with a 1" overlap, shaved or scarfed as needed. Adjust all clothespins for the final time and insert cable ties for a snug rim.
14. **Waxed Linen Lashing.** This thread is the lashing material best used when there are many spoke ends and spokes are very close together. Lash with a tapestry needle or curved needle and 4-ply or 7-ply waxed linen. Measure a long lasher approximately five times the distance around the rim of the basket. To begin, tie one end of the waxed linen around a vertical spoke below the Rim Row and above the last weaver. Leave a 5" tail, bring the waxed linen lasher from the inside around to the front of the basket, moving to the right on a diagonal. Lash with waxed linen in this one direction around the entire rim of the basket. Pull tight to keep the rim snug and cut cable ties out of the way. At the starting place, end the waxed linen lasher by tying it to the beginning end of the lasher, trim and tuck the ends under the inside rim.
15. Diamonds All Around begins as a square base and gradually rounds out, creating an indented neck and round flared rim opening. Re-wet the basket as necessary to make any adjustments in the overall shape or to maintain the base to rest flat on the surface.
16. This basket can remain with the original natural weavers and dyed red reed for great contrast and traditional Cherokee colors. The natural weavers will darken over time to a golden oak color.
17. As an alternative, finish the basket with a natural walnut hull stain or dye. (Refer to the recipe in chapter 2.) This process gives the basket an aged appearance and enhances its beauty. Or spray the finished basket with a commercially available stain.

BECOMING BLUE SKIES

The tallest Becoming Blue Skies design earned a 2nd Place ribbon at the North Carolina Basket Association Convention, NCBA, 2006 Exhibit in the Professional Wicker Category. Becoming Blue Skies was accepted in the smaller design size in The National Basketry Organization Exhibit at the Bascom Louise Gallery in Highlands, North Carolina. This basket, using the slanted rim design, was juried in the 20th Annual Juried Exhibit in 2008 at the South Carolina State Museum in Columbia and was also juried in the Pickens Museum of Art and History, Pickens, South Carolina Annual Exhibit.

Discover Five-Rod Wale and the Blending technique woven in shades of denim blue as photographed. Begin with a 4" or 6" round, slotted wood base. Create a unique design of bands, in varying shades of blue that blend into one another and create a new shade of that color. Finish the rim in flat oval reed, round reed rim filler, and a waxed linen lasher. Rinse the finished basket in a light shade of the accent color for a "wash" over the natural reed. This basket can be woven in three sizes by changing the height and altering the rim opening of the finished basket.

Intermediate round reed design.

Approximate Size: 8" to 9" (h) with 6" to 7" rim opening, 9" to 11" at widest diameter
Taller basket: 20" (h) × 14" at widest diameter

Materials

- 4" or 6" round, slotted wood base, pre-finished with stain and urethane
- ¼" flat oval reed cut for spokes: 29 spokes at 16" long, 45' or 28" for tall basket
- #1 or #2 round reed, natural, or dyed lightest accent color; Continuous Twine, 6' base and around the Rim, 40'
- #2.5 or #3 round reed, natural or dyed lightest accent color, Three Rod Wale, 3 rows near the base, 35'
- #2.5 or #3 round reed, dyed accent dark denim, Five Rod Wale, 12 to 15 rows, 160'–200'
- #2.5 or #3 round reed, Five Rod Wale, 20 rows, Blending, 300'
- #3 round reed, Blending and Five Rod Wale, 20 to 30 rows, dyed, 300'–400'
- ½" flat oval reed, medium blue, Rim, 6'
- #6 round reed, dyed, Rim Filler, 3'
- Blue waxed linen, Lasher, approximately 12'
- Tapestry needle

The Becoming Blue Skies Trio design is woven in three sizes.

Instructions

1. **Base**. Pre-finish the round wood base; sand and stain the wood then allow it to dry. Apply three coats of urethane allowing each to dry completely between coats.

   See chapter 3 for details of this process.
2. For the weaving technique used in this basket to work correctly the number of spokes used must be divisible by 5 minus 1 and also by 3 minus 1.

   Cut base spokes as indicated in the Materials list. With ¼" flat oval reed, cut 29 spokes at 16" long, or longer for the tallest version of this basket.
3. Divide the wood base into four quadrants or quarters. With a pencil, mark the quadrants' centers near the edge of the base to assist inserting spokes with equal distance between each spoke within each quadrant. From paper, cut a template the same size as the wood base. Fold the template in half, then fold it in half once again. Next place the open template on the wood base and mark the four quadrants. You may also do this by approximating if you choose.

   Check the slotted grooved opening before inserting spokes into the base. If the groove is narrow and the spokes fit tight, do not wet them. If the groove is wider and your spokes move about and are loose, wet the spokes briefly. When water is absorbed, it will temporarily enlarge the spokes, causing them to stay in place. If these steps do not solve the movement issue, apply a small amount of fast-drying gel glue before inserting the end of the spoke into the groove.

   Insert base spokes rough side facing up. Check your spacing, creating an equal distance between each spoke. Push all spokes firmly into the slot or groove. When finished, count the total number of spokes to be sure the accurate number are in place. (Refer to chapter 3 for additional instructions.)
4. **Continuous Weave.** Soak #1 round reed, natural or dyed in the lightest accent color, for weaving around the wood base. Insert the first base spoke, rough side up, at one of the center marks at the fold. Insert half of the base spokes, spacing them approximately ¼" apart, into one half of the base. Continue to insert all of the ¼" spokes. Check to be sure there are 29 spokes in the base before proceeding. Begin to Continuous Weave with the #1 round reed. Crimp, then insert the end of the round reed weaver into the groove in the base. Begin weaving over the first spoke, under, and over moving around the base. When you reach the Starting Spoke, mark it with a pencil, with the letters SS or cut the end of the spoke to a point to mark this for future reference. Continue to weave over and under using the Continuous Weave technique, for **6 rows;** with three over strokes on each spoke. Keep this weaver tight against the wood base and continue to keep it packed as you weave these rows near the base. Tuck the end of the round reed under the round reed at the Starting Spoke and trim it to end. Re-wet all spokes before moving to the next step.
5. **Three Rod Wale** is also known as Triple Twine. Weave **3 rows** of Three Rod Wale from the right side of the basket and gently begin to upsett the spokes to a slight flare. You may choose to place the basket base on its side to begin weaving. See chapter 4, Weaving Techniques, for this Continuous Weave technique. It is important to pack each row as it is woven.

   Place 3 weavers of #2.5 or #3 round reed, 1 behind each of 3 consecutive spokes.

   Weaver #1 is on the far left side, under or behind the Starting Spoke. Weave with this left-most weaver, over 2 spokes to the right, under 1 spoke, and bring it out to the front of the basket.

   Weaver #2 and **Weaver #3** will continue this technique. Weave around the basket for **3 rows.** Step-up to end these 3 weavers. The Step-up is done as follows: Stop weaving to the left of your Starting Spoke and weave, with your right-most weaver, over 2 spokes, and under 1 spoke. Bring the weaver out to the front of the basket. Continue in this way with the next two weavers. Do not cut the round reed weavers, these weavers will be used in the next step.

Becoming Blue Skies gradually transforms from a lighter shade of blue and blends into a darker shade of the same color.

The Five Rod Wale weaving technique uses 5 weavers; each is woven over 3 spokes and under 2 spokes.

Replace one weaver with the new dark Dyed Weaver #1 behind the Starting Spoke.

The new dark Dyed Weaver #1 continues the Five Rod Wale technique, over 3 spokes and under 2 spokes.

6. **Five Rod Wale** needs two additional round reed weavers matching in color with your original weavers; insert these behind/under the next two consecutive spokes to the right, spokes #4 and #5. Begin Five Rod Wale at the Starting Spoke with the left-most weaver, weaving over 3 spokes, under 2 spokes, and out to the front. Continue with each of the round reed weavers, using this Continuous Weave technique. Pack each row as you weave. Be sure the spokes remain equal distant apart. Check the overall shape of your basket after three or four rows of weaving to keep the spokes in a gentle flare; use left hand pressure and gently tug on weavers to assist the gentle upsett. Place a clothespin to hold tension on your weaver. Complete **12 rows** with five round reed weavers. Approximately 2½" of weaving is added with a circumference of approximately 27" and a diameter of approximately 8".
7. **Blending technique.** Continue the design in denim blue dyed accent reed or the accent color of your choice. Insert **Dark Denim Dyed Weaver #1** behind the Starting Spoke after the last of your five original weavers finishes the over 3 spokes, under 2 weaving. Trim the original round reed weaver behind the Starting Spoke and replace it with one dark weaver. The other four weavers remain the same. Place a twist tie wire or a cable tie around this first dark dyed round reed weaver to be able to more easily count the number of rows later. Weave Five Rod Wale for **4 rows with 1 dark dyed weaver and 4 original light accent weavers**.
8. Insert **Dark Denim Dyed Weaver #2** at the beginning of Row 5 of this Blending technique. Mark this place with a twist tie wire to enable easy counting of rows. Be sure all five weavers have completed weaving over 3 spokes, and under 2 spokes passed the Starting Spoke. Then replace the original weaver behind the Starting Spoke, which comes just after Dyed Dark Weaver #1. Weave Five Rod Wale for **4 rows with 2 dark dyed weavers and 3 original light accent weavers.** Check the overall shape of your basket as the sides continue to gradually flare toward the widest diameter.
9. **Dark Denim Dyed Weaver #3** replaces the original round reed weaver that follows the two dark dyed weavers. At the Starting Spoke, mark this third weaver with a twist tie wire and weave **3 or more rows with 3 dark dyed weavers and 2 original light accent weavers**. You now have reached the widest point in your basket, 9" to 11" wide or 14" wide in the tallest basket design. This creates more dark dyed reed accent in this area. If you weave additional rows for the tallest design, then delay the decreasing of the rim opening for height.

Re-wet the spoke ends and begin to decrease the size of the basket by pushing in on the spokes using left hand pressure as you weave. Place a clip or clothespin on your weaver to maintain tension and enhance shaping as you decrease in this part of the basket.

10. **Dark Denim Dyed Weaver #4** is added behind the Starting Spoke after the 3 dark weavers are woven over 3 spokes, and under 2 spokes passed the Starting Spoke. Mark this new weaver with a twist tie wire and weave **3 rows with the 4 dark dyed weavers and 1 original light accent weaver**. Continue decreasing the size of the rim opening with pressure from your left hand as you weave. Gently tug on the round reed weaver to encourage a smaller rim opening. Be sure to keep your spokes upright, equal distant apart, and clothespin or clamp your weaver to maintain the tension. Dyed weavers must stay in consecutive order to create the blending design.
11. **Dark Denim Dyed Weaver #5** is added one spoke to the right of the Starting Spoke or after all dark weavers are woven over 3 spokes and under 2. At this point, trim the last of the original weavers. Mark this new weaver with a twist tie wire and weave with **5 dark dyed weavers for 5 or more rows** before the next step begins. This step is also a good place to weave additional rows to increase the height of the tallest basket design.

Mark each new dark dyed weaver with a twist tie wire to be able to count the number of rows easily.

Replace the next weaver with dark Dyed Weaver #4.

The new dark dyed weaver continues the Five Rod Wale technique, over 3 spokes and under 2 spokes.

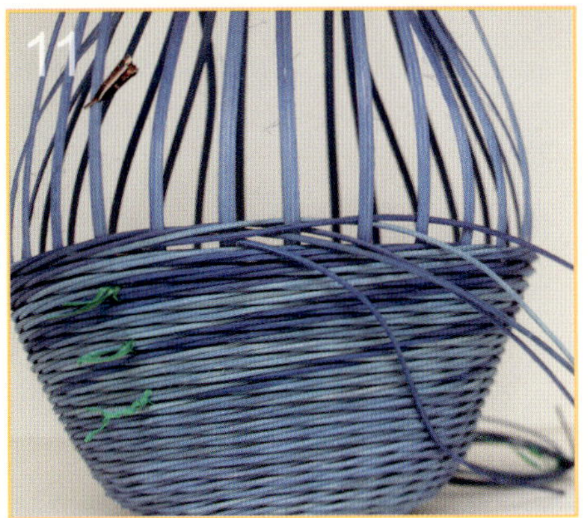

Nearing the widest diameter of Becoming Blue Skies, weave with four dark dyed weavers and one original weaver for three rows.

12. **Reversing the pattern.** In this step, gradually add the natural or light dyed round reed weavers and weave in the opposite direction. Continue the Five Rod Wale weaving technique by replacing the dark dyed weavers with your original light accent color weavers.

    New Original Light Accent Weaver #1 is inserted at the same place the original weaver ended previously, one spoke to the right of your original Starting Spoke. **Weave 4 rows using 1 original light accent weaver and 4 dark weavers**.

    New Original Light Accent Weaver #2 starts at the beginning of the 5th row, one spoke to the right of the original Starting Spoke. Continue to mark each new weaver with a twist tie wire making counting rows easier. **Weave 3 rows with 2 original light accent weavers and 3 dark weavers** or to the desired height.

    New Original Light Accent Weaver #3 starts at the beginning of the 4th row. **Weave 3 rows using 3 original light accent weavers and 2 dark weavers.**

    New Original Light Accent Weaver #4 begins at the 4th row, under or behind 1 spoke to the left of the Starting Spoke. Weave with **four original light weavers and 1 dark weaver for 3 or more rows.** All natural weavers are behind consecutive spokes. The basket is approximately 8 inches across in diameter and continues to decrease in size to the final rim.

    New Original Light Accent Weaver #5 is placed 2 spokes to the left of the Starting Spoke. **Weave 5 or more rows** to reach your desired height, approximately 8 inches to 8½ inches tall and 6 inches to 7½ inches across the rim. Step up to end all 5 weavers. Trim your ends and tuck them on the inside of the basket.

Option: Becoming Blue Skies with Slanted Rim Opening

13. To create the varying sizes of this design, increase one woven side of the rim to be taller than the opposite side. Insert short weavers of natural or original light accent weavers and weave Five Rod Wale using one half the vertical spokes. With each new row, use 2 spokes fewer to decrease the number of spokes being used, thus increasing the height on only one side of the basket. The tall design of **Becoming Blue Skies with Slanted Opening** begins with longer, 28 inch spokes. Increase weaving the number of rows in each section of your dyed and natural weavers until you reach the height you desire for your basket. Then, increase one side of the basket as above.
    Option: Choose to weave to your desired finished height keeping a level rim. Then trim half of the spoke ends on a diagonal to create the slanted rim opening. (Refer to chapter 5, Rim Borders.) Use clothespins to keep the weavers packed.
14. **Rim.** The last or top rows of weavers will be the Rim Rows for this basket.
    Re-wet all of the spoke ends. The spokes are upright, not flared out, for ease in working with the rim. Trim and tuck every other spoke to the inside of the basket under two rows of weaving.
15. **Rim Preparation**. Measure and cut two rim pieces from dyed flat oval reed. Soak these along with the round reed Rim Filler. Use clothespins to temporarily secure the flat oval rims to the basket. Distribute the overlaps, insert the Rim Filler and adjust clothespins or clamps as needed. Add cable ties to secure rim pieces.
16. **Waxed Linen Lashing**. Lash with a tapestry needle or curved needle and 4-ply or 7-ply waxed linen. Measure a long lasher approximately five times the distance around the rim of the basket. To begin, tie one end of the waxed linen around a vertical spoke below the Rim Row and above the last weaver. Leave a 5" tail, bring the waxed linen lasher from the inside around to the front of the basket, moving to the right on a diagonal. Lash with waxed linen in this one direction around the entire rim of the basket. Pull tight to keep the rim snug and cut cable ties out of the way. At the starting place, end the waxed linen lasher by tying it to the beginning end of the lasher, trim and tuck the ends under the inside rim.
17. Rinse the finished Becoming Blue Skies Basket in a light shade of denim blue or your choice of accent color for a wash. This will also cover any natural reed. Turn the basket upside down with the base side up and allow the basket to dry completely.
18. **Personalize** the wood base with a wood burning pen or a permanent fine line marker for future reference. Sign your name or initials, the date or the year the basket was made, and the number assigned from your list of completed baskets. (Refer to chapter 6, Finishing Touches.)

The largest Becoming Blue Skies design measures 20" tall and has a unique slanted rim opening.

The slanted rim opening, a unique finish to Becoming Blue Skies, is lashed with waxed linen thread.

Becoming Blue Skies design #3 is woven in the Five Rod Wale and Blending techniques. The bands of color change from lighter dyed accent reed and blend into the darker dyed reed, remaining the darker color to the slanted rim opening.

SPIRALS CHANGE

This round reed basket was awarded a First Place Ribbon at the North Carolina Basket Association Convention, NCBA, 2009 Exhibit in the Professional Wicker Category.

Spirals Change was juried in the 2009 North Charleston Cultural Arts Exhibition and was on loan for one year, 2009–2010, to the South Carolina State Museum Palmetto Hands Traveling Art Exhibit.

Intermediate/Advanced Round reed design.

Approximate Size: 4" to 10" diameter × 10" (h)

Materials

- 4" round wood base, pre-finished with stain and urethane
- ¼" flat or flat oval reed, natural, cut as follows for base spokes: 32 spokes at 15" long
- #1 round reed, natural, Base Weavers
- #2.5 or #3 round reed, natural, Weavers
- #2.5 or #3 round reed, dyed rust and cocoa, or any 2 contrasting colors, Weavers
- ¼" half round reed, dyed cocoa, Outside Rim
- #6 round reed, dyed cocoa, Inside Rim and Rim Filler
- Brown waxed linen, Lasher
- Tapestry needle

Spirals Change, a graceful vessel, earned a First Place Ribbon and traveled for one year with the South Carolina State Museum Palmetto Hands Art Exhibit.

Instructions

1. **Base**. Pre-finish the round wood base; sand and stain the wood then allow it to dry. Apply three coats of urethane allowing each to dry completely between coats. See chapter 3 for details of this process.
2. With ¼" flat oval reed, cut base spokes as indicated in the Materials list: 32 spokes at 15" long. (Or use any number of spokes that is divisible by 3, then subtract 1. For example, for 29 spokes, start with 30—a number divisible by 3—then subtract 1. This equals 29 spokes. Or for 27 spokes, which is divisible by 3, subtract 1. This equals 26 spokes.)
3. **Wood Base Spoke Preparation**. Divide the wood base into four quadrants or quarters. With a pencil, mark the quadrants' centers near the edge of the base to assist inserting spokes with equal distance between each spoke within each quadrant. From paper, cut a template the same size as the wood base. Fold the template in half then, fold it in half once again. Next place the open template on the wood base and mark the four quadrants. You may also do this by approximating if you choose.

   Check the slotted grooved opening before inserting spokes into the base. If the groove is narrow and the spokes fit tight, do not wet them; insert dry spokes, and then spray with water. If the groove is wider and your spokes move about and are loose, wet the spokes briefly and then insert them. When water is absorbed, it will temporarily enlarge the spokes, causing them to stay in place. Or, insert a 1" piece of cane on top of the spoke then insert into the groove. If these steps do not solve the movement issue, apply a small amount of fast-drying gel glue to the end of the spoke. Insert it into the groove, and hold it there long enough for the gel glue to thoroughly dry. Refer to chapter 3 for additional hints.
4. Insert the first base spoke, rough side up, at or near one of the center marks. Insert one quarter or one half of the base spokes within the marks. Check your spacing, and then continue to insert all spokes rough side up, creating an equal distance, approximately ⅛" between each. Push all spokes firmly into the slot or groove. When finished, count the total number of spokes to be sure the accurate number are in place. You can include 26, 29, or 32 base spokes, numbers that work with the techniques in this basket. Choose the amount of spokes depending on your ease working with a tight technique. Insert 8 spokes or less in the first quadrant. Add more spokes spaced ⅛" apart until all spokes are in place.
5. Soak #1 round reed for weaving near the base.
6. **Chase Weave** with an **even number** of spokes, 32 or 26 spokes. Or, **Continuous Weave** with an **uneven number**, 29 spokes.

   Chase Weave with a long round reed Weaver #1 for **4 rows**. Crimp or bend one end of this reed about ⅜" and insert it into the base groove. Begin weaving over and under each spoke. Now, insert round reed Weaver #2 into the base groove one spoke before, or to the left of your first weaver, and weave over and under the base spokes in a pattern that is opposite that used for round reed Weaver #1.

   If you are using 29 spokes, **Continuous Weave** with dyed or natural #1 round reed. Crimp or bend the weaver for ⅜" on one end and insert this end, between two spokes, into the groove in the wood base. Weave over, then under spokes as close to the base as possible. Push spokes into the base if needed. Use a small tool to assist in packing the round reed weaver(s); this tool also serves as a measuring tool for the space between spokes. Weave very close to the base, gently lift spokes up and weave around them for 4 rows. Tuck the end(s) of your round reed weavers under the previous row and at the starting place.

   Turn the base over to the opposite side.
7. Briefly wet #2.5 or #3 round reed in natural and dyed reed of two contrasting colors such as cocoa brown and rust, or colors of your choice. To remove any excess dye, gently pull the dyed reed through a towel several times.

   Re-wet the spokes to allow for a rounded, gentle upsett. Use clothespins to hold several spoke ends together to help the sidewalls of the basket. Allow the spokes to stay relaxed with a gentle flare or angle.

Nearing its widest diameter, Spirals Change will change direction in shape as well as change direction in spiral.

To finish a spiral weave, end with a Step-up. Stop weaving when the lead weaver is in the space to the left of the Starting Spoke. Now you are ready to do the Step-up.

The Reverse Spiral technique begins behind the same spokes in which you ended the spiral and Step-up. The rust weaver is inserted behind the Starting Spoke and moving to the left. You will weave left-handed in this Reverse Spiral.

8. **Outside Spiral technique** uses a number of spoke ends divisible by 3 minus 1 and is one of the variations in Three Rod Wale. Begin by marking a Starting Spoke, then insert three weavers of #2.5 or #3 round reed behind, under three consecutive spokes. Start with dyed accent **#1 rust Dyed Weaver #1** behind the Starting Spoke. **Dyed Weaver #2 cocoa brown** is behind the next spoke to the right, Spoke #2.

   Weaver #3 is natural reed and starts under the next spoke to the right, or at Spoke #3. Weave with the left-most weaver, Dyed Weaver #1, rust. Weave over 2 spokes, under 1 spoke in the **Three Rod Wale technique for about 2" or approximately 20 rows.** At this widest point in the basket, the circumference is 24 inches, the diameter is approximately 7 inches and measures 6 inches tall. Create a spiral with a gentle flare outward. This is a Continuous Weave and rows are packed as woven. There is no Step-up until the last row of this technique.
9. The next **5 rows** of this **Three Rod Wale** technique are woven to allow the spokes to stand upright then begin to flare inward.
10. Re-wet all spoke ends and gently bend them to the inside of the basket; clothespin several spoke ends together. Allow your basket to dry in this position if you have difficulty shaping the basket. Using left hand pressure to assist in shaping, continue **Three Rod Wale for 10 rows, or approximately 1½ inches, reaching approximately 6 inches** in height at this point in the basket. Gently and consistently tug on your weavers to decrease the basket diameter.
11. End the round reed weavers with a Step-up on the last of these 10 rows. When your right-most weaver reaches the space to the left of the Starting Spoke, use this reed and weave over 2, under 1, and trim to stay inside the basket. If necessary, refer to chapter 4, Weaving Techniques. Crimp and tuck the end of each weaver under and along the next spoke to the right, or trim it with a back cut. When the weaver rests behind the next spoke to its right, hold the scissors at an angle, cut the dyed reed end so the natural cut shows at the bottom and is not seen from the top of the basket. (Refer to the photo on page 66 in chapter 6, Weaving Hints.)
12. A Pattern Change is now necessary to reverse the Outside Spiral with **Reverse Three Rod Wale**. Start 3 new weavers behind or under the Starting Spoke where your last weavers ended. Match your dyed accent color, with ends of weavers to the left rather than to the right. You may choose to crimp and tuck these new weavers, or you may place them behind the 3 consecutive spokes. Weave left-handed to reverse the Outside Spiral so it moves to the left. Begin with your right-most weaver,

rather than your left-most weaver as is usual in weaving a regular Three Rod Wale. This right-most weaver is **Dyed Weaver #1 rust**, and it will move to the left. **Dyed Weaver #2 cocoa brown** is behind the next spoke to the left, and **Weaver #3 natural** is to the left of the first 2 weavers. Right-most Weaver #1 is woven over two spokes to the left and under 1. Continue with the next weaver to create arrows in this first transition row. Your dyed and natural weavers will form individual matching arrows. Continue Reverse Three Rod Wale Spiral for **10 Rows** or 1¼" tall.

13. Emphasis is now on shaping with hand pressure. Gradually decrease the size of the diameter of the basket by gently tugging on the weavers to assist shaping. Spokes stay upright and an equal distance apart, about ⅜". As spokes move closer together, taper them to allow room to be able to continue weaving. End the spiral with a Step-up in the last row of Reverse Spiral, moving to the left; trim all ends and tuck them to the inside.
14. Wet 3 pieces of natural #2.5 or #3 round reed. Choose a new Starting Spoke and insert 3 new natural weavers to weave **Three Rod Wale for 3 rows**. With one hand inside the basket, push out on the spokes to help flare outward as you weave these 3 rows. There is no Step-up and do not trim or tuck your weavers just yet.
15. **Single Spiral technique for 3 rows**. At the Starting Spoke, replace 1 natural weaver with 1 dyed cocoa brown weaver. Continue to weave Three Rod Wale with **1 dyed weaver and 2 natural weavers**. Use hand pressure to keep spokes upright and/or flared out, your choice. There is no Step-Up at the end of the third row of the Single Spiral technique. Continue weaving 3 spokes past the Starting Spoke to complete 3 rows. The circumference at the neck of the basket is approximately 13½" and the diameter about 4¼".

    Hint: Another method to increase the distance between spokes and increase the diameter to assist in weaving this section is to weave with the basket base facing up and spoke ends flaring out and touching the table.
16. Replace the 1 dyed cocoa brown weaver with 1 natural weaver and complete **2 or more rows of Three Rod Wale** with all 3 weavers in natural reed.
17. **Single Spiral technique for 3 rows**. Replace natural Weaver #3 with the contrasting dyed rust weaver. Continue to push out on spokes while weaving Three Rod Wale with 1 dyed rust weaver and 2 natural weavers. Keep your spokes wet to assist in shaping.
18. Replace the dyed rust weaver with a natural reed and finish **3 rows of Three Rod Wale** with all 3 natural reed weavers. You may choose to end each row with a Step-up or end only the third row with a Step-Up. Trim and tuck

The Reverse Spiral technique creates arrows. In this transition row, the rust weaver makes the first arrow.

At the neck, the narrowest diameter in Spirals Change, three rows of Reverse Spiral create the Single Spiral. Replace one of the natural weavers with a cocoa brown dyed weaver for this graceful design element.

all spoke ends for a neat finish. (Refer to the photos on page 45 in chapter 4, Weaving Techniques.)

19. Wet #1 natural round reed, then twine 3 rows as Rim Rows in preparation for the rim. Pack all rows of weavers and adjust the shape as needed. Then soak your spoke ends until the reed is flexible. Trim every other spoke even with the top rim opening. Tuck the remaining spokes to the outside of the basket when the rim opening has a wide flare. Tuck these under the first rows of weavers.
20. **Rim** your basket with dyed reed and lash with waxed linen. Prepare ¼" half round outside rim, in cocoa brown or natural reed. Measure the outside rim, adding 2" for the overlap. Shave or scarf one end of the half round rim to half its thickness for a neat 2" overlap and soak this until flexible. Measure the inside rim, adding 2" for overlap and cut #5 round reed dyed cocoa brown for the inside rim and the rim filler. Soak these along with the half round outside rim.

    Use clothespins to temporarily secure the rim pieces to the basket. Distribute the overlaps, insert the Rim Filler and adjust clothespins or clamps as needed. Add cable ties to secure rim pieces.
21. **Waxed Linen Lashing**. Lash with a tapestry needle or curved needle and 4-ply or 7-ply brown waxed linen. Measure a long lasher approximately five times the distance around the rim of the basket. To begin, tie one end of the waxed linen around a vertical spoke below the Rim Row and above the last weaver. Leave a 5" tail, bring the waxed linen lasher from the inside around to the front of the basket, moving to the right on a diagonal. Lash with waxed linen in this one direction around the entire rim of the basket. Pull tight to keep the rim snug and cut cable ties out of the way. At the starting place, end the waxed linen lasher by tying it to the beginning end of the lasher, trim and tuck the ends under the inside rim.
22. **Stain**. Finish Spirals Change with a natural walnut hull stain or dye. (Refer to the recipe in chapter 2.) Or, spray the finished basket with a commercially available stain. I prefer to keep this basket with its natural weavers in contrast to the dyed cocoa and rust reed.
23. Allow your finished basket to completely air dry; turn the basket upside down with the base side up.
24. **Personalize** the woven or wood base with a wood burning pen or a permanent fine line marker for future reference. Sign your name or initials, the date or the year the basket was made, and the number assigned from your list of completed baskets. (Refer to chapter 6, Finishing Touches.)

Weaving Summary

Rows 1–4:-------- #1 Round reed, natural, Chase Weave at base
Rows 5–24: ------ #2.5 or #3 Round reed, cocoa, rust, natural, Outside Spiral, 20 Rows
Rows 25–29:----- #2.5 or #3 Round reed, cocoa, rust, natural, Outside Spiral, 5 Rows
Rows 30–39:----- #2.5 or #3 Round reed, cocoa, rust, natural, Outside Spiral, 10 Rows
Rows 40–49:----- #2.5 or #3 Round reed, Reverse Three Rod Wale, 10 Rows
Rows 50–53:----- #2.5 or #3 Round reed, natural, Three Rod Wale, 4 Rows
Rows 54–56:----- #2.5 or #3 Round reed, Single Color Cocoa Spiral, 3 Rows
Rows 57–58:----- #2.5 or #3 Round reed, natural, Three Rod Wale, 2 Rows
Rows 59–61:----- #2.5 or #3 Round reed, Single Color Rust Spiral, 3 Rows
Rows 62–64:----- #2.5 or #3 Round reed, natural, Three Rod Wale, 2 Rows
Rows 65–67:----- #1 Round reed, natural, Twine, 3 Rim Rows

Several round reed weaving techniques are included in Spirals Change: Chase Weave, Three Rod Wale, Outside Spiral, Reverse Spiral, and Single Spiral.

RIBBONS TO REMEMBER

This award winning breast cancer awareness basket earned a 3rd Place Ribbon at the North Carolina Basket Association Convention, NCBA, 2010 Exhibit in the Professional Wicker Category.

Ribbons to Remember is the third in a series of Breast Cancer Ribbon Baskets I have designed and dedicated to my mother, Bertha McMahon Smith. This basket was created in honor of the fifteenth anniversary of her battle with breast cancer. To personalize, use all pink ribbons to symbolize breast cancer, or you may insert many colorful ribbons to honor a variety of health issues.

Intermediate Round Reed design.

Approximate Size: 4" to 10" diameter × 10½" (h); 12" with handles

Materials

- 4" round slotted wood base, pre-finished with stain and urethane
- ¼" flat oval reed, dyed pink, cut as follows for the base: 32 spokes at 24" long
- #0 or #1 round reed, natural, or dyed, Base Weave, 36', Handles, pink, 25'
- #2.5 or #3 round reed, dyed, Three Rod Wale in teal with Single Spiral Weave in purple, or colors of your choice
- Center Arrow, wine, pink, and purple
- Dyed round reed amounts:
  - teal: 210'
  - purple: 95'
  - pink: 70'
  - wine: 95'
- 3⁄16" flat oval reed, dyed pink, Weavers, 2 rows
- 3⁄16" or 1/4" flat oval reed, dyed pink, wine, purple, or teal, for Ribbons, 64 pieces at 8" long

A round reed design, Ribbons to Remember, honors our loved ones who battle cancer and other health issues. The ribbon color denotes the health concern.

Instructions

1. **Base**. Pre-finish the round wood base; sand and stain the wood then allow it to dry. Apply three coats of urethane allowing each to dry completely between coats. See chapter 3 for details of this process.
2. Cut 32 base spokes at 24" long with ¼" flat oval reed dyed **accent #1 pink,** or in the color of your choice.
3. Divide the wood base into four quadrants or quarters. With a pencil, mark the quadrants' centers near the edge of the base to assist inserting spokes with equal distance between each spoke within each quadrant. From paper, cut a template the same size as the wood base. Fold the template in half, then fold it in half once again. Next place the open template on the wood base and mark the four quadrants.
   You may also do this by approximating if you choose.
   Check the slotted grooved opening in the round wood base before inserting spokes. If the groove is narrow and the spokes fit tight, do not wet them; insert dry spokes, and then spray with water. If the groove is wider and your spokes move about and are loose, wet the spokes briefly and then insert them. When water is absorbed, it will temporarily enlarge the spokes, causing them to stay in place. Or, insert a one inch piece of cane on top of the spoke then insert into the groove. If these steps do not solve the movement issue, apply a small amount of fast-drying gel glue to the end of the spoke. Insert it into the groove, and hold it there long enough for the gel glue to thoroughly dry.
   Insert the first base spoke, rough side up, at or near one of the center marks.
   Insert one quarter or one half of the base spokes within the marks. Check your spacing, and then continue to insert all spokes rough side up, creating an equal distance between each, approximately ⅛" apart. Push all spokes firmly into the slot or groove. When finished, count the total number of spokes to be sure the accurate number are in place. (Refer to chapter 3, Base Techniques.)
4. **Chase Weave** with the 32 spokes. Use #0 or #1 natural or dyed round reed. Wet, crimp, and then insert one end of this round reed **Weaver #1** into the groove. Bend it to the right and weave over and under each base spoke, keeping the weaver as close as possible to the base. Before reaching your starting place, insert round reed **Weaver #2** in the space before or to the left of the original weaver. Weave opposite Weaver #1, over and under. To avoid round reed tangle, keep each piece of round reed in a small coil with a twist tie or a plastic bobbin as you weave for a total of **4 rows**; count 4 overs showing on each spoke. Tuck the ends of the round reed weavers under the previous row at their respective starting places and trim them to end.
5. Spray the spokes, at the same time protecting the wood base. You will wish to keep it from absorbing too much moisture. Now, gently bend and upsett the spokes. Clothespin three to five spoke ends together all the way around the basket. This step helps shape the sides of the basket. Spoke ends can also be held upright by using a wide rubber band. Allow to air dry to assist in shaping.
6. **Rows 1 to 8 Three Rod Wale** with #2.5 or #3 round reed dyed **accent #2 teal**, or the accent color of your choice. Wet, and lightly wipe the dyed weavers through a towel to remove excess dye. Mark any spoke with SS, for your Starting Spoke, or clip the spoke end to a point for future reference. Weave from the outside, the right side of the basket. Beginning rows of weavers shape the sidewalls of the basket with a gentle flare. With three pieces of dyed round reed of the same color, tuck one each behind or under three consecutive spokes. With the left-most weaver of the 3, weave over 2 spokes, under 1 spoke, in the Three Rod Wale technique for 1¾" or approximately 8 rows, creating a gentle flare outward as you progress. This is a Continuous Weave with rows packed as they are woven. Choose to either Step-up at the end of each row, as I did or, you may Step-up at the end of these 8 rows.
   To **Step-up and end the weavers**, you will work with the right-most weaver rather than the left-most weaver you have used in the Three Rod Wale technique. The Step-up begins once a weaver reaches the opening to the left of that spoke you have designated as the Starting Spoke, (SS). See chapter 4, Weaving Techniques, if needed.
   At the end of Row 8, the basket start has a 22 inch circumference and is approximately 1 inch tall from the work surface including the wood base and the first 8 rows of weaving.
7. **Rows 9 to 11 Single Color Spiral.** At the Starting Spoke on Row 9, introduce a single round reed dyed in **accent #3 purple**, or the color of your choice. Insert the new purple weaver before pushing the original weaver back into the inside of the basket to be tucked and trimmed later. This insures the new weaver is in the correct position. Weave Three Rod Wale for **3 rows with 1 purple weaver and 2 teal weavers**. Step-up at the end of the third row to end this Single Spiral.

8. **Rows 12 to 15 Three Rod Wale Rows.** At the Starting Spoke at the end of Row 11, beginning Row 12, replace the single purple spiral weaver with teal, or one of your original dyed accent color. Weave in Three Rod Wale **for 4 rows with all 3 weavers in the same dyed accent, teal** as before. End each row with a Step-up. Trim and tuck all ends after these four rows are complete.
9. **Rows 16 to 17 Three Rod Wale.** At the Starting Spoke at the end of Row 15, begin Row 16 by replacing all 3 teal weavers with all dyed accent **#3 purple** weavers, or weavers dyed the accent color of your choice. Three Rod Wale **for 2 rows with all 3 weavers in the same dyed accent, purple**. End each row with a Step-up. Trim and tuck these round reed weavers to end the second row.
10. Mark every other spoke with a light pencil mark in two places: ¾" above the last row of weaving, and ¾" above this first mark.

    Row 18 Over and Under, Start and Stop. On the first ¾" mark, weave with 3/16" or ¼" flat oval pink dyed reed**.** The spaces are left open below and above the flat oval weaver. This weaver serves as an anchor for the ribbons, which are added last. After Row 18, at the beginning of the open weave area, the circumference is at 27½ inches and the basket is approximately 2½ inches in height.
11. **Center Arrow technique** begins with Three Rod Wale as a border in dyed accent **#4 wine** for **Rows 19 to 20,** with a Step-up to end each row. Insert 3 wine dyed weavers behind 3 consecutive spokes for Three Rod Wale working to the right.

    Rows 21 to 23 Three Rod Wale. Weave 3 rows with wine, pink, and purple round reed weavers as in the photograph for the upward stroke of the arrow. Step-up at the end of the third row; trim and tuck the ends. This is the center of the arrow, the widest part of the basket. It has a 33" circumference, is 9" to 10" diameter, and stands 5¼" in height.
12. **Rows 24 to 26 Reverse Three Rod Wale.** To complete the arrow, weave 3 rows in the opposite direction. Weave to the left, matching the dyed weavers in the same position as in the previous row. Begin weaving with the right-most weaver, rather than the left-most weaver as is usual in regular Three Rod Wale. This right-most weaver is Dyed Weaver #1 and will move to the left. Dyed Weaver #2 is behind the next spoke to the left, and Dyed Weaver #3 is to the left of these. Begin to decrease the size of the rim opening with these rows weaving to the left. Re-wet two inches above the weaving to assist you in shaping; use hand pressure, pushing down and in on the spokes as you weave. Gently tug

The Single Spiral technique is woven near the base and near the rim of the Ribbons to Remember Basket. Introduce one new dyed weaver and replace an original accent weaver to create a spiral in the new color.

An inside view of the open areas for ribbon placement in Ribbons to Remember. The flat oval weaver serves as an anchor for the ribbons, which are added later.

The arrow in the center of Ribbons to Remember is woven with three dyed accent colors in Three Rod Wale and Reverse Three Rod Wale.

A Single Spiral in purple changes to a Single Spiral in pink near the rim of Ribbons to Remember.

on weavers as needed, being careful to keep all vertical spokes upright. Use a clothespin to maintain tension on the weaver. Finish these 3 rows with a Step-up; trim and tuck all round reed ends.

13. **Rows 27 and 28 Three Rod Wale.** With wine round reed, **reverse the weaving** and work to the right for 2 rows. Step-up at the end of each row. This repeats the border woven below and prior to the arrow.
14. Above the center arrow section, mark spokes in two places, ¾" apart, as in Step 10.

    Row 29 Over and Under, Start and Stop On the first ¾" mark, weave with 3⁄16" or ¼" flat oval reed, dyed pink. Again, this will be the anchor for ribbons, which are added last. At the top of this last open weave area, the circumference of the rim opening decreases to approximately 28 inches, and the basket is 7½ inches tall. Re-wet the spoke ends as needed. To continue shaping, encourage spokes with your hand pressure to decrease the circumference of the basket.
15. **Rows 30 and 31 Three Rod Wale.** Weave 2 rows with purple weavers and Step-up at the end of each row to stack, rather than spiral, these rows. Replace these with three dyed weavers in teal, or your original dyed accent color, in preparation for the next step.
16. **Rows 32 to 34 Three Rod Wale.** Weave 3 rows with teal dyed reed**.** No Step-up is needed to end these rows as you will replace only one of the weavers for the next Single Spiral.
17. **Rows 35 to 37 Single Color Spiral.** Weave 3 rows with 2 teal and 1 purple weaver. See Step 7.
18. **Rows 38 and 39 Three Rod Wale.** Weave 2 rows with all 3 weavers in teal dyed reed. Then, replace one of the three teal weavers with one pink weaver.
19. **Rows 40 to 42 Single Color Spiral.** Weave 3 rows with 1 pink and 2 teal weavers. Then, replace two teal weavers with two pink weavers.
20. **Rows 43 and 44 Three Rod Wale.** To complete the weaving, weave 2 rows with 3 pink weavers to match the color of the spoke ends used in the folded rim. Step-up in each of these two rows of pink.

    The rim opening is approximately 22½ inches in circumference, 6 inches to 6½ inches in diameter, and the basket height is 10 inches.

Weaving Summary

Rows 1–8:-------- Teal, 8 rows, Three Rod Wale
Rows 9–11: ------ Purple, 3 rows, Single Color Spiral
Rows 12–15:----- Teal, 4 rows, Three Rod Wale
Rows 16–17:----- Purple, 2 rows, Three Rod Wale
Row 18: ---------- Pink Flat oval reed, 1 row, Over and Under, Start and Stop
Rows 19–20:----- Wine, 2 rows, Three Rod Wale
Rows 21–23:----- Wine, Pink, Purple, 3 rows, Three Rod Wale Arrow
Rows 24–26:----- Wine, Pink, Purple, 3 rows, Reverse Three Rod Wale Arrow
Rows 27–28:----- Wine, 2 rows, Three Rod Wale
Row 29: ---------- Pink Flat oval reed, 1 row, Over and Under, Start and Stop
Rows 30–31:----- Purple, 2 rows, Three Rod Wale
Rows 32–34:----- Teal, 3 rows, Three Rod Wale
Rows 35–37:----- 2 Teal, 1 Purple, 3 rows, Single Color Spiral
Rows 38–39:----- Teal, 2 rows, Three Rod Wale
Rows 40–42:----- 1 Pink, 2 Teal, 3 rows, Single Color Spiral
Rows 43–44:----- Pink, 2 rows, Three Rod Wale

Pati's Fold and No-Tuck Rim Border Technique

21. Re-wet the spoke ends until they become flexible enough to avoid reed breakage while constructing the border. Adjust all the spokes to be sure they are in an upright position and equal distance apart.

Step 1: Choose five consecutive spokes on opposite sides of the basket and mark these for handles. Do not include these in the folded rim. With a small clip or twist tie wire, mark a Starting Spoke at a point close to the last row of weaving. Work to the right with this Starting Spoke and move under one spoke to the right, bring the spoke end up to the top rim of the basket.

Step 2: Gently bend the same spoke end over one spoke to the left. This is the same spoke you just passed it under. Push down and in to the inside of the basket. The spoke end will tuck under and lay along the underside of the flat-top rim. Trim it to 1" or so and continue in this same way all around the border. Gently bend under one spoke to the right, fold over one spoke to the left, and push it down and

The Fold and No-Tuck Rim Border is a two-step technique. The spoke end moves under one spoke to the right and up. The second step moves the spoke end to the left, over the same spoke you just passed under, and then into the opening on the left of this spoke.

inside. You may choose to do Step 1, under one spoke to the right and up for four or more spokes before going back and doing Step 2, over one spoke to the left, tucking down and inside the keyhole opening. Continue folding and tucking until all spoke ends are included in the border, with the exception of the handle spokes.

The folded rim border is complete with five spoke ends for the handle.

Ribbons to Remember has two woven side handles. Each handle is made up of five spoke ends on opposite sides of the basket.

Each woven handle is inserted and secured inside the basket at the reed ribbon opening.

22. **Handles.** On each side of the basket, use the five consecutive spokes marked for each handle. These spokes remain upright while finishing the fold and no-tuck rim border. Or you can weave the handles first and then complete the folded border.
To weave the handles, soak #1 round reed dyed pink to match the spoke ends and the rim. A **Continuous Weave, Over and Under** will be used. Begin by tucking the end of the dyed round reed weaver down into the top rows of pink Three Rod Wale. Weave over 1 spoke, under 1 spoke, over 1 spoke, and under 1 spoke and at the last of the five spokes, re-wet and then crimp the round reed weaver with needle nose pliers or crimping tool. Then turn this weaver back and continue to weave over and under until you reach the last spoke on the opposite side of the handle. Continue weaving, decreasing the width of the handle by moving the five handle spokes closer together until the handle is approximately 1½ inches across. Continuous Weave, Over and Under, in this manner for **26 Rows.**
Then, in the next **9 rows**, weave over 1 spoke at the edge of the handle, weave under 3 spokes in the middle of the handle, and then over 1 spoke at the edge of the handle at the opposite side. Re-wet your reed. Now crimp your weaver and weave around to the back side, under 1 spoke at the handle edge, over 3 middle spokes, and under 1 spoke at the opposite edge. This technique decreases your handle width.
To end the handle, re-wet and shape the handle in preparation for turning it downward. Stack all five spoke ends on top of each other to create one thick spoke. Tuck this spoke of five spoke ends into one of the ¾" openings where reed ribbons are inserted. Trim the spoke ends leaving a 2" tail, and secure all 5 spokes to the adjacent spoke by tying with waxed linen. Repeat this on the opposite side of the basket to complete the second handle.

23. **Ribbon Accents** are added when the basket is completely woven. Cut 64 reed ribbons at 8" long from ¼" flat oval reed dyed pink or the colors of your choice. Wet each ribbon, gently wipe excess dye, and bend it to create a hairpin shape. At the lower open area on the basket, insert the ribbon from inside of the basket, hairpin around a vertical spoke and the flat oval weaver in the open area, through the space on each side. Tuck the left side of the ribbon under the round reed weavers at the bottom of the open area. Cross the right side of the ribbon over the left side. Finish by tucking this end under the same row, one vertical spoke to the left. Trim the ends of each ribbon if necessary. Continue to insert the remaining ribbons until each vertical spoke has been included. Repeat this step in the open area above the center arrow weavers.
24. **Personalize** the wood base with a wood burning pen or a permanent fine line marker for future reference. Sign your name or initials, the date or the year the basket was made, and the number assigned from your list of completed baskets. (Refer to chapter 6, Finishing Touches.)
25. **Stain**. No additional stain or dye is needed to finish the Ribbons to Remember Basket. This basket is woven completely in dyed reed.

The ribbons in this basket are ¼" flat oval dyed reed in pink for breast cancer and several other colors representing a variety of health issues.

Insert the hairpin-shaped reed ribbon around a vertical spoke and the flat oval weaver in the open area.

Dyed reed ribbons embellish and add a three-dimensional charm to the Ribbons to Remember Basket.

HOPI-INSPIRED GRAND CANYON AND RAIN CLOUDS

Awarded a Third Place Ribbon in the North Carolina Basket Association Convention, NCBA, 2007 Exhibit Professional Wicker Category, this Hopi-inspired plaque or tray is woven in all round reed.

This Grand Canyon and Rain Clouds plaque or tray was inspired by the Native American baskets in my personal collection. After vacationing in Arizona and the Southwest, I felt the need to use many colors in this traditional woven plaque, as many bright hues are found in the Hopi baskets displayed at the Grand Canyon gift shop, museums, trading posts, and various other locations of that area.

Hopi wicker weavers gather natural materials such as siwi, yucca, scrub sumac, willow, and rabbitbrush found growing in their area. For dye colors, they also use many naturally available materials. For example, red and yellow dyes come from flower blossoms of these colors, and blue comes from indigo plants. Green stems, white clay, and black sunflower seeds are other commonly used natural materials. In addition, hohoisi or Hopi tea is often incorporated for an orange-red color. Commercial aniline dyes are also often used to create many of the colors that are common today.

The Hopi wicker weavers create plaques and trays that are as pretty on the right side as on the reverse or back side of the plaque. This requires practice and patience. Plaques made by the Hopi people are for sale at tourist destinations while other plaques are given as a form of payment for services rendered. Some of these woven treasures are kept in the family given to infants, young children, and women. They are often found in Hopi basket dances and other ceremonies.

This Hopi-inspired plaque measures approximately 12½" in diameter. The yayni base is a traditional start to a Hopi plaque and is similar in construction to a Hopi wicker tray in the book *Handmade Baskets*.[2]

Advanced round reed basket design.

Approximate Size: 12½" diameter

Materials

- #3 round reed, dyed golden yellow, cut as follows:
  - 16 base spokes, 36" long
  - 2 sets of 8 Bi-Spokes, 18" long
  - 2 sets of 24 Bi-Spokes, 14" long
- #0 or #1 round reed, natural and dyed, for Weavers

(Dye colors are golden yellow, spring green, rust, royal blue, and black)

This Hopi-Inspired Grand Canyon and Rain Clouds Plaque begins with a traditional Hopi yayni, cross-warp base.

Instructions

1. **Base**. Two separate bases are woven and then put together to make one base. In Hopi, this process is known as yayni. With #3 round reed, cut 16 spokes at 36" long, dyed golden yellow, or in the color of your choice. Wet spokes before marking each with a pencil in the center and 1 inch on each side of the center mark.
2. **Base #1** Place 8 spokes horizontally, parallel on the table with two spokes paired together to be treated as one base spoke. This is four spokes of two pieces each; each pair approximately ½ inch apart. The base will measure two inches across. Use spoke weights and/or tape to secure to the table and keep these spokes in place while weaving.
3. **Continuous Weave** with a long, wet #0 or #1 round reed weaver of the same dyed accent color, **#1 golden yellow,** as the base spokes.

   Start **Base #1** with a 3 inch tail and **Continuous Weave** from the right side of the base at the 1" mark from the center. Weave over, under, over, under and around the end spoke. Re-wet and slightly crimp the weaver each time it turns back around the end spoke to avoid cracking the round reed. Continue weaving over, under, over, under and around the opposite side. Continuous Weave from the 1" mark to the opposite 1" mark until the woven base is 2 inch × 2 inch square. Pack each row as you weave. Coil the remaining round reed weaver and clothespin it to this first base for now.
4. **Base #2** in this traditional start to a Hopi plaque repeats Step 2 and Step 3 in a Continuous Weave with the remaining spokes at 36" long.
5. These two separate bases combine to become one base. Place the bases on top of one another, perpendicular to each other, at right angles so that the horizontal spokes in Base #1 make one side of the combined base. Base #2, with its spokes positioned vertically, is placed on top of Base #1. By placing these two yayni in this crossed position, we have created what is known as a cross-warp base start. Weaving with the same round reed weavers from before holds the two bases together. Use clothespins to temporarily keep the bases together. The round reed weavers should be on the same side and opposite ends of the combined base. If the over/under sequence does not work out on the second side of the base, weave the 3 inch tail to make the correction.

Start a Hopi base with four spokes, each spoke consists of two pieces of #3 round reed together to be treated as one. Continuous Weave with #0 or #1 round reed in the same accent color.

The round reed weaver is crimped each time it goes around an end spoke. Use needle nose pliers or a crimping tool to keep the reed from cracking.

After the weaver is crimped, resume the over and under Continuous Weave to the opposite edge of the base.

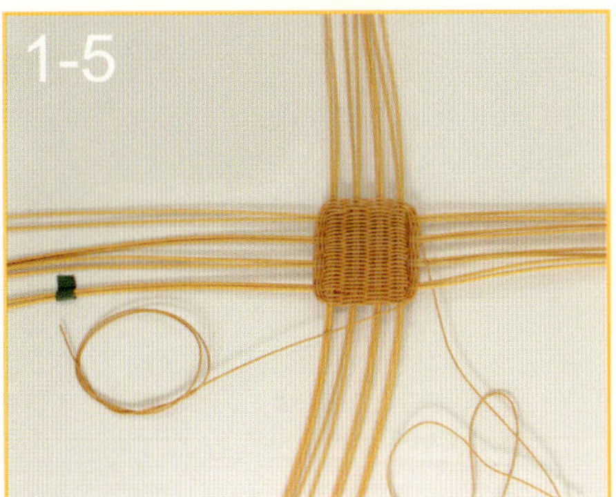

Two woven bases are combined; place one base perpendicular to and on top of the other. One side of the base is vertical while the opposite side is horizontal. Two bases in this crossed position is known as a cross-warp base.

Chase Weave for three rows around the cross-warp base with the same base weavers as before.

Insert an awl at the corner spoke to prepare a space for the Bi-spoke.

Taper one end of a Bi-spoke and add this new spoke into the base between the corner spoke. This separates the two original pieces of round reed that made up this paired spoke.

A Bi-spoke is added at each corner to help change the square base into a round tray.

6. **Chase Weave** beginning with the round reed weaver from Base #2. Begin weaving over and under, around the spokes, treating the two spokes from two bases as one pair. When this weaver reaches the weaver from Base #1, stop, but do not cut the weaver. Start to Chase Weave with this second weaver. Continue under and over, alternating around the spokes. Pack continuous weavers, as you weave, to keep a tight finish. Chase Weave for approximately **3 rows** with each weaver. When a new weaver is needed, crimp the new weaver and insert it down alongside the previous spoke. Trim, crimp, and tuck the old weaver to the back.
7. **Bi-Spoke** with the original dyed accent reed, #1 golden yellow. These are short spokes that are inserted in the base alongside an original base spoke. This step assists in shaping the corners as this base starts as a square and becomes more round with each color change. Wet the **8 bi-spokes at 18" long**. Bi-spoke, add one new spoke, in between each corner spoke separating the original two pieces that made up this paired spoke. Use side cutters or scissors to taper one end of each bi-spoke at an angle. Then insert an awl between the corner spokes and slide the new bi-spoke in and up against the original base.

8. When inserting this first set of 8 bi-spokes, the original over and under weave will change. Start with the weaver that is closest to the base and near the corner. Weave over 2 spokes as one pair (one spoke is the new bi-spoke); then weave under 1 spoke as a single spoke and over 1 spoke as a single spoke. Continue under the next paired spoke. Then weave over and under the paired spokes until almost reaching the second weaver.
9. Begin to weave with the second weaver, opposite the first. Continue to Chase Weave around the base for **5 rows,** alternating weavers and over/under.
10. Additional **bi-spokes** are added as the plaque increases in diameter. When the round reed weavers do not hold their position in the row, it is again time to insert new bi-spokes.
11. At each corner, insert a new golden yellow 18" bi-spoke where the corner spoke is a single spoke. Once this is done, it becomes a paired spoke again. Two new spokes will be added at each corner, as before, use the second set of **8 new bi-spokes at 18".** Chase Weave including these new spokes, for **5 rows**. End the golden yellow weaver by crimping and tucking in alongside the next spoke for about ½ inch. At this point, the base is no longer square; it has become rounded at the corners and is almost a circle. Now it is time to change dyed weavers, to add a new accent color and additional new bi-spokes at the same time.
12. Wet **24 new golden yellow bi-spokes at 14" long** and insert these between the remaining paired spokes.

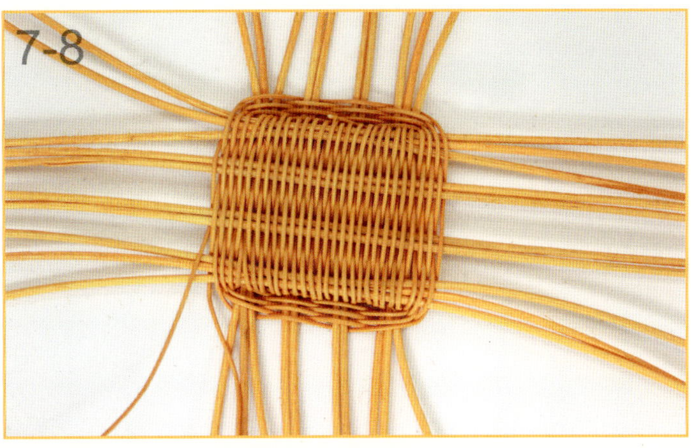

The horizontal side of the Hopi base shows a Bi-Spoke at every corner.

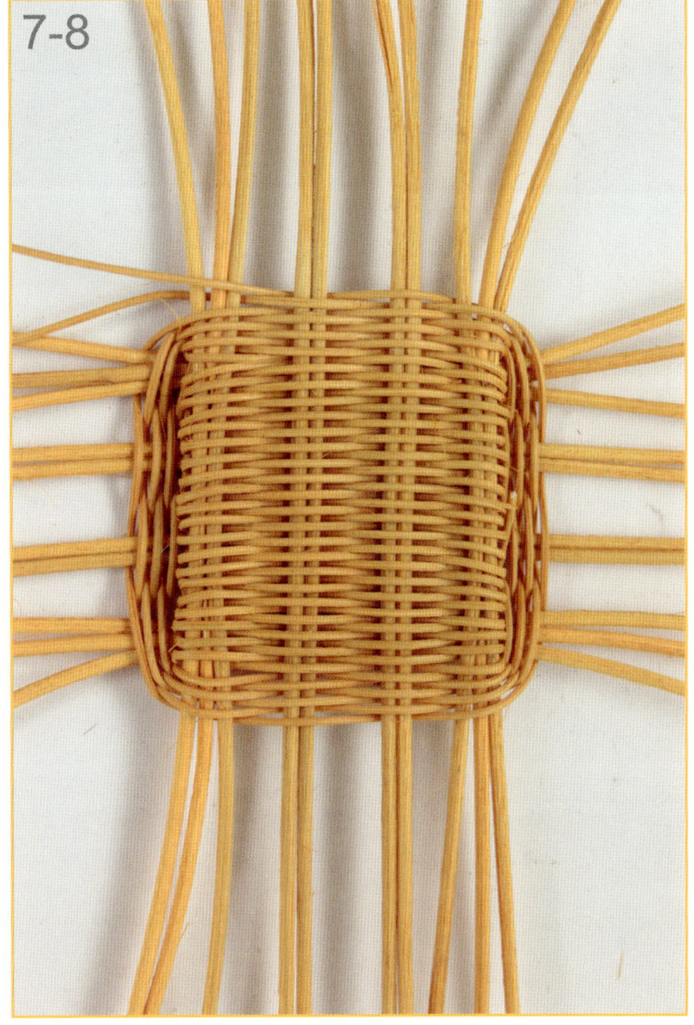

The vertical side of the Hopi base shows a Bi-Spoke at every corner.

The Hopi base begins to take on a round shape as the weaving progresses. Additional Bi-spokes and colorful weavers enhance the design.

Two green canyons are woven in Continuous Weave with Turnbacks on opposite sides of the base.

The Turnback technique allows the round reed weaver to continue the design without stopping each row. Crimp the round reed each time you weave over the end spoke to keep the reed from breaking.

13. **Color Change.** Replace one golden yellow weaver with **1 Row** of dyed accent reed **color, #2 black**, including the new bi-spoke, along with the old pair for this row. At the starting place, crimp this weaver and tuck it in and alongside the adjacent spoke. Replace the golden yellow weaver #2 with a **black** weaver #2 and weave **1 Row.** Trim, crimp and tuck this weaver. Change to accent reed **#3 natural**, **1 Row,** and continue to replace the weavers to repeat **black** weavers for the next **2 rows**. This produces two rows of black, one row of natural reed, and two rows of black.
14. Wet the second set of **24 new golden yellow bi-spokes at 14" long.** These are the final bi-spokes of the project. Insert a new bi-spoke along the right side of the previous spokes, now in groups of three spokes, to make each spoke four pieces.
15. **Color Change.** Wet two weavers in dyed accent reed **color, #4 green.** Crimp and insert these alongside the previous row; bend to start the new weavers. **Chase Weave** for **3 Rows in green,** using all four pieces as one spoke for these rows.
16. At this point in the plaque, the pattern changes from Chase Weave to Continuous Weave with turnbacks. This allows the design to develop the green and rust colors found in the canyons of the Southwest. Changing dyed reed colors several times will add black and natural rain clouds and blue sky.
17. Continue weaving with 1 green round reed weaver; end the shorter weaver by crimping and tucking. To create the green area of the canyon, choose 18 spokes along the horizontal base side. These will become four spokes, made up of four pieces each, and two additional from the next spoke. Mark these with a pencil to indicate where to begin and end.
18. **Continuous Weave** with dyed accent reed **color #4 green,** under and over, separating the spokes with four pieces into spokes of two pieces. When reaching the end of the 18 spoke section, re-wet the weaver, crimp and **turnback** by weaving around and back to the front in the same manner as the start to the original yayni bases. Weave over and under until reaching the end of the 18 spoke section on the opposite side. Turnback and continue weaving for **10 rows**. Do not end this weaver; keep it for the continuation of this canyon later. Repeat this same step on the opposite side of the plaque to create the second green canyon.
19. Turn your work to a side of the plaque that has no additional green weavers or turnbacks. In this area, change to dyed accent reed **color #2 black weaver** for **3 Rows. Continuous Weave** from the spokes that are next to the green canyon and the turnbacks. From side

to side, weaving over and under around 30 spoke ends, or 15 paired spokes of two pieces each. Separate the spokes made up of four pieces into paired spokes of two pieces while weaving this step. Do not end this black weaver. Add a new **natural weaver for 1 row.** Do not end this natural weaver. Alternate with **1 Row black, 1 Row natural, and finish weaving with 3 Rows in black reed**.

20. With dyed accent reed **color #5 rust**, weave above the black and natural sections for **3 rows,** using all 30 spoke ends as 15 paired spokes. Begin to weave with rust on either side of the center spoke above the black weaver. Continue weaving with the rust weaver for approximately **9 rows** using the turnback technique. This time, turnback one spoke sooner near the center spoke on every other row, to create a taller woven section. Use the **Increasing technique** as discussed in chapter 4, Weaving Techniques. The result creates a deep rust canyon. The turnbacks on the green side of the plaque continue at the same spoke. Repeat the same number of rows on the opposite side of the center spoke on the rust section of the plaque. This creates a lower area in the rust section, allowing room for the black and natural rain clouds to be woven later. Repeat this same rust canyon weaving on the opposite side of the plaque between the previous green weavers.
21. Return to one **green** canyon side of the plaque. Continuous Weave with dyed accent reed **color #4 green**. Turnbacks match the tall side of the rust canyon for approximately **12 Rows** and you will turnback 1 spoke sooner at every other row on the center spoke side. Repeat this step to create a complete green canyon and then turn to the opposite side of the plaque and repeat this step to construct a second green canyon.
22. **Rain clouds** are woven with black and natural weavers above each of the 4 canyons, 2 rust and 2 green canyons. Begin on any side of the plaque weaving **2 rows** of **black on the same center spoke** at the lowest point in the canyon. Then add a **natural** weaver and alternate weaving with natural and black. Turnback 1 spoke to the right and left of the center spoke, weaving 2 rows of each color. Every 2 rows creates an alternating pattern: 2 rows black reed and 2 rows natural reed. Continue in this way until you have 2 rows of natural reed about 3 spokes to the right and 3 spokes to the left of the center spoke and 2 rows of black reed about 4 spokes to the right and left of the center spoke. You will have woven approximately **12 Rows, alternating black and natural** weavers. This is the widest part of the rain cloud.

Now you are ready to begin the **Decreasing technique**, using the turnback technique discussed in

Continuous Weave with Turnbacks creates the rust canyons on two opposite sides of the basket. These canyons fill in the space between the green canyons.

Rain clouds are woven in black and natural weavers in the Increasing and Decreasing technique.

Weave four rain clouds, one on each side of the plaque, above the green and rust canyons.

The Hopi-Inspired Grand Canyon and Rain Clouds Plaque has a golden center with grassy green and rust canyons, black and natural rain clouds, and a royal blue sky.

The round reed border on the Hopi plaque is a two-step technique. In Step #1, the spoke moves to the right and under two spokes, then out to the front.

The two-step border continues with the spoke end moving to the right and over two spokes.

End the two-step border by inserting the spoke end into the back side of the plaque, between the border and the last row of black round reed weavers.

chapter 4. Turn 1 spoke sooner every 2 rows as you move toward the center spoke. This will complete the rain cloud, which resembles a diamond shape. Repeat this step above each of the remaining 3 canyons.

23. **Blue Sky** is the last dyed accent reed **color #6 royal blue.** Between any 2 rain clouds, begin to **Continuous Weave** above the rust weavers. Weave until reaching the black in the rain cloud. Then turnback and weave to the next rain cloud and turnback again at the black weavers. This increases the Blue Sky 1 spoke for every 2 rows. Weave with turnbacks for approximately **10 rows** until the blue weaver lines up with the last row of the rain cloud.

    Repeat this step above each of the rust canyons between the rain clouds. To complete the Blue Sky portion of the plaque, **Continuous Weave** for approximately **10 rows** above the rain clouds and around the entire plaque without turnbacks.
24. Return to Continuous Weave with **black** reed for **3 Rows**. Change to weave **1 row of natural reed, followed by 1 Row of black reed, and then 1 Row of natural reed.**
25. At this point, you may choose to dye all the spoke ends black, being careful to keep the black dye from bleeding onto the last 2 natural rows. Finish by weaving **6 Rows of black reed** around the plaque.
26. In each of the paired spokes, cut the right piece even with the last row of black weavers to prepare for the border.
27. **Rim Border.** With spoke ends wet and flexible, begin the 2-step woven border by marking a Starting Spoke with a green twist tie wire or a scrap of reed in a contrasting color. Begin weaving at this Starting Spoke and move to the right, under or behind 2 spokes and out to the front. Pick up the next spoke to the right and repeat, placing it under 2 spokes to the right and bringing it out to the front. Repeat until you have used each spoke. The last spoke will go under the Starting Spoke, which must be lifted to allow enough room for the last spoke to fit. Now weave with the Starting Spoke, over the next 2 spokes to the right. Push the Starting Spoke through to the back side, in between the 2 spokes to the right, through the opening between the border and the last row of black round reed weavers. Continue around the border until you reach the marked Starting Spoke. The last spoke will go through the opening to the right of the Starting Spoke.

28. **Weaving Summary**

This summary gives brief row-by-row directions, beginning when the 2 bases are combined and become a cross-warp base.

Golden yellow accent #1:-- Chase Weave, 3 Rows
Bi-Spoke, Chase Weave, 5 Rows
Bi-Spoke, Chase Weave, 5 Rows
Black accent #2:------------- Bi-Spoke, Chase Weave, 1 Row with each weaver, total of 2 Rows
Natural accent #3:----------- Chase Weave, 1 Row
Black accent #2:------------- Chase Weave, 2 Rows
Green accent #4: ------------ Bi-Spoke, Chase Weave, 3 Rows
Continuous weave with turnbacks, 10 Rows
Black accent #2:------------- Continuous Weave with turnbacks, 3 Rows
Natural accent #3:----------- Continuous Weave with turnbacks, 1 Row
Black accent #2:------------- Continuous Weave with turnbacks, 1 Row
Black accent #2:------------- Continuous Weave with turnbacks, 3 Rows
Rust accent #5: -------------- Continuous Weave with turnbacks using 30 spoke ends for 3 Rows
Continuous Weave with turnbacks
Increasing/Decreasing technique, 9 Rows
Green accent #4: ------------ Continuous Weave with turnbacks, 12 Rows
Black accent #2:------------- Continuous Weave, 2 rows around 1 center spoke
Black and Natural accents: Alternate Black and Natural for the rain clouds with the Increasing/Decreasing technique, 12 Rows
Blue accent #6: -------------- Continuous Weave with turnbacks, 10 to 12 Rows
Repeat rain cloud above each rust and green canyon
Continuous Weave without turnbacks, 10 Rows
Black accent #2:------------- Continuous Weave without turnbacks, 3 Rows
Natural accent #3:----------- Start and Stop technique, 1 Row
Black accent #2:------------- Start and Stop technique, 1 Row
Natural accent #3:----------- Start and Stop technique, 1 Row
Black accent #2:------------- Continuous Weave without turnbacks, 3 or more rows
Border: ---------------------- 2-Step border using the spoke ends (see Step 27)

The Hopi-Inspired Grand Canyon and Rain Clouds Plaque and Tray changes color several times to illustrate the Southwest landscape.

29. Crimp, trim, and tuck any weavers on the back side of the plaque for a neater finish. To keep the finished plaque flat, allow it to dry with spoke weights resting across the ends.
30. To hang your finished plaque, use clear thread or fishing line. Tie a piece around several spokes before the rim border. Hang this beautiful plaque out of direct sunlight to avoid fading the dyed accent reed.

AUTUMN'S DRESS

Autumn's Dress was inspired by the array of colors I see when looking out my studio windows. This woven art piece earned 2nd Place at the annual North Carolina Basket Association Convention, NCBA, 2011 Exhibit in the Professional Wicker Category.

A variety of round reed techniques are shared in this advanced design. Autumn colors, a three-color combination, may be changed from cocoa brown, rust, and gold, to blue, green, and purple for Spring colors. Finish with a slanted rim opening and philodendron sheaths.

Advanced Round Reed design.

Approximate Size: 14" diameter at widest × 25" (h); 6" rim opening

Materials

- 6" round slotted wood base, pre-finished with stain and urethane
- ¼" flat oval reed, natural or dyed walnut, cut for the base: 44 spokes at 32" long
- #0 or #1 round reed, dyed cocoa brown, base weave
- #2.5 or #3 round reed, dyed cocoa brown, rust, and gold, for Weavers
- Philodendron sheaths, 2 or more, Rim
- Waxed linen, butterscotch, Rim Lasher
- Tapestry or curved needle

Autumn's Dress is a design featuring a variety of round reed techniques which add color, texture, and interest to this shapely vessel. From the base to the rim, techniques blend into a sampler patchwork resembling a lady's dress with open cross over area for the belt and philodendron sheath as the collar.

Instructions

1. **Base**. Pre-finish the 6" round wood base; sand and stain the wood then allow it to dry. Apply three coats of urethane allowing each to dry completely between coats. See chapter 3 for details of this process.
2. Check the slotted grooved opening on the base before inserting 44 spokes; 22 spokes, spaced approximately ⅛" apart will fit in each half of the base. If the groove is narrow, add the spokes dry. If it is wider, wet the spokes or apply gel glue at the end of spokes to secure them as needed. Wet #0 or #1 round reed for weaving next to the base.
3. **Chase Weave** when using an even number of spokes; use two weavers in #0 or #1 round reed dyed **accent #1 cocoa brown**. Weave **4 rows** or more with each weaver to secure all spokes in the base. Trim and tuck these weavers under their Starting Spoke.
4. This is an advanced round reed basket design that includes a variety of techniques; some of these techniques are used in other projects within this text, while some of the weaving techniques are introduced for the first time with this basket. (Refer to the detailed instructions in chapter 4, Weaving Techniques, as necessary.)
5. Weave with #2.5 or #3 round reed in dyed **accent #1 cocoa brown** or the color of your choice. Mark a Starting Spoke and begin with this darkest color accent near the base. Weave **9 Rows in Three Rod Wale technique**, with a Step-up at the end of each row, for the weavers to stack rather than spiral.
6. **Blending or Becoming technique, a variation of Five Rod Wale**. Introduce dyed **accent #2 gold**, in the Blending technique. When all the weavers have passed the Starting Spoke, add one gold weaver behind the Starting Spoke, and one new cocoa weaver behind Spoke #5. Weave with 1 gold and 4 cocoa brown weavers in this **Five Rod Wale for 3 rows**. (There is no Step-up until you finish the last rows of Five Rod Wale in Step 9).
7. Continue **Five Rod Wale for 2 more rows** after you replace the second cocoa weaver with 1 gold weaver. Weave now with 2 gold and 3 cocoa brown weavers.
8. **Five Rod Wale for 2 rows,** weaving with 3 gold and 2 cocoa brown weavers.
9. **Five Rod Wale for 2 rows** with 4 gold weavers and 1 cocoa brown weaver.
10. Finish this **Five Rod Wale technique for 2 rows**, using all 5 gold weavers. Step-up at the end of this second row; trim and tuck your ends to the inside of the basket.
11. **Horizontal Bands of Color**. Return to **Three Rod Wale for 5 rows** using 3 rust weavers and Step-up at the end of every row. At the end of the fifth row, trim

From Three Rod Wale to Five Rod Wale Blending techniques, cocoa brown weavers blend into golden yellow.

Replace one cocoa brown weaver with one golden yellow weaver and continue to blend additional golden yellow weavers until you are weaving with all five pieces in yellow.

The Double Braid Weave technique has three weavers behind three consecutive spokes. Each weaver consists of two pieces of dyed round reed as one double weaver.

The Large Arrow in rust and golden yellow weavers begins with an Outside Spiral. When the weaving changes to Reverse Outside Spiral Three Rod Wale, weave left-handed in the opposite direction.

and tuck ends to the inside; crimp and tuck these alongside the next spoke, or tuck them under the previous row. This creates a horizontal band of color with rows stacked rather than in a spiral.

12. **Three Rod Wale for 3 rows** weaving with 3 cocoa brown weavers. Step-up to end each row. Trim and tuck the ends of your round reed weavers.
13. Repeat Step #11, weaving **5 rows** in all rust weavers. Step-up at the end of each row.
14. **Double Braid** Weave for **5 rows** as a Continuous Weave. See chapter 4, Weaving Techniques, for braid weave instructions. Combine two weavers of the same color to make one double weaver. Weaver #1 is two pieces of gold round reed as one weaver. Weaver #2 is two cocoa brown weavers as one weaver, and Weaver #3 is rust.

    Hint: For the rows of braid to line up horizontally in matching color accent, treat two adjacent vertical spokes as one spoke to create 43 spoke ends for this step of 5 rows of Double Braid Weave. Return to 44 spokes for Step 15.
15. **Horizontal Bands of Color** continue in **Three Rod Wale for 3 rows** with 3 cocoa brown weavers. Step-up at the end of each row for horizontal bands of color. Re-wet spokes for the 2" above the finished woven section. Use left hand pressure to assist in shaping the sidewalls. Begin to decrease the size of the rim opening.
16. **Three Rod Wale for 2 rows** with all gold weavers; Step-up each row.
17. Repeat Step #15, **Three Rod Wale for 3 rows** in cocoa brown. Step-up each row.
18. The **Large Arrow is an Outside Spiral Three Rod Wale technique for 6 rows,** weaving with 2 gold weavers and 1 rust weaver.

    To create the arrow, allow these rows to spiral with no Step-up until the end of the sixth row. Trim and tuck these three weavers to the inside of the basket.
19. The next technique is **Reverse Three Rod Wale.** Weave to the left for **6 rows** as in left-handed. Insert 3 weavers, 2 gold and 1 rust, behind the same spokes where weavers ended in Step 18, matching the colors in the previous row. Weave with weaver ends to the left, over 2 spokes and under 1 spoke, working with the right-most weaver rather than the left-most weaver as in regular Three Rod Wale.

    At the end of the sixth row, Step-up, beginning with the left-most weaver. This completes the top part of the arrow.
20. Return to weaving to the right. Repeat Steps 11, 12, and 13. Weave **Three Rod Wale** with a Step-up on each row. Weave **5 rust rows**; end these and replace weavers weaving for **3 rows** in cocoa brown, and then repeat weaving **5 rows** in rust reed.

21. At this point in the project, spokes are moving inward with hand pressure used to aid in decreasing the size of the rim opening. Re-wet all spokes before the next step.
22. The **Cross Over Open Area** was inspired by the need to create a belt for this Autumn's Dress. Begin with any spoke; cross it over to the left on top of the adjacent spoke, creating a long X with the 2 spokes. Continue creating an X with pairs of spokes. Use clothespins as needed to keep the tops of the X close together so that each pair now becomes 1 spoke for the remainder of the project. By decreasing the number of spoke ends, the size of the rim opening also decreases.
23. **Bargello Arrow technique** was inspired by an embroidery stitch. With one weaver of each accent color, weave **Three Rod Wale for 1 row** and then **Reverse Three Rod Wale for 1 row**. Alternating rows in this way creates **5 rows of complete arrows**, 10 rows of weaving. See chapter 4, Weaving Techniques.
24. **Three Rod Wale 3 rows,** with all cocoa brown weavers, and a Step-up to end each row. This creates stacked rows or **Horizontal Bands of Color**.
25. **Three Rod Wale** with all gold weavers for **2 Rows**. Step-up on every row.
26. At this point in the project re-wet your spokes to avoid any reed damage as the spokes are now encouraged to flare out. Repeat Step 15 for **3 rows** with cocoa brown. Using hand pressure from the inside, push out to increase the size of the rim opening and create the bust area of Autumn's Dress.
27. Border the next technique in **2 rows** rust **Three Rod Wale** with a Step-up at the end of each row.
28. A **Feathered Arrow** is woven next. At the Starting Spoke, replace 1 rust weaver with 1 gold weaver in **Three Rod Wale**. Weave **1 row** with 1 gold and 2 rust weavers; no Step-up is needed.
29. Replace 1 rust weaver with 1 gold to weave **1 row** with 2 gold weavers and 1 rust weaver and no Step-up.
30. The center of the Feathered Arrow is woven with all three gold weavers for **1 row** with a Step-up to end this row. Trim and tuck ends to the inside of the basket.
31. The next rows are woven left-handed, moving the weavers to the left to create the top portion of the Feathered Arrow technique. Begin this **Reverse Three Rod Wale** by inserting 1 rust weaver for 1 gold and weave **1 row** with 2 gold and 1 rust weaver.

    This is a repeat of the previous rows, or a mirror image. See chapter 4, Weaving Techniques, which describes the Reverse Three Rod Wale technique in detail.
32. Weave **1 row** with 1 gold and 2 rust weavers. Replace the next gold weaver with rust in preparation for the next step.

Create a belt for Autumn's Dress; in the Cross Over Open Area, cross one spoke over to the left and on top of the adjacent spoke forming an X.

The Cross Over Open Area brings two spokes together which become one spoke for the remainder of the project. This decreases the number of spoke ends and aids in decreasing the size of the rim opening.

A Feathered Arrow is a variation of Three Rod Wale. Replace rust weavers with yellow weavers; the arrow emerges as you weave left-handed in Reverse Three Rod Wale.

33. Weave **2 rows** with all rust weavers as a border (as in Step 27).
34. Return to right-handed weaving for the remainder of the basket. Re-wet the spoke ends to allow your hand pressure to encourage spokes to move inward to decrease the size of the rim opening in the following rows. Gently tug on the weavers with equal tension to aid in decreasing the rim circumference.
35. **Three Rod Wale for 3 rows** in cocoa weavers ending each row with a Step-up.
36. **Three Rod Wale for 2 rows** in rust weavers ending each row with a Step-up.
37. **Three Rod Wale for 3 rows** in cocoa weavers ending each row with a Step-up as before.
38. Carefully soak two or more long philodendron sheaths in warm water for one hour or longer, to soften and prepare for the rim border.
39. **Outside Spiral**, a Three Rod Wale technique, is woven with one weaver of each accent color: rust, gold, and cocoa brown. Continue to decrease the rim opening during these **10 rows** of Continuous Weave. The Step-up is at the end of the last row of the Outside Spiral.
40. **Three Rod Wale for 3 rows** using gold weavers and ending each row with a Step-up.
41. Weave **2 rows Three Rod Wale** in cocoa brown; end each row with a Step-up.
42. Repeat Step 40, **Three Rod Wale for 3 rows** using gold weavers.
43. **Five Rod Wale for 1 row** using 5 rust weavers. This is the beginning of the Blending or Becoming technique. There is no Step-up until the very last row. See chapter 4, Weaving Techniques, if necessary.
44. To begin to change the dyed accent color from rust to cocoa brown, replace 1 rust weaver with 1 cocoa brown; now weave with the 1 cocoa brown and 4 rust weavers for **2 rows in Five Rod Wale**.
45. Continue to blend the cocoa brown with the rust by weaving **2 rows Five Rod Wale** using 2 cocoa brown weavers and 3 rust weavers.
46. Continue with this pattern replacing 1 rust weaver each time. Weave **2 rows** of **Five Rod Wale** using 3 cocoa brown weavers and 2 rust weavers.
47. At this point, the neck of the basket has the vertical spokes upright to finish. Weave **2 rows Five Rod Wale** with 4 cocoa brown weavers and 1 rust weaver.
48. Weave with 5 cocoa brown weavers in the **Five Rod Wale technique for 8 rows** or more, to your desired height. Step-up to end the very last row.

The rim opening continues to decrease in size at the Three Rod Wale Outside Spiral.

Five Rod Wale and the Blending technique make the neck in Autumn's Dress.

49. **Rim** preparation begins with soaking the spoke ends until they are flexible. To create the slanted rim opening, trim the last 8 rows of weavers on an angle dipping to the center of the basket. Or, you can back weave, un-weave one row at a time, for part of the way around the basket. Trim each row one spoke sooner to create the angle.
50. Trim every other spoke even with the final row of weavers. Trim and tuck the remaining spokes down into two rows of weavers.
51. **Philodendron** sheaths are carefully removed from the water and placed in a towel to absorb excess water. Handle this natural material delicately. Apply the first sheath at the dip in the front of the basket. Use large clothespins or cable ties to secure sheath to the basket rim. Gently fold the sheath in half lengthwise. Place the fold at the top of the rim and allow the sheath to cover several of the last rows of weavers on the inside and the outside of the basket. Apply additional philodendron sheath as needed to cover the rim. With a tapestry needle and 6 feet of butterscotch, rust, or any matching color waxed linen, tie this waxed linen lasher around a vertical spoke at the rim. Lash around the basket at 1 inch intervals or as needed. Allow the philodendron sheath to overlap in the front and extend one end to create a collar for Autumn's Dress. End the waxed linen lasher as it was started; tie a knot with the beginning end of the lasher, trim and tuck the ends under the inside philodendron rim.

    Adjust the philodendron sheath at the rim as needed. Encourage the wet material in the direction you prefer; curl it or bend it up or down to create the neck or collar of Autumn's Dress.
52. Trim any remaining round reed ends on the inside of the woven vessel by inspecting the various weaving techniques used in this project.
53. **Personalize** the wood base with a wood burning pen or a permanent fine line marker for future reference. Sign your name or initials, the date or the year the basket was made, and the number assigned from your list of completed baskets. (Refer to chapter 6, Finishing Touches.)

Autumn's Dress is finished with philodendron sheaths. Gently place this natural material to cross over and curl or bend into the neck or collar.

CHAPTER EIGHT

JURIED EXHIBIT BASKET PROJECTS

WREN HOUSE WILLIAMSBURG BASKET

The Wren House Williamsburg Basket was displayed for one year at The Wren House, a *Southern Living Magazine* Showcase Home at The South Carolina Botanical Garden, Clemson University.

A sturdy square base rounds and flares out as the sides of the basket grow. Let the Williamsburg handle, which increases in width from the bottom up, guide you in shaping this woven basket. It is important to make all four sides flare evenly. This practical basket holds towels rolled up for guests, stores magazines standing upright, or holds your favorite fruits and snacks. Filled with pinecones or silk or dried flowers, this becomes a decorative basket as well.

Beginner Basket design

Approximate Size: 7" × 7" Base × 7"(h), 13" with handle, 12" rim diameter

Materials

- 7" Williamsburg handle
- ½" flat reed, natural or dyed, cut as follows: 13 spokes at 30" long, 36'
- #2 round reed, Twine, Base & Rim, 30'
- ½" flat reed, natural, Weavers, 45'
- ¼" flat or flat oval reed, Weavers, natural 40', dyed 40'
- ¼" flat natural reed or cane, Rim Lasher, 18'
- ⅜" flat reed, Rim Row/False Weaver option, 4'
- ½" flat oval reed, Rim, 8'
- #3 seagrass, Rim Filler, 4'
- Optional handle wrap technique materials

Displayed for one year at The Wren House *Southern Living* Showcase Home, this Williamsburg Basket features alternating navy and walnut dyed weavers.

An inside view of The Wren House Williamsburg Basket features an open weave base.

Instructions

1. **Base**. With ½" flat reed, cut 13 spokes at 30" long; dye navy or color of your choice. Wet these spokes along with #2 round reed for twining around the base. Remove from the water and wipe through a towel to remove excess water or dye.
2. Mark spokes in the center on the wrong or rough side of the reed. Mark the center of the handle also.
3. Next, place seven spokes horizontally, spaced approximately ½ inch apart, with the center marks lined up. Then, weave the wood handle vertically on top of three original spokes. Four spokes are on top of the handle including the two spokes nearest the handle. The woven base now has three spokes under the handle, while four spokes are on top of the handle.
4. Weave the six remaining vertical spokes through the original horizontal spokes. Start on the right side of the handle, weave over the first spoke, then under the next spoke, over, under, over, under, over and pull the spoke through about 10" beyond the woven base. The next spoke is woven on the left side of the handle, following the same over, under pattern as above. To finish the base, weave a total of three spokes on each side of the handle, alternating under and over.
5. Adjust the base to measure approximately 7 inches × 7 inches square. Be sure to measure the spoke ends that extend beyond the base so all are about the same length. Adjust where needed then, place a clothespin at each corner. (Refer to chapter 3, Base Techniques.)
6. Twine with #2 round reed. Find the center of the round reed, bend it in half and loop the fold around the second or third spoke from a corner. Twine around each spoke for one row. Keep the round reed close to the base. Square off each corner, trim and tuck the round reed ends to secure round reed under the loop and the next spoke to the right. (Refer to chapter 3.)
7. Re-wet the woven base, then bend the spokes to form the side walls of the basket in a gently relaxed upsett. Bend each spoke over your thumb and gently crease or crimp it. Secure several spokes together with clothespins at the ends of the spokes to help the shaping process.
8. **Weave Over and Under Start and Stop technique**. Row #1 begins with the smooth side of the reed facing out. Place the ½" weaver over or on the outside near a corner spoke, weave under the next spoke, over and under around the basket. Do not square off the corners; allow these to flare out to help shape the Williamsburg design. To end the weaver, overlap four spokes, trim on a diagonal and hide behind the fourth spoke. Place clothespins as necessary to keep rows packed down; at the handle, the corners, and in between spokes. To shape the basket, spray the inside and use left hand pressure pushing out on the sides of the basket without the handle to keep the

flared shape. The Wren House Williamsburg Basket design has alternating rows of ½" natural reed and ¼" dyed accent reed as pictured above. Remember to alternate over and under as you begin each new weaver and alternate the starting place to avoid build-up on one side. Continue to weave approximately eight or nine rows with each size reed, alternating ½" natural weavers and ¼" dyed weavers. Weave to a height of approximately 7 inches.

9. Inspect the overall shape of the basket; make adjustments as needed. The more left hand pressure pushing out and down on the spokes from the inside of the basket, the wider the rim will be on the finished basket.
10. **Rim Rows.** With #2 round reed, twine for three rows around the rim of the basket. Or, weave one Rim Row with ⅜" flat reed as an option.
11. Re-wet the spoke ends and carefully trim every other spoke even with the rim. Trim the remaining spokes on a diagonal before tucking each spoke under one of the top rows of weavers. Push in from the outside while tucking spokes or use a weaving tool to create an opening. Look at the last row of weaving; when the weaver is over the vertical spoke, trim it even with the rim. When the last weaver is under the vertical spoke, tuck that spoke.
12. **Rim Preparation**. Measure and cut two rim pieces from flat oval reed. Soak these along with the Rim Lasher. Include seagrass as the Rim Filler, which does not get wet. Use clothespins to temporarily secure the flat oval rims to the basket. Distribute the overlaps, insert the Rim Filler and adjust clothespins or clamps as needed. Add cable ties to secure rim pieces. (Refer to chapter 5, Rim Borders.)
13. Lash with medium chair cane or narrow flat reed. Tuck the end of the lasher up under the inside rim at or near the handle. Be sure the right, shiny side of the lasher is facing out. Lash around the basket on a diagonal to the right. Pull the lasher tight to keep rim pieces together and use clothespins or clamps to hold the tension.

    When the lasher reaches the starting place, finish by tucking the end of the lasher under the inside basket rim at your starting place.

    Or, reverse the lasher and Double Lash to the left to create an X as the rim border. End the lasher at the starting place. (Refer to chapter 5, Rim Borders, for additional instruction.)
14. **Stain**. Finish the basket with a natural walnut hull stain or dye. (Refer to the recipe in chapter 2.) Or, spray the finished basket with a commercially available stain. This process gives the basket an aged appearance and enhances its beauty.
15. **Personalize** the woven base with a wood burning pen or a permanent fine line marker for future reference. Sign your name or initials, the date or the year the basket was made, and the number assigned from your list of completed baskets. (Refer to chapter 6, Finishing Touches.)

The Wren House Williamsburg Basket is a traditional design updated with dyed reed for an eye-catching pattern.

COTTON LAUNDRY BASKET WITH OVERLAYS

A reproduction of an antique basket uncovered at an estate sale, this basket was juried for the Upper South Carolina Basketmakers Guild Weave-In Convention. The Cotton Basket hamper was a very common basket found on many farms; it was used for a variety of farm and home uses. Traditionally this basket was made wider at the rim and narrower at the base to easily empty cotton. Today the large basket serves as a laundry basket, for toy storage, for quilts, and many other practical uses. I add color accent and overlays for an updated design.

Beginner/Intermediate design.

Approximate Size: 12" × 12" Base × 14¾" (h)

Materials

- ¾" flat reed cut as follows: 20 spokes 52"
- #2 round reed, Twine Base and Rim, 40'
- ⅝" flat reed for weavers, natural, 23 rows or less
- ⅜" flat reed, dyed, Weavers, 10 rows
- ¼" flat reed, dyed, Weavers, 11 rows
- ⅝" flat oval reed, Rim, 12'
- #5 seagrass, Rim Filler, 5½'
- ¼" or 7 mm flat reed, Lasher, handle wrap, overlays

A large Cotton Laundry Basket design inspired by an antique cotton basket uncovered at an estate sale in Fairplay, South Carolina. It has a traditional wide rim opening for ease in emptying its contents.

Instructions

1. **Base**. Cut 20 spokes at 52" long from ¾" flat reed for the base of the Cotton Basket. Soak all of the spokes, #2 round reed for twining, and ⅝" flat reed for weavers. When spokes are flexible, remove from the water and mark the center on the rough side of each spoke.
2. Place ten spokes horizontally on the table. Weave the remaining ten spokes vertically through the original spokes, alternating over and under at the start of each spoke. Weave five spokes to the right of the center marks and five spokes to the left of the center marks. The base spokes will extend beyond the woven base for approximately 20" on each side.
3. The Open Weave Base measures 12 inches × 12 inches square. Make any needed adjustments, then clothespin the corners to keep your measurements accurate.
4. With a long piece of #2 round reed or two pieces of round reed behind two consecutive spokes, twine one row around the base. Trim and tuck ends under the original loop.
5. Re-wet the base; carefully bend spokes up for a gentle upsett. To help form the side walls of the basket, place a clothespin near the spoke ends including two from each side at the corners and clothespin several spokes together in between. At this point, the basket seems large and floppy without a handle for support.
6. **Over and Under Start and Stop Weave technique**. Push the long ends of the spokes up and away from you towards the inside of the basket. With ⅝" flat reed, weave **3 Rows** beginning on the left side of the basket, over on the outside of the second spoke from the left. Use clothespins to keep the weaver packed down. See chapter 4, Weaving Techniques.
7. Rotate the basket a one-quarter turn after each row of weaving to avoid a thick build-up on one side. Overlap two or four spokes as you end each row.
8. After Row 3, check the shape of the basket. Work towards a gradual relaxed flare to achieve the wider rim. From the inside of the basket, push spokes outward to help in shaping. In addition, begin to round out the corners rather than keep them square for the Cotton Laundry Basket. Re-wet the basket as needed. Follow the Weaving Summary.

9. **Cotton Laundry Basket Weaving Summary**

Rows 1–3:-------- ⅝" Flat reed, natural, 3 rows
Rows 4–8:-------- ⅜" Flat reed, dyed, 5 rows
Rows 9–11: ------ ⅝" Flat reed, natural, 3 rows
Rows 12–22:----- ¼" Flat reed, dyed, 11 rows
Rows 23–25:----- ⅝" Flat natural reed, 3 rows
Rows 26–30:----- ⅜" Flat reed, 5 rows
Rows 31–32:----- ⅝" Flat reed, natural; these are half rows with spokes tucked down for side handles

Bands of dyed reed add color to this Cotton Basket design. I updated the traditional pattern with three-dimensional overlays for texture.

An inside view shows the Built-in Handle opening in the Cotton Basket.

A Plain Handle Wrap covers the opening for a comfortable handle grip on the Cotton Basket.

10. **Built-in Side Handles.** The last two rows of ⅝" flat reed, Rows 31 and 32 are not complete rows. To create two side handles, choose two opposite sides of the basket and re-wet the two center vertical spokes, #5 and #6. Crimp, then slowly bend these vertical spokes and tuck them to the inside of the basket under one or more rows of weavers. Repeat on the opposite side of the basket to form the second handle. With ⅝" flat reed, weave 2 rows on each side of the handle. These are woven half-way around the basket; use the turnback technique at the handle areas.

    Re-wet, crimp and then slowly bend the end of the weaver back for 5". Weave this end and tuck behind the second or third spoke.
11. **Rim.** With #2 round reed, twine around the entire basket rim for three rows; include the handle area in the twining.

    Option: Add pottery handles or leather handles with the first of three rows of twining at the rim.

    Soak spoke ends until flexible. Trim and tuck every other spoke to the inside of the basket under the third row of weavers near the rim. See chapter 5 for additional instruction.
12. Measure around the inside and outside rim, add 3" to each measurement. Cut rim pieces of ⅝" flat oval reed. Shave or scarf the oval side from one end to create a smooth overlap. Soak rim pieces until flexible. Place inside rim piece to the left of a handle opening; clothespin or clamp the shaved edge. Secure the outside rim piece near the opposite handle and overlap it for 3". Add the seagrass rim filler adjusting clothespins where necessary.

    Optional Pottery Handles are included with the outside rim and are used in place of the handle wrap described in the next step. Slide the flat oval outside rim through the pottery handle opening and line up with the built-in opening.
13. Lash the rim with ¼" or 7 mm flat reed. Wet a long piece of reed and begin by tucking the end of the lasher up under the inside rim near the handle. Be sure the right, shiny side of the lasher is facing out. Lash around the basket on a diagonal to the right. Pull the lasher tight to keep rim pieces together and use clothespins or clamps to hold the tension. Continue around the basket rim until you reach the handle opening. Re-wet the lasher and continue to wrap the handle. Place the lasher right next to the previous row of wrapping. These wrapped rows need to touch; however they do not overlap. At the end of the handle, continue to lash until the opposite handle is reached. Repeat the handle wrap as before, then continue lashing to the starting place. Re-wet the lasher as needed. To end, tuck the lasher under the inside basket rim.

14. The traditional Cotton Basket design is updated with three sections of dyed accent reed in two different overlay techniques.

    Cross-Stitch Overlay is woven by placing flat reed, right side to the basket. Twist the reed so the right side faces you, then twist once more before tucking under the next spoke to the right. This overlay is worked in one direction and reverses to form the cross-stitch X design. Add the overlays to the dyed accent weavers near the bottom and top of the basket.

    The Diamond Overlay is woven as two separate rows of smocking. Place the right side of the reed to the basket under the second spoke from the left. Bring the end out to the left and continue on the outside of the basket, over the dyed accent weavers to the right, and up to the right-hand side of the sixth row of dyed accent weavers (the middle row of color). Tuck the overlay reed under this row and pull it to the left and around on a diagonal down to the right and under the first row of dyed accent weavers. Continue around the basket alternating the up and down smocking overlay. Trim and tuck the end under at the starting place.

    The top row of the diamond overlay is another smocking row. Start under at the sixth row of accent color, move up to the right, around the spoke, and down to the next spoke to the right to complete the diamond.
15. **Stain**. Finish the basket with a natural walnut hull stain or dye. (Refer to the recipe in chapter 2.) Or, spray the finished basket with a commercially available stain. This process gives the basket an aged appearance and enhances its beauty.
16. **Personalize** the woven base with a wood burning pen or a permanent fine line marker for future reference. Sign your name or initials, the date or the year the basket was made, and the number assigned from your list of completed baskets. (Refer to chapter 6, Finishing Touches.)

A woven X overlay is stitched onto the finished Cotton Basket.

As the center focal point, a Diamond overlay is stitched in two separate steps.

SEAGRASS EGG BASKET

The Ribbed Egg Basket is also known as a Fanny Basket, Buttocks Basket, Cheek Basket, Bowtie Basket, Gizzard Basket, Melon Basket, or Hip Basket as the shape rests nicely on the hip or on the back of a horse or mule. Pouches or nests on each side of the basket protect eggs, separate, and disperse the weight. Two round wood hoops are joined with the "ojo de Dios" or God's Eye, a four-point technique where the handle meets the rim. The round reed ribs determine the graceful shape in this historical and decorative basket. This basket was juried for Guilder's Weave Convention in Newport News, Virginia.

Beginner/Intermediate design.

Approximate Size: 6" (w) × 8" (l) × 6" (h)

Materials

- Two 6" round wood hoops
- Waxed linen thread, 2 pieces, 2' each
- #6 round reed, cut into 2 of each length below, for Ribs:
  - #1: $9\frac{3}{4}$"
  - #2: 11"
  - #3: $11\frac{3}{4}$"
  - #4: 11"
  - #5: 10"
  - #6: $8\frac{3}{4}$"
- $\frac{3}{16}$", $\frac{1}{4}$", or 7 mm flat reed, natural and dyed, God's Eye: 2 pieces, 10' each
- #0, #1 or #2 round reed, dyed, Weavers
- #00, #0, #1, or #2 seagrass, Weavers

This ribbed Egg Basket has a two-color God's Eye and is woven of seagrass.

Instructions

1. **Base**. While you assemble the wood hoops, soak two long pieces of flat reed, natural or dyed, for the God's Eye. Weave with seagrass or soak two long strands of round reed or additional flat reed.
2. On the 6" round wood hoops, find the place where the ends are joined and mark one inch away from this place. Then, measure to find the center of the hoop and mark it with a pencil.
3. Put the two hoops together by placing one over the other perpendicular to each other. The top of the basket is the hoop that is on the outside; mark this to assist in keeping the basket upright. Keep the glued, joined places on opposite sides of the basket. Tie the hoops together with thread or waxed linen at their intersections.
4. Before weaving the God's Eye, you may need to adjust the hoops. Measure the rim from one side of the hoop to the other; each side should be the same length.
5. **Traditional God's Eye**. With a long piece of wet flat reed, wrap around the hoops in sequence, with a clockwise turn after each wrap. Place the wrong side of the reed under the hoop, below the hoop that is now considered the rim. Wrap the smooth side of the reed over the rim hoop from the top left of the handle intersection, down on a diagonal to the right, then bring under the rim hoop to the left side. Finish the X by placing reed over the intersection on a diagonal up to the right and back to the starting point. Continue around in this way, moving the hoops clockwise and one-quarter turn and wrap over and under the hoop just crossed with a diagonal. Keep the wrong side of the weaver to the inside of the hoop; the smooth side overlaps the edges of the weaver slightly so each wrap lays on top of the preceding one on the right side of the basket. Make 5 or 6 wraps towards the outside of the basket to the desired size. Change the reed color for a contrasting outline to this four-point God's Eye. To finish, tuck the end under the last wrap at the starting place on the inside of the basket frame. You may need to use a bent end tool or flat screwdriver to allow the reed to pass under a previous wrap. Trim to end on the inside. (Refer to chapter 7 for God's Eye and the Plaid Carryall Basket.)
6. **Ribs**. Using #6 round reed, cut two each of the ribs as described in the Materials List. With a pencil, write the number on the center of each rib as it is cut. Sharpen each end of the ribs with a pencil sharpener to a blunt point, to allow insertion in the God's Eye. Use twist ties to secure numbered pairs of ribs together then, soak them until flexible.

An inside view of the God's Eye illustrates where ribs are inserted in the Seagrass Egg Basket.

7. Carefully bend each rib into a U-shape and place the sharpened end of Rib #1 under and into the God's Eye just below the rim.
8. Place Ribs #2, #3, #4, #5, and #6 in the same manner as described for Rib #1. Each rib is to be placed below the previous one to form the basic shape of one side of the Egg Basket. Continue to place ribs alternating from side to opposite side of the basket in the same way. Rib #1 is nearest the rim while Rib #6 is nearest the bottom of the handle hoop. After all 12 ribs are inserted, look at the outline of the shape of the basket to be sure it is desirable. Adjust or trim the ribs where needed to create the rounded pouches. Numbers on the ribs assist in identifying the placement as you weave, (especially if a rib pops out). Glue ribs into the God's Eye if necessary.
9. Begin weaving next to the God's Eye with #00, #0 seagrass, #0, #1, or #2 round reed, or narrow flat reed. Be sure the reed is wet and flexible; do not wet seagrass. To avoid breakage when bending over the top rim hoop, crimp the weaver as it reaches that place.
10. **Continuous Weave.** Leave a short one inch tail end of the weaver on the inside of the Egg Basket frame. Start weaving on the left side of the basket, close to the God's Eye. Weave under Rib #4, over Rib #5, under Rib #6 and over the bottom hoop. Continue on the right side of the basket, under Rib #6, over Rib #5, alternating in a Continuous Weave. At the rim hoop spray the weaver or use a sponge to keep the reed wet as you bend it over the wood hoop. Seagrass offers an advantage in that you can weave this basket anywhere without the need for water. Keep the weaver snug at the turn around and over the wood hoop. Weave back to the opposite side, alternating over and under in this Continuous Weave technique. Check rib numbers to be sure they are in the correct sequence.
11. When the weaver runs out or has turned over the rim hoop three or more times, turn the Egg Basket to the opposite side and start weaving with a new weaver. Always alternate sides of the Egg Basket to enhance the shape and keep consistent tension.
12. To add a new weaver, hide the new end under the last few ribs of weaving at the end of the old weaver near the bottom of the basket; this end is trimmed later.

    Weave with dyed round reed, flat reed, or seagrass. If the space between Rib #6 and the wood hoop becomes too large, add Secondary Spokes near the bottom hoop; one on each side. Weave it in the same pattern as Rib #6. Treat these two ribs as one for this row; then separate them and weave over and under in the following rows.
13. Periodically check the basket shape to keep it as symmetrical as possible on both sides.
14. **Filling in** may be necessary if you no longer have room on the hoops to turn over and around. To fill in, continue weaving over and under, turn on Rib #1 near the hoop, just be sure not to turn on the same rib two times in a row. Weave until the two weavers meet near the center of the basket.
15. Finish the seagrass basket with a few adjustments. Trim any seagrass or reed weaver ends close to the inside of the basket. Glue ends down if needed.

    Re-wet the ribs to make adjustments so the basket rests level. If needed, place a heavy object inside the wet basket and allow it to dry overnight.
16. **Stain**. Finish the basket with a natural walnut hull stain or dye. (Refer to the recipe in chapter 2.) Or, spray the finished basket with a commercially available stain. This process gives the basket an aged appearance and enhances its beauty.
17. **Personalize** the basket on the bottom wood hoop with a wood burning pen or a permanent fine line marker for future reference. Sign your name or initials, the date or the year the basket was made, and the number assigned from your list of completed baskets. (Refer to chapter 6, Finishing Touches.)

Seagrass offers two advantages in the Egg Basket; you can weave this basket anywhere without the need for water and the flexible material keeps the weaver snug at the turn around and over the wood hoop.

OVAL BARGELLO BASKET

The Oval Bargello Basket was juried for the South Carolina State Museum Triennial Exhibition in Columbia, South Carolina, from November 2004 through February 2005, and was juried to teach at two state conventions: Georgia Basket Association and North Carolina Basket Association, 2005.

Intermediate Basket design.

Approximate Size: 7" (w) × 11" (l) × 5" (h), 11" with handle

Materials

- 5" × 8" oval slotted wood base
- Round-top swing handle with wooden or brass knobs, 6"
- ¼" flat oval spokes: cut 48 at 9" long
- #1 round reed, natural, Chase Weave, Base, 20'
- #2 or #2.5 round reed, natural, Three Rod Wale, 25', Bargello, 50', and Rim Rows, 25'
- #2 or #2.5 round reed, dyed, Bargello Arrow; 50' each of 2 colors, optional Rim Filler
- 11/64" flat oval, Weavers, 5 rows
- 3/16" flat oval, Weavers, 8 rows
- ½" flat oval reed, Rim, 6'
- ⅜" flat reed, Rim Row option
- #3 seagrass, Rim Filler
- Medium cane, Rim Lasher

A round-top swing handle with wood knobs allows easy access to the Oval Bargello Basket and its contents.

Instructions

1. **Base**. Pre-finish the oval wood base; sand and stain the wood then allow it to dry. Apply three coats of urethane allowing each to dry completely between coats.
   See chapter 3 for details of this process.
2. With ¼" flat oval reed, cut 48 base spokes 9" long for the 5" × 8" Oval Bargello base. The number of spokes is a number divisible by 3 for this Bargello arrow design. Divide the wood base into four quadrants or quarters. With a pencil, mark the centers near the edge of the base to assist inserting spokes with equal distance between each spoke within each quadrant. From paper, cut a template the same size as the wood base. Fold the template in half, then fold it in half once again. Next place the open template on the wood base and mark the four quadrants.
   You may also do this by approximating if you choose.
   Check the slotted grooved opening before inserting spokes into the base. If the groove is narrow and the spokes fit tight, do not wet them; insert dry spokes, and then spray with water. If the groove is wider and your spokes move about and are loose, wet the spokes briefly and then insert them. When water is absorbed, it will temporarily enlarge the spokes, causing them to stay in place. If these steps do not solve the movement issue, apply a small amount of fast-drying gel glue to the end of the spoke. Insert it into the groove, and hold it there long enough for the gel glue to thoroughly dry.
   Insert the first base spoke, rough side up, at or near one of the center marks.
   Insert one quarter or one half of the base spokes within the marks. Check your spacing, approximately ¼" apart, and then continue to insert all spokes rough side up, creating an equal distance between each one. Push all spokes firmly into the slot or groove. When finished, count the total number of spokes to be sure the accurate number are in place.
3. **Chase Weave** beginning with one piece of #1 round reed, on the long side of the wood base and as close to the base as possible. Crimp and bend the end of round reed Weaver #1 and insert it into the slot in the base between two spokes. Weave over, then under and continue weaving around the base stopping two spokes before reaching the starting point. Push spokes into the base as necessary to keep in place; use a small weaving tool to push the round reed weaver close to the base.
4. Chase Weave with a second piece of #1 round reed, Weaver #2. See chapter 3. Insert the end into the slotted wood base in the space before and to the left of round reed Weaver #1. Weave over and under, opposite the first weaver, around the wood base until you are two spokes away from the first weaver. Pick up Weaver #1 and continue to weave over and under around the wood base. Chase Weave for a total of four rows. Check the spacing between spokes often. Tuck the ends of the round reed weavers under the previous row, and trim ends.

5. **Oval Bargello Basket Weaving Summary**

Rows 1–5:--------	11/64" Flat oval reed, natural, Over and Under Start and Stop, 5 rows
Rows 6–8:--------	3/16" Flat oval reed, natural, Over and Under Start and Stop, 3 rows
Row 9:------------	#2 Round reed, natural, Three Rod Wale (Triple Twine), 1 row
Rows 10–15:-----	#2 or #2.5 Round reed, natural and dyed, Bargello Pattern, 6 rows
Row 16: ----------	2 mm Round reed, natural, Three Rod Wale (Triple Twine), 1 row
Rows 17–21:-----	3/16" Flat oval reed, Over and Under Start and Stop, 5 rows
Rows 22–24:-----	#2 Round reed, natural, Twine, Rim Rows or 3/8" Flat reed, 1 Rim Row

6. **Over and Under, Start and Stop Weave technique**. With 11⁄64" flat oval reed, weave **Rows #1 and #2** from the inside of the basket, flat side of reed faces up, the oval side is on the outside of the basket. Weave over and under around the basket; end with a four spoke overlap to allow for adjustments later. Shave one oval end of the weaver at the overlap for ease in packing. Spray spokes from the inside, cover the wood base to avoid getting it wet. Gently upsett and bend spokes upward. Place clothespins at the ends of several spokes to help shape the side walls of the basket. Now, you will transition to weave from the outside, the right side of the basket.
7. Continue to weave three more rows, for a total of **5 rows** with 11⁄64" flat oval reed. Then change to the next size larger reed and weave an additional 3 rows with 3⁄16" flat oval reed. These beginning rows are gradually shaping the side walls of the basket with a relaxed, gentle flare outward in contrast to the upsett technique in a market-style basket. Pack weavers before moving on to Step 8.
8. **Three Rod Wale (Triple Twine)**. Mark your Starting Spoke. Weave one row in Three Rod Wale as a border for the Bargello pattern to follow. With #2 round reed, begin this step by placing three round reed weavers, one each

behind three consecutive spokes, and behind the marked Starting Spoke. (Refer to chapter 4, Weaving Techniques.)

To end this row, weave a Step-Up to complete the pattern. Stop the Three Rod Wale in the space to the left of the Starting Spoke. Weave with the right-most round reed weaver. (Refer to chapter 4 for details.)

9. **Bargello Arrow**, a Chase Weave technique. Form the Bargello Arrow with a Chase Weave including one row of Three Rod Wale (Triple Twine) followed by or chased by one row Reverse Three Rod Wale.

   Begin with Three Rod Wale, round reed Weaver #1 natural, round reed Weaver #2 wine, round reed Weaver #3 navy. Weave one row of Three Rod Wale with these colors behind the first three consecutive spokes. Stop weaving three spokes before your Starting Spoke. Do not cut or tuck these weavers; secure this set of three round reed weavers with twist ties while not in use. (No step-up until the final row).

   The Chase Weave starts here. Reverse Three Rod Arrow begins with three round reed weavers one each behind three consecutive spokes beginning one spoke to the left of the original 3 spokes. The color sequence is navy, natural, wine to create the arrow. Take the left weaver (navy), weave under two weavers instead of weaving over two round reed weavers as in Three Rod Wale. Move these two out of the way with your left hand, continue the left-most (navy) weaver over two vertical spokes, under, behind the next vertical spoke, and out to the front. Continue this sequence around the Oval Bargello Basket until you nearly reach the original three round reed weavers Three Rod Wale. Continue to alternate Three Rod Wale and Reverse Three Rod Wale. Mark each coil to distinguish which step you are weaving. Each time around the basket you will change to the chase weave in a slightly different place since you stop three spokes back each time. The Three Rod Wale part of the arrow is a diagonal from bottom up to the right and the Reverse Three Rod Wale part of the arrow is a diagonal from the top down to the right. Weave three rows of arrows then, begin to decrease the size of the basket by applying left hand pressure, pushing in on spokes and gently tugging on the round reed weaver. Complete a total of 6 rows of arrows. Be sure each individual arrow matches in color. Arrows will be vertical rows matching in color as well.

10. To end the Bargello pattern, the last row of Three Rod Wale has a Step-up. (Refer to chapter 5.) The last row of Reverse Three Rod Wale arrow does not have a Step-up; complete each arrow, matching colors as before. End two spokes to the right of your Starting Spoke. Bring round reed to the inside of the basket, and trim or tuck under the previous row.

The Bargello arrow design was inspired by the embroidery stitch. It is a Three Rod Wale and Reverse Three Rod Wale Chase Weave.

11. **Three Rod Wale, Triple Twine.** Weave one row of Three Rod Wale as a border for the Bargello pattern with three natural round reed weavers.
12. **Handle Insertion.** Find the center spoke on the two long sides of the basket and insert the end of the handle ear into one or more rows of weavers on the inside of the basket. To decrease any stress on the wood knobs of the handle, you may need to wet the round top of the handle, not the wooden knobs. Then gently stretch the handle ends to the desired size to fit the handle inside the rim of the basket. Use a twist tie wire to keep the handle ear and the spoke together; treat as one for the remainder of the basket.

An inside view of this add-in swing handle shows the lasher wrapping several times to help secure it.

The Double X or Double Cross adds detail next to the wooden knob and swing handle.

13. **Over and Under, Start and Stop Weave technique.** Re-wet the ends of the vertical spokes. With 3/16" flat oval natural reed, weave Over and Under, Start and Stop for **5 rows.** Push spokes down and to the inside of the basket and increase tension on the weavers to decrease the shape of the side walls of the basket. Check for handle fit while weaving these last rows of the basket. Adjust weavers as necessary to fit the 6" round top Swing Handle.
14. With #2 round reed, Twine for 3 rows around the top of the basket as your Rim Rows. Or, weave one Rim Row with 3/8" flat reed.
15. **Rim** Application. Re-wet spoke ends, trim and tuck every other spoke to the inside of the basket. Trim the remaining vertical spokes even with the top row of Twine, Rim Row.
16. Measure and cut two rim pieces from flat oval reed. Soak these along with the Rim Lasher and round reed Rim Filler. Or include seagrass as the Rim Filler, which does not get wet.
17. Use clothespins to temporarily secure the flat oval rims to the basket. Distribute the overlaps, to the left and right of the handle on the same side of the basket. Insert the Rim Filler and adjust clothespins or clamps as needed. Add cable ties to secure all rim pieces.
18. **Lash** with medium chair cane or narrow flat reed. Tuck the end of the lasher up under the inside rim at or near the handle. Be sure the right, shiny side of the lasher is facing out. Lash around the basket on a diagonal to the right. Pull the lasher tight to keep rim pieces together and use clothespins or clamps to hold the tension.
    When the lasher reaches the starting place, finish by tucking the end of the lasher under the inside basket rim at your starting place.
    Or, reverse the lasher and Double Lash to the left to create an X as the rim border. Weave a Double X, also known as a Cross-Knot, at each handle as you reach it for the final time. (Refer to chapter 5, Rim Borders, for additional instruction.)
19. Use the back cut technique and trim any ends of round reed for a neat finished appearance.
20. **Stain.** Finish the basket with a natural walnut hull stain or dye. (Refer to the recipe in chapter 2.) Or, spray the finished basket with a commercially available stain. This process gives the basket an aged appearance and enhances its beauty.
21. **Personalize** the wood base with a wood burning pen or a permanent fine line marker for future reference. Sign your name or initials, the date or the year the basket was made, and the number assigned from your list of completed baskets. (Refer to chapter 6, Finishing Touches.)

RECTANGLE SAMPLER BASKET

The Rectangle Sampler Basket incorporates eight different techniques beginning at the base and continuing to the cable stitch rim. This pattern, created especially for teaching the Upper South Carolina Basket Makers Guild, was juried for exhibit in the South Carolina State Museum Palmetto Hands Exhibit.

Intermediate pattern.

Approximate Size: 8" (w) × 14" (l) × 8½" (h)

Materials

- Leather handles or pottery handles, 1 pair
- ½" flat reed, natural, cut for Base Spokes: 8 at 38" and 13 at 32"
- ¼" flat oval reed, natural, cut for Filler spokes: 14 at 20"
- #2 round reed, natural, Twine base and Rim Rows, 40'
- ¼" flat oval reed, natural and dyed, Weavers: French Randing, 42 pieces, dyed, 7½" long, 35'. Braid Weave, two dyed colors, 25' each, natural, 25'
- ¼" flat reed, dyed, Ti-Twining, 3 long pieces, 40'
- #2.5 or #3 round reed, natural, Double Four Rod Wale, 16 pieces, 5' each
- #2.5 or #3 round reed, dyed, Three Rod Wale 12 pieces, and Rim Filler
- ⅜" flat reed, Weavers and Rim Row option, 45'
- ½" flat oval reed, Rim, 9'
- #3 seagrass, Rim Filler option
- Medium cane or $^{3}/_{16}$" flat reed, Cable Rim Border, 20'

The Rectangle Sampler Basket has a functional filled-in base with eight techniques to weave into one basket.

Instructions

Filled-in Base Sampler technique #1

1. Cut spokes as indicated in the Materials list and soak along with #2 round reed for Twine around the base. Mark the centers on the rough side of all spokes.
2. Place 8 spokes of ½" flat reed at 38" long horizontally on your work surface. Alternate these with a pair of flat oval filler spokes in between each of the ½" spokes, for a total of 14 filler spokes. Line up all of the center marks.
3. Use spoke weights to anchor fillers and spokes.
4. With 32" spokes, weave the center vertical spoke at the center marks, begin under the ½" spokes and over the pairs of filler spokes. Continue to weave a total of 6 spokes on each side of the center spoke, alternating over and under, for a total of 13 vertical spokes. The last vertical spokes are the same as the center spoke, under the ½" spokes and over the pairs of fillers.
5. Measure the filled-in woven base and adjust to an 8" × 14" rectangle. Re-wet the filler spokes, crimp, and slowly bend each to the inside of the basket base and split the pair tucking one spoke above and one below. Trim and tuck these ends under the second spoke.
6. Twine Row #1 around the base with #2 round reed. Tuck ends under the starting loop and trim close to the base. Place a clothespin at each corner.
7. Re-wet the base and upsett the sides of the basket.

8. **Rectangle Sampler Basket Weaving Summary**

Row 1:------------ #2 Round reed, natural, Twine, 1 row
Rows 2–3:-------- 3/8" Flat reed, natural, Over & Under, Start and Stop, 2 rows
Row 4:------------ #3 Round reed, dyed, Three Rod Wale, 1 row
Rows 5–6:-------- 1/4" Flat oval or Flat reed, dyed, French Randing, 2 rows
Row 7:------------ #3 Round reed, dyed, Three Rod Wale, 1 row
Row 8:------------ 3/8" Flat reed, Over & Under, Start and Stop, 1 row
Row 9:------------ #3 Round reed, natural, Double Four Rod Wale, 1 row
Rows 10–12:----- 3/8" Flat reed, natural, Over & Under Start and Stop with Ti-Twining, 1/4" Flat reed, dyed, 3 rows
Row 13: ---------- #3 Round reed, natural, Double Four Rod Wale, 1 row
Row 14: ---------- 3/8" Flat reed, Over & Under, Start and Stop, 1 row
Row 15: ---------- #3 Round reed, dyed, Three Rod Wale, 1 row
Rows 16–18:----- 1/4" Flat oval reed, natural and dyed, Braid Weave, 3 rows
Row 19: ---------- #3 Round reed, dyed, Three Rod Wale, 1 row
Row 20: ---------- 3/8" Flat reed, natural, Over and Under, Start and Stop, 1 row
Rows 21–23:----- #2 Round Reed, Twine, 3 rows Or 3/8" Flat reed, natural, Rim Row option
Cable Border

9. **Rows 2–3: Over and Under, Start and Stop**. Weave 2 rows with ⅜" flat reed. Overlap at the Starting Spoke for four spokes, then trim and tuck the weaver under the fourth spoke. To distribute the weaver overlap, give the basket a one-quarter turn and begin Row 3 on the next side of the basket. Check corners for straight vertical sides and keep equal space between spokes. Adjust clothespins as needed.
10. **Three Rod Wale Sampler technique #2.** Weave with #3 Round reed, dyed, for one row and Step-up to end. This serves as a border for the next step. (Refer to chapter 4, Weaving Techniques.)

11. **French Randing Sampler technique #3.** Woven with ¼" flat or flat oval dyed reed, this is a good technique to use up your scraps. Insert a 7½" piece behind every vertical spoke. Begin by placing the first short weaver behind any spoke, tuck it under the previous row of round reed Three Rod Wale. Mark this the Starting Spoke, "SS." Weave from left to right at a diagonal over 1 spoke, under, behind 1 spoke, and out to the front. Place the next diagonal weaver to the left of the Starting Spoke and weave over 1, under 1, and out to the front. Continue French Randing in this way by placing a diagonal weaver to the left of each spoke until you reach the Starting Spoke. This completes one row. Check to be sure you have placed a diagonal weaver behind every vertical spoke, 42 pieces in all.
12. **French Randing Row 2**. Begin at the Starting Spoke and continue to weave the short diagonal weaver over 1 spoke, under 1, and out to the front as before. Continue around the basket working with the next spoke to the left each time. Pack these short weavers as needed. To end, trim each diagonal weaver and be sure it rests on the inside of the basket to the right of the vertical spoke. Each diagonal weaver will use seven spokes: under 1, over 1, under 1, over 1, under 1, over 1; trim and bring under 1 to the inside of the basket.
13. Three Rod Wale for one row, see Step 10. Check the overall shape of the basket be sure the corners are square and spokes are upright. Keep clothespins at the corners to assist in shaping. Re-wet the basket as needed. With ⅜" flat reed weave one row, Over & Under, Start & Stop.
14. **Double Three Rod Wale Sampler technique #4.** Soak #3 round reed, 6 pieces, 5' long. Double Three Rod Wale begins with two weavers of round reed put together as one pair or Double Weaver. Three pairs are needed. Begin by placing pairs of round reed near the left side of the basket and behind three consecutive vertical spokes. (Refer to chapter 4 as needed.) Weave around the basket alternating weavers, then stop one spoke before reaching your Starting Spoke; do not trim.
15. Step-up to end these weavers and complete this row.
16. **Ti-Twine Sampler technique #5**. Weavers are ⅜" flat reed and ¼" flat or flat oval dyed accent reed as the flexible weaver. The flexible weaver is the Ti-Twine wrapper, which wraps around the ⅜" weaver on a diagonal. Begin Ti-Twine **Row 1** with the ⅜" flat weaver, weave over, under, over; then tuck ¼" dyed accent weaver under the previous row (Double Three Rod Wale). Bring the ¼" Ti-Twine wrapper from inside the basket, over on a diagonal to the right from top left to bottom right. Weave over the vertical spoke to the right where the ⅜" weaver is in the under position.

The French Randing technique has a small piece of dyed or natural reed behind every spoke; the design works on a diagonal.

A flat weaver wrapped with a dyed flexible weaver is found in the Ti-Twine technique.

Ti-Twine and Braid Weave are two of the samples in this Rectangle Sampler Basket.

17. The Ti-Twine wrapper, a flexible dyed accent, is woven to the inside of the basket, on a diagonal, under and behind the next vertical spoke to the right. Continue with the ⅜" weaver, over, under, over, then, repeat the diagonal weave with the ¼" Ti-Twine Wrapper. Continue to alternate weaving with ⅜" reed in the Over and Under, Start and Stop technique. Followed by the ¼" Ti-Twine wrapper. To end Row 1, overlap the ⅜" weaver for 4 spokes, trim and tuck under. Do not trim the ¼" wrapper since this is a Continuous Wrap technique. (Refer to chapter 4.)
18. A second method to achieve the Ti-Twine design is to weave one row in ⅜" flat reed. Then, wrap around this weaver in the Ti-Twine technique, which is similar to lashing at the rim of a basket. Resume weaving with ⅜" and repeat for three rows.

    Row 2. Start the next ⅜" weaver, over, under, over as before, continue the ¼" Ti-Twine wrapper by bringing it up a row on the inside of the basket. On the outside of the basket, the ¼" Ti-Twine Wrapper is over the vertical spoke that has the ⅜" weaver in the under position; while the ¼" Ti-Twine Wrapper is under and inside the basket where the ⅜" weaver is over the vertical spoke. Complete three rows in the Ti-Twine technique.
19. **Double Three Rod Wale Sampler technique**. One row is woven above the Ti-Twine as a border to accent this design in the center of the basket. This adds a rope-like, textural dimension. See Step 14 or refer to chapter 4.
20. With ⅜" flat reed, weave one row in the **Over and Under, Start & Stop** technique. Adjust corners if needed.
21. **Three Rod Wale**. With three pieces of #3 dyed round reed, weave one row with a Step-up to end. This one border row is found in Step 2 of this pattern. See chapter 4 if needed.
22. **Braid Weave Sampler technique #6.** Weave with ¼" flat oval reed, two dyed accent weavers and one natural weaver.
23. To start the Continuous Braid Weave, taper the ends of three weavers for 6". Place two weavers behind two consecutive spokes on one of the long sides of the basket. Mark the Starting Spoke, SS. (Refer to chapter 4.)

    Weaver #1 moves over 2 spokes to the right, then under 1 spoke, and out to the front of the basket.

    Next, Weaver #2 also moves over 2 spokes, under 1 spoke, and to the front.

    Weaver #3 actually begins the braid and it is placed above the first two weavers and behind the third consecutive vertical spoke. The first two weavers form an arrow, and Weaver #2 moves over 2 spokes, then in between the arrow, continue under the third vertical spoke, and out to the front. This is a Continuous Weave, where the weaver on the far left goes over two spokes, between the arrow, then under the next spoke to the right and out to the front of the basket.

24. After each Braid row, look on the inside of the basket to check for accuracy. The braided weavers will alternate slanting up or down on each base spoke. This diagonal slant will stay the same all the way up the spoke. Check for correct positioning; if a spoke has diagonal slants in both directions, go back and adjust where necessary.
25. Pack each row of the braid as you continuously weave around the basket. To finish the braid pattern, taper each weaver for 6" and end each weaver under its starting place on the same side of the basket it originated.
26. **Three Rod Wale** with #3 dyed round reed for one border row above the braid weave matching the border below the braid.
27. **Over and Under Start and Stop**. Weave one row with ⅜" flat reed.
28. Rim Row(s). Twine 3 rows with #2 round reed or one Rim Row with ⅜" flat reed.
29. **Rim**. Re-wet spoke ends until flexible. Trim and tuck every other spoke to the inside of the basket. Trim the remaining spokes even with the top row of twining, or Rim Rows. See chapter 5 as needed. Use clothespins to secure the inside flat oval rim before Step 30.
30. **Handles, Sampler technique #7.** Choose to include two leather handles or pottery handles. These are added as you apply the outside flat oval rim. Thread the flat oval reed through the leather handle openings or loops. Place handles at the center of the short sides of the basket, near spokes 3 and 6. Insert both leather handles; then continue to add the rim filler. Adjust clothespins as needed and add cable ties to secure all rim pieces to the basket.
31. **Lash** with medium chair cane or narrow flat reed. Tuck the end of the lasher up under the inside rim at or near the handle. Be sure the right, shiny side of the lasher is facing out. Lash around the basket on a diagonal to the right. Pull the lasher tight to keep rim pieces together and use clothespins or clamps to hold the tension.

    When the lasher reaches the starting place, finish by tucking the end of the lasher under the inside basket rim at your starting place.
32. **Cable Border, technique #8.** The Cable Stitch takes the lasher in reverse and wraps over, under and around the previous lasher working to the left. The lasher stays on the outside of the rim and continues to wrap over, under, and around each original lasher wrap. To finish, tuck the end of your lasher under the inside basket rim. (Refer to chapter 5, Rim Borders.)

Leather Handle is attached with the outside rim before lashing begins. Cable Stitch rim lashing is a two-step technique in cane.

33. While the basket is damp, make any necessary adjustments. Pinch the corners for a crisp rectangle shape. Push up on the base where needed to allow the basket to rest flat and level on the surface.
34. **Stain**. Finish the basket with a natural walnut hull stain or dye. (Refer to the recipe in chapter 2.) Or, spray the finished basket with a commercially available stain. This process gives the basket an aged appearance and enhances its beauty.
35. **Personalize** the woven base with a wood burning pen or a permanent fine line marker for future reference. Sign your name or initials, the date or the year the basket was made, and the number assigned from your list of completed baskets. (Refer to chapter 6, Finishing Touches.)

CHAPTER NINE

GALLERY OF CONTRIBUTING ARTISTS

Artists in the twenty-first century bring new and innovative ideas to their artwork. Enjoy the talents of these eight artists in this sampling of woven art. From baskets based on our traditional designs with a new twist, to the most contemporary, abstract woven vessels, here is a peek into today's fine craftsmanship and art in combination.

Baskets have evolved from the most functional designs to a fascinating array of contemporary art pieces. The weavers acknowledge the techniques of our ancestors and intertwine them with a variety of natural materials. Each artist shares a connection to their chosen materials and their vision to create the new baskets.

I have had the pleasure of teaching alongside these artists at many conventions and seminars. It has been my privilege to weave in class under their instruction. If you find the opportunity to weave with these artists, you're sure to learn from your instructor's enthusiasm and love for their art.

JOANN KELLY CATSOS

JoAnn Kelly Catsos is an award-winning black ash splint basketmaker and teacher who teaches her basketry designs at craft schools and conferences across the country. She and her husband, Steve, harvest the black ash logs near their home in the Berkshire Mountains of Massachusetts, process the logs into splint, and make the wooden molds, handles, and rims needed for each basket.

Originally based upon traditional Shaker and native New England utilitarian styles, JoAnn's baskets have evolved into smaller, more finely woven intricately patterned vessels.

JoAnn has won numerous awards during her thirty-year basketry career, and her baskets are in many private and public collections. In 2013 her sewing basket was included in the Cole-Ware Collection of American Baskets exhibition at the Renwick Gallery of the Smithsonian American Art Museum. Her work has been published many times, including in the book *500 Baskets*, and in October 2012 her work graced the cover of the *Crafts Report* magazine. In 1999, JoAnn was honored to have an ornament on the official White House Christmas Tree. In 2003, she received the Certificate of Excellence in Basketmaking: Level I, from the Handweavers Guild of America. JoAnn has juried national basketry exhibitions and is a past board member of the National Basketry Organization.

Snowflake Sewing Basket by JoAnn Kelly Catsos. 9¾" dia. × 8" h. Materials used are stained and natural black ash splint with maple rims. The large basket is mold woven and plaited with an original design on the lid. Interior baskets are mold woven in a hexagonal weave. *Courtesy of David Wiechnicki.*

Prestidigitation by JoAnn Kelly Catsos. 7" dia. × 10" h. Materials including stained and natural black ash splint and maple rims are used in this mold woven, plaited twill pattern. *Courtesy of Jeff Magidson.*

Jubilique by JoAnn Kelly Catsos. 9¾" dia. × 13½" h. Stained and natural black ash splint, maple rims and handle are mold woven and plaited with an original twill pattern on the lid. *Courtesy of David Wiechnicki.*

Jubilation by JoAnn Kelly Catsos. 6" dia. × 8" h.Stained and natural pounded black ash splint, maple for the rims, and waxed linen lashing materials are used in this basket. The techniques are mold woven and plaited in an original twill design. *Courtesy of Jeff Magidson.*

FLO HOPPE

Flo Hoppe is a full-time studio artist, teacher, and author. She began her career in 1971 teaching herself basketmaking from a small booklet published in 1924. Her main emphasis is on wicker basketry and Japanese basketry.

She lived in Japan from 1968 to 1971 and on a return trip to Japan in 1994, Flo studied with two master basketmakers.

Her published books are titled *Wicker Basketry, Contemporary Wicker Basketry* (which has been translated into German), and *Plaited Basketry with Birch Bark*, co-authored with Vladimir Yarish and Jim Widess.

She teaches and exhibits worldwide, with teaching venues in England, Canada, Japan, Russia, and Australia.

She was one of three basket artists to receive the prestigious Lifetime Achievement Award given for the first time by the National Basketry Organization in 2013.

Divertimento by Flo Hoppe. 10½" dia. × 9" h. Materials used in this tall basket with surface embellishment are dyed rattan, randing, Indonesian cane, and dyed Japanese cane; with twining, figure-8 weave, and the cretan stitch techniques. *Courtesy of Ray Bolton.*

Homage I by Flo Hoppe. 10" dia. × 9" h. Dyed rattan, dyed Indonesian cane, and dyed Japanese cane are woven into this tall basket with overlays. Twining, randing, figure-8 weave and Japanese raindrop border techniques. *Courtesy of Ray Bolton.*

Khamari by Flo Hoppe. 10½" dia. × 8" h. Dyed rattan, tiger bamboo, Indonesian cane, and dyed Japanese cane are woven into this medium size basket with overlays and surface embellishment using twining, randing, square knots, and the figure-8 weave techniques. *Courtesy of Ray Bolton.*

Intermezzo by Flo Hoppe. 13" dia. × 7" h. Materials include dyed rattan, Indonesian cane, and dyed Japanese cane. This low round basket has twining, randing, square knots, and the figure-8 weave techniques. *Courtesy of Ray Bolton.*

BILLY OWENS

Billy Owens is a second-generation White Oak basketmaker from the Ozark hills of southwest Missouri. His father, Dale Owens, was the first of the Owens family to take up basketweaving. He was self-taught as a child, but did not begin taking it seriously until he was grown. In the early 1980s, Dale began making white oak baskets for sale in Branson, Missouri. In the mid-1990s, Dale and his son, Billy, opened their white oak basket shop in Branson.

All the material used in their baskets comes from white oak trees that they have selected, cut, and prepared by hand in the "Ozark Method" using a handmade tool called a split knife, designed and made by Dale. They closed the shop in 2008 and since then, Billy has traveled across the United States to teach his Ozark Method of white oak basketry full-time.

Billy has taught at conventions and workshops in Alabama, Arkansas, Connecticut, Delaware, Florida, Georgia, Illinois, Indiana, Iowa, Kansas, Kentucky, Maryland, Michigan, Minnesota, Missouri, New Jersey, North Carolina, Oklahoma, Ohio, Pennsylvania, South Carolina, Tennessee, Texas, Vermont, Virginia, West Virginia, and Wisconsin. In his classes, he enjoys sharing with folks everything concerning white oak, from selecting the right tree to how to prepare the weaving material. It is his goal that first and foremost, the weavers in his class have an enjoyable time, gain an understanding of the Ozark culture and basketry, as well as leave with a finished white oak basket that they will enjoy and that will last them a lifetime.

Now there are a third and even a fourth generation of Owens white oak basketmakers. They make the distinction between being a basket "maker" and a basket "weaver."

"We make them from scratch," Billy says. "We don't buy the material and cut it to length; we cut down the tree, load it in a truck, haul it home, and then prepare the material the way it's been done for generations here in the Ozarks."

Large Williamsburg by Billy Owens. The material used in this large basket is white oak from the Ozark Mountains of Missouri. *Courtesy of Billy Owens.*

Market Baskets and Large Round Cotton Basket by Billy Owens. White oak is the material used in this trio of baskets. The weaving technique is known as the Ozark Method using a handmade tool called a split knife. *Courtesy of Billy Owens.*

NATHAN TAYLOR

Nathan Taylor is a master craftsman, educator, author, designer, and historian. Shaker baskets had become a lost art and would have remained lost except for the efforts of Nathan Taylor and Martha Wetherbee. Together they recreated the system and opened the first Shaker basket shop in America since the Shakers had stopped making baskets over one hundred years ago.

In his fifteenth year of basket making, Nathan's interest in Nantucket baskets grew, due in part to its similarity to Shaker basketmaking. He was the first to develop and offer a total system for other basket makers to follow.

Now in his thirty-ninth year, he also designs and makes his own line, which he calls Cape Cod Baskets. Continuing in the tradition as a master basketmaker, he and his wife Kathy, have moved to Hohenwald, Tennessee, where he teaches and supplies others nationwide.

Sweetheart Picnic Basket by Nathan Taylor. 15" l × 10" w × 7½" h, 12" with handles. Weaving materials are ash with cherry wood accents. The handles swing on brass and bone findings and brass hinges accent the cherry lid. Using the latest technology in slotted rims, this woven lid mates perfectly with the single piece rim. *Courtesy of Mark S. Johnson.*

Quadrifoil Lidded Purse by Nathan Taylor. 6" dia. × 5½" h, 8" with handle. This lidded purse is woven with hand-pounded black ash, cherry base, cherry rims, and cherry handle. Combining Nantucket and Shaker techniques, this small purse was designed by Nathan for his wife, Kathy. *Courtesy of Mark S. Johnson.*

Shaker Nesting Set of Three Kittenheads by Nathan Taylor. Small: 1" dia. × ¾" h, 1½" with handle. Middle: 2" dia. × 1" h, 2¼" with handle. Large: 2¾" dia. × 1½" h, 3" with handle. All of the material used in the weaving of this nesting set is hand-pounded black ash. The Shakers were known as the most progressive and among the highest quality basketmakers in the world. These baskets represent exacting copies of their work in a miniature scale. The Shakers' materials and techniques are applied in the making of these exquisite miniatures. *Courtesy of Mark S. Johnson.*

Mini Mt. Lebanon Carrier by Nathan Taylor. 2⅝" l × 1¾" w × 1" h, 1¾" with handle. Made of hand-pounded black ash with the Shaker techniques. *Courtesy of Mark S. Johnson.*

KATHY TESSLER

A simple apple basket was the beginning of a career in basketmaking for Kathy Tessler of Howell, Michigan. It was a six-hour class offered through the Bridgeport, Michigan, Community Education Program.

Kathy's goal as a teacher is to fill her students' heads with as many tips and techniques as she possibly can. She also hopes that they leave class with a basket they really love!

Most of Kathy's baskets are functional, strong designs. She specialized in double base/double wall baskets for many years and has lots of patterns for these designs in basketry shops nationwide and online. She also designs totes that feature her leather handles.

Kathy has been a member of the Association of Michigan Basketmakers since 1985 and has taught at every AMB Convention since 1987. Kathy also teaches at several other conventions and gatherings in the Midwest, East, and South.

Cherokee Tote Basket by Kathy Tessler. 15" l × 6½" w × 14½" h × 43" circumference. A tote basket woven with commercial reed in dyed and natural and Kathy's leather strap handles. *Courtesy of Andrew E. Tessler.*

Celebration in Ash by Kathy Tessler. 6" dia. × 4" h. Featured in *Basket Bits Magazine* in August 2004, this double base/double wall basket is woven on a cathead mold with brown ash hand processed by Bob Coker. The inner basket features three continuous dyed weavers in a twill pattern. The outer wall of the basket has dyed spokes and a unique shifting twill design with curl accents. *Courtesy of Andrew E. Tessler.*

Blue Diamonds v. 1 & v. 2 by Kathy Tessler. Blue Diamonds v. 1, 3½" dia. × 4½" h with handle. An award-winning double base/double wall basket for Best Traditional Basket at the 2007 Association of Michigan Basketmakers Convention. Woven with brown ash hand processed by Bob Coker and woven on a cathead mold in a quatrefoil design. Blue Diamonds v. 2, 6" dia. × 8" h with handle. Woven with brown ash hand processed by Bob Coker using a cathead mold, dyed and natural spokes and weavers in a quatrefoil design. *Courtesy of Andrew E. Tessler.*

Reversals by Kathy Tessler. 14" h × 55" circumference. This large double base/double wall basket is woven using commercial reed, natural and dyed. *Courtesy of Andrew E. Tessler.*

MATT TOMMEY

Matt Tommey's handcrafted baskets are a whimsical collaboration of traditional weaving techniques, vines, bark, branches, and recycled metal. Since the early 1990s, Matt's interpretation has offered a heartfelt nod to his roots in Appalachian basketry while offering a contemporary expression that is all his own. Matt's most recent work focuses on the use of a wide variety of locally available southeastern invasive species, encaustic wax and recycled metal in the creation of sculptural art vessels.

> It has been said that all creativity happens at the edge of chaos and order. For me, the chaos just happens to look like tangles, gnarly vines wrapped tightly around strangled trees and laurel, pods and cones littering the forest floor, the order like a beautiful sculptural basket that reminds me of its source. Somewhere in the middle is where the magic happens, where creativity broods over the chaos and new life begins; beauty is born. A simple walk through the forest explodes into a symphony of possibilities; back breaking in giddy glee as I carry the treasures toward their purpose. What once was dead is now alive, that which was hated is now desired, that which had no breath suddenly heaves with hope afresh. The weaving is the easy part; it's seeing beauty while it's still hidden that is the adventure. Even though these woven creations seem to simply form in the hands of their maker, as if to say it is only skill that brings them to life, it must always be remembered that every basket begins with a walk in the woods. It's time to take a walk.

As a professional craft artist, Matt is a leader in the contemporary basketry movement, serving on the Board of Directors of the National Basketry Organization from 2011 to 2014, the River Arts District in 2013, and as an instructor at schools, guilds, and conventions around the country including Arrowmont, the John C. Campbell Folk School, and the North Carolina Basketmakers Association Convention. He is also the founder of an international arts organization, The Worship Studio, committed to helping artists make the connection between creativity and spirituality.

Sculptural Vessel by Matt Tommey. 20" dia. × 15" h. Made from honeysuckle, kudzu, willow, poplar bark, and mimosa bark nestled in mountain laurel branches and stained with black walnut dye. This woven vessel is created in a Random weave technique.

Sculptural Vessel by Matt Tommey. 6" dia. × 12" h. Made from poplar bark, royal paulownia bark, and mimosa bark. *Courtesy of Tim Barnwell.*

Sculptural Freeform Vessel by Matt Tommey. 13" dia. × 12" h. Made from kudzu, copper wire, and poplar bark, covered in encaustic wax. *Courtesy of Tim Barnwell.*

Sculptural Vessel by Matt Tommey. 15" dia. × 16" h. Made from kudzu, poplar bark, encaustic wax, and copper nails nested in mountain laurel branches. *Courtesy of Tim Barnwell.*

LAURA LEE ZANGER

Laura Lee Zanger is from Augusta, Georgia. She has been designing baskets and writing patterns since October, 2000 and began teaching classes on the basketry circuit in 2002. Laura Lee enjoys expressing her creativity using Cherokee, Choctaw, and Chitimacha techniques. She shares her excitement and enthusiasm for twills with everyone she encounters, maintaining the fascination of a child with every new idea, lesson and experience. Her goal is to enlighten everyone on the thrill of twill, weaving in the Southeastern Native American tradition of the single and double woven baskets.

Laura Lee is self-published and the author of a series of mini books filled with techniques. She has written a fictional story, "Old Woman and the Legend of the Doublewoven Basket."

Midnight Sky Tray by Laura Lee Zanger. 15" l × 14" w × 2" h. Materials are rattan in natural and dyed dark blue to resemble the stars at midnight, are woven into this Chitimacha-style tray using the Muscadine Rind design. The Chitimacha have a unique numbering system in their twill designs that uses the number one as a design element recognized in their weaving. *Courtesy of Laura Lee Zanger.*

Large 1-3-5 Twill Sampler Mat by Laura Lee Zanger. 44" l × 25" w. Woven of natural and dyed rattan, this very large mat is a sampler of 16 Cherokee twill designs made with number combinations of 1s, 3s, and 5s to allow one design to flow effortlessly into the next. This mat was designed for display at the Traditional and Contemporary Woven Art Exhibit at the Pickens Museum of Art and History in Pickens, South Carolina. The designs are (from left to right): Chief's Daughter, Peace Pipes, Rivers and Streams, Unbroken Friendship, Double Chief's Daughter in a Diamond, Cherokee Hearts, Arrows or Fish Bones, Chief's Coffin, Cross on the Hill, Bird Eyes, Noon Day Sun, Evening Star, Indian Arc, Four Principle Directions, Field of Crosses, Birds Eyes again, Mountains and Valleys, and Chief's Daughter in a Diamond Chain. *Courtesy of Laura Lee Zanger.*

Toxaway Double Woven Basket by Laura Lee Zanger. 10" dia. × 9" h. Made of rattan in a rainbow of colors, this basket has a brim at the rim and is woven in the tradition of the ancient double woven technique. This technique is thousands of years old and continues today with the Cherokee, Choctaw, and Chitimacha weavers. It is the most intriguing design of all their baskets; since it is woven in one continuous weaving process. The material in which it begins is all that is used to make double the bases and double the sides making it difficult to see where it begins or ends. *Courtesy of Laura Lee Zanger.*

Sacred Fire by Laura Lee Zanger. 17" l × 6½" w × 21" h. In dyed rattan with the colors of fire, this basket is made in the Choctaw Elbow Basket style. With an artistic flair, the ends of the elbow represent the flames of the Sacred Fire of the Native Americans. Fire is a necessity for light and survival and is never allowed to burn out. The technique used is a 4-block twill that transitions into a 4, 4 twill out to the ends. *Courtesy of Laura Lee Zanger.*

JUDY ZUGISH

Judy Zugish began experimenting with cultivating fibers and using them to invent contemporary, sculptural basket forms nearly thirty-five years ago. As her notable fiber arts garden grew, so also her basketmaking, teaching, and studio work developed maturity, expanding to national and international exhibitions and teaching in many cultures.

Judy's delight in the irregular kindles the creative in her students and together they find their own hidden gardens of expression.

She is co-founder of Fishsticks Basketry School, a field study education resource, bringing local, national and international weavers to her celebrated nursery garden to workshop, to laugh, and to learn.

A deep respect for the historical place of basketry has inspired study travels in Japan, England, Germany, Thailand, Ireland, Mexico and Australia. In 2011, she traveled into the willow forests of Denmark. She led a group of weavers to France and Denmark in 2013 and to Scotland in 2014.

Judy's connection with materials she grows and processes means each woven piece becomes a thought filled container; she has begun writing the poetry of each basket as its companion.

One of Judy's sculpted willow bark pieces was included in the book *500 Baskets*. Her gardens are featured in *Landscaping with Herbs* and *Snohomish County, Treasure of the Northwest.*

Grandmother's Buttons Made Me Dance by Judy Zugish. 32" h × 12" × 18". Made of willow barks, peeled cedar root, and buttons stitched and woven and wrapped. "A story piece recalling childhood times with Granny, her sewing machine, our chatter, the magical buttons in her box, our joy and laughter." *Courtesy of Barb Chase.*

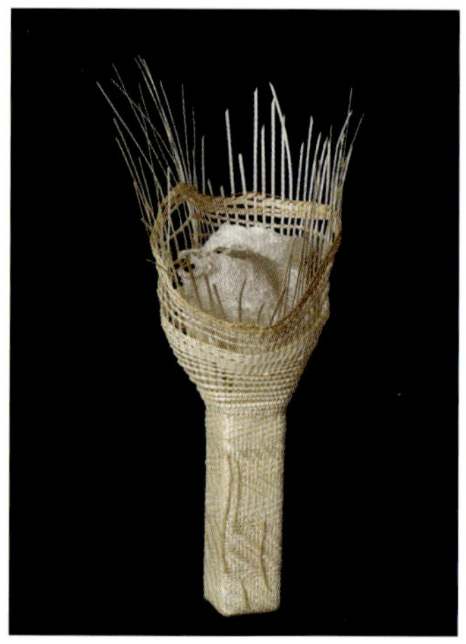

Whispers and Shouts, Speaking Out by Judy Zugish. 16" h × 6" × 7". Materials include hand-skeined willow and abaca fibers in this twill pattern with open stitching created as a public election piece "about community, speaking your heart, from contained within to bravely out." *Courtesy of Barb Chase.*

Float by Judy Zugish. 12" h × 6" l × 6" w. Materials include hand-skeined natural and buff willow in twill patterns and sculpting spiral weaves with skip stitch lines. "This woven vessel is autobiographical; the shaping and mis-shaping of a vessel with no forward, no aft, pulled up, and made to accept a tossing sea." *Courtesy of Barb Chase.*

Moving Spirit by Judy Zugish. 9" h × 15" × 18". Hand-skeined willow and peeled spruce root are used in this undulating twill weave with open wrap. "A suspended, sculptural open weave that carries and loosely contains the spirit of flexibility. Lightly moving, it casts the elongated shadows of the unknown beyond." *Courtesy of Barb Chase.*

CHAPTER TEN

DISPLAY AND CARE OF BASKETS

HOW TO DISPLAY BASKETS

At home there are numerous ways in which you can display your handwoven baskets. Make use of furniture and other items you already have in your décor. Shelves at any level provide a resting place for any basket. Depending on the size of the basket and the height and depth of the shelf, test a basket's location in several places before deciding where it fits best. An entertainment center provides display space and the baskets can also serve as storage containers for various electronics.

Above kitchen cabinets is a common place to display baskets, especially those art pieces that are not often removed from display for functional purposes.

One of my favorite ways to exhibit baskets is by hanging them on a basket tree. Several wrought-iron basket trees in my home are covered with baskets. Place the basket-filled tree in a corner and instantly your eye is drawn to the interesting textures and colors. This manner of display makes it easy to select the perfect basket when needed.

Wall groupings are more permanent locations for basket display. Plan the group by selecting wall baskets, woven bowls, plaques, and trays that work to your liking. Measure the wall space and mark hanging locations based on the basket dimensions chosen. Display these baskets in a part of the room that receives no direct sunlight or direct heat source, to reduce color fading.

The kitchen countertop, tables, bathroom vanity, windowsills, and many other places around your home are other locations to display and use your favorite baskets.

At craft shows, art galleries, and gift shops, baskets are enhanced by the use of several display techniques.

At craft shows, cover your tables with cloth in a compatible color. Try using burlap or other tablecloths for seasonal displays.

Make use of any vertical space in the craft booth for hanging baskets above and at eye level. Shelves in varying heights allow the consumer to visualize baskets in their home environment. Ladders, boxes, and clear plastic storage containers in different sizes help add interest to the display.

At a gallery or craft shop, baskets display nicely on glass or wood shelves. Handwoven pieces are accented with ample lighting; however, avoid direct sunlight from storefront windows.

At any exhibit or display opportunity, include your business cards and brochures publicizing your art.

HOW TO CARE FOR BASKETS

Our environment provides our basketweaving materials, and our environment is also important in the care of baskets. Every three to six months, examine your baskets and clean those that are in need.

To remove dust, use a hairdryer or soft-bristle paintbrush.

Baskets displayed in the kitchen and those used for food storage and transporting may need inspection more often. Remove any food particles that may attract insects using a soft-bristle paintbrush. Stubborn areas can be cleaned with warm water and a small amount of mild dishwashing liquid. (Test a small area on the basket for dye bleeding before using water.) Rinse several times with warm to cool water, then allow the basket to air dry overnight.

To keep color accents from fading, avoid direct sunlight and direct fluorescent lighting. Use blinds or shades to control the amount of light near baskets.

Provide moderate humidity at 40% to 60%; too much moisture would lead to mold or mildew. Supply a constant temperature between 60 and 75 degrees Fahrenheit (15 to 23 degrees Celsius).

Avoid display areas near heat and air circulation vents to prevent basket materials from becoming dry or brittle.

The ideal condition to display your most special baskets and antique woven treasures is under glass in an enclosed glass case that provides the correct environment described above.

One additional important factor in preserving and caring for your baskets is to handle them with clean hands, free of any oils or lotions, which may cause staining. To protect antique baskets, handle them very delicately, wearing white cotton gloves or latex-free gloves.

Periodically, rotate your baskets to a different location to avoid overexposure to damaging environmental factors and for variety and interest. Most of all, enjoy your beautiful handwoven baskets every day.

WEAVING SUPPLIERS

August Moon Basketry
4702 Airport Road
Pageland, SC 29728
843-672-3534
www.augustmoonbasketry.com

Basket Bases by Rusty
280 Dasali Way
Murphy, NC 28906
828-644-5365
www.basketbasesbyrusty.com

BasketWeavingSupplies.com
11 Baywood Drive
Shirley, MA 01464
866-928-5430
www.Basketweavingsupplies.com

The Country Seat
1013 Old Philly Pike
Kempton, PA 19529-9321
610-756-6124
www.countryseat.com

Feix Family Baskets
321 E. Somers Street
Eaton, OH 45320
937-456-6067
www.feixbaskets-crafts.com

Inter-Mares Trading Co., Inc.
1064 Route 109
P.O. Box 617
Lindenhurst, NY 11757-0617
631-957-3467
800-229-2263
www.canefish.com

K-n-K Creations
254 Pine Bluff Road
Waynesboro, VA 22980
540-292-1669
www.knkcreations.com

Suzanne Moore's N. C. Basket Works, Inc.
130 Main Street
P.O. Box 744
Vass, NC 28394
910-245-3049
800-338-4972
www.ncbasketworks.com

P. L. Butte, Inc.
44 West Park Avenue, 2nd Floor
Long Beach, NY 11561
516-889-1190
800-289-1049
www.plbutte.com

Royalwood, Ltd.
517 Woodville Road
Mansfield, OH 44907
419-526-1630
800-526-1630
www.RoyalwoodLtd.com

GLOSSARY

Arrow: design element made of two rows of weaving; a pictorial design found in Native American baskets.

Awl: sharp, pointed tool for making openings in the weaving or to pierce holes in spokes.

Back Weave: unweave or take out the last rows of weavers to correct an error or try something new.

Bargello: arrow and zigzag design made of two rows of weaving, Three Rod Wale and Reverse Three Rod Wale; similar to the embroidery stitch by the same name.

Base: foundation or bottom of a woven basket; also a wooden base with slots or grooves for spoke placement.

Basket: woven container made of fiber, wood, or other natural or manmade materials.

Bi-spokes: added alongside base spokes after the basket is started to help form the sides.

Border: the finished rim at the top of a basket.

Burden basket: type of basket carried on one's back for transporting heavy items or small children.

Cable ties: plastic zip ties used to hold rim pieces in place when lashing.

Cane: inner bark of rattan palm.

Cathead: basket shape resembles a cat when base is turned upside down.

Chain Weave: three consecutive rows of dyed weavers resembles a chain or belt buckle.

Chase Weave: a continuous weave with two weavers; one chases the other but does not pass the first.

Coil: bundle of reed; a weaving technique as in sweetgrass baskets.

Continuous Weave: weaving technique does not stop to end each row, keeps weaving around the basket.

Cross-warp base: two wicker bases joined together to make one rigid base.

Crimp: bend and compress fibers with crimping tool, needle-nosed pliers.

Cut and Tuck: at the rim of the basket, trim spoke ends to tuck inside the basket.

Double Lashing: lash in one direction around the basket rim, reverse and lash around to the starting place creating an X rim border.

Double Three Rod Wale: two pieces of round reed put together to make one double weaver, one of three double weavers needed in this technique. The left-most weaver moves over two spokes and under one spoke then out to the front.

Dye: substance used to add color to basket reed.

Ear: wood extension on swing handles and other add-in handles, stays under the rim to keep the handle secure.

Embellishment: added to the surface of a basket for decorative finish.

Feet: wood extensions added to create height to a basket and to lift base off the floor.

Filled-in base: woven base with filler spokes; all spokes are as close together as possible.

Five Rod Wale: weaving technique using five weavers.

Flat reed: common type of basket material commercially prepared; flat on both sides.

Flat oval reed: commercially prepared basket material, flat on one side and raised oval on the other side.

Folded Rim: spoke ends are folded, bent, and ended as a rim option.

Four Rod Wale: weaving technique using four weavers.

French Randing: weaving technique using a short piece of reed behind every spoke, woven on a diagonal.

God's Eye: decorative design to secure two handles or hoops together, most often found in ribbed baskets.

Half round reed: round reed split in half lengthwise, sturdy material used for rims.

Handle: wood or other material used to carry the basket.

Handle anchor: reed used to secure handle wrap techniques.

Handle wrap: a design to enhance the beauty of a basket, material encircles the handle making a comfortable grip.

Hoop: wood, bent into a circle, glued together for ribbed baskets.

Increasing Technique: weaving adds height to one or more sides of the basket.

Lasher: flexible material, cane or narrow reed, which wraps around all rim pieces and secures them to the basket rim.

Notch: a cut-out area on handles; wooden ledge that secures an add-in handle to the rim and the basket.

Over and Under, Start and Stop: a weaving technique moving over one spoke, under one spoke; also known as plain weave or randing.

Overlap: place where weaver or rim pieces end.

Overlay: material or decoration added to the basket surface for design element as in embellishment.

Pack: push or move rows of weavers close together.

Philodendron: plant that grows in warm climates; its sheaths are used as rim borders and other embellishments.

Plain weave: over one spoke and under one spoke.

Rattan: also called reed, comes from the genera Calamus and Daemonorhops (which together include several hundred species), a climbing vine-like palm that is found in the tropical areas of Southeast Asia.

Reed: rattan, the inner core of a rattan palm processed commercially then woven into baskets.

Reed gauge: tool with marked openings to measure reed sizes.

Reverse Spiral: Three Rod Wale technique introduces a dyed weaver for three rows, woven in the opposite direction from previous weavers.

Rib: round reed spoke that reaches from one side of the basket to the other side forming the frame of the basket.

Ribbon: reed bent and turned in an open space and inserted under weavers (this can be an embellishment with color significance, i.e., pink for breast cancer, other colors for other health issues).

Rim: materials, usually flat oval reed, used for the inside and outside bands which cover the top rows of weavers.

Rim Filler: material sandwiched between inside and outside rim pieces fills in any gap and covers the cut and tuck location of spokes.

Round reed: commercially prepared basket material from the inner core of the rattan plant.

Row: weaving material making one complete movement around the base or basket.

Scarf: the place where two ends meet, overlap on a slant or angle for a tight and smooth overlap.

Seagrass: natural marshy grasses, gathered and twisted into a ropelike weaving material, most commonly used as a rim filler, and woven as textural accent.

Shaker tape: a textile or thick fabric often woven from the base of a basket or at the basket rim to create inexpensive, flexible handles for various baskets.

Space dyed reed: two, three, or more dyed colors distributed around a coil of reed creating multiple colors on each piece.

Spiral Weave: Three Rod Wale technique woven over two spokes and under one using a total number of spoke ends divisible by three minus one; a twill weave over two spokes and under two spokes over an odd number of spoke ends.

Spokes: reed or other material which makes the rigid frame from the base up the sides of a basket.

Spoke weight: metal ruler or other heavy object which holds spokes in place while weaving the base.

Stain: a liquid preparation of coloring or dye applied to baskets and other woods.

Step-up: an ending technique for Three Rod Wale and other weaves; this makes each row complete and a smooth transition.

Taper: trim or thin the width of a weaver in the beginning and ending of a continuous weaver to keep the basket level.

Template: a pattern or shape cut from paper to the size of the wood base; assists inserting spokes equal distance apart.

Three Rod Wale: Triple Twine Weave technique uses three round reed weavers working with the left-most weaver over two spokes, under one, and out.

Turnback: weaving technique used to increase, decrease, or fill in an area in a basket.

Twill: weaver passes over and under using a different number of spokes, going over in groups of two or more, creating diagonal patterns around the basket.

Twining: a strong weaving technique that alternates two or more weavers and twists around and in between spokes; also known as pairing.

Upsett: British term for bending spokes into correct position or angle to set the shape then weave the side walls of the basket.

Wale or Waling: a twining technique woven over any number of spokes where the left-most weaver of three or more weavers moves over a given number of spokes, under one spoke and out to the front for a textural component.

Walnut hull stain: natural dye made from dried outer covering of walnuts.

Waxed linen: thread processed with a wax covering in several thickness: 2-ply, 4-ply, 7-ply, and 12-ply.

Weaver: reed or other material interlaced in and out around the basket.

Wicker: baskets and furniture made with round materials such as round reed or willow.

Yayni: Hopi term used for a cross-warp base where two woven bases are combined to make one rigid beginning to a woven plaque.

BIBLIOGRAPHY

Barnes, Marianne. *New and Different Materials for Weaving and Coiling*. Atglen, PA: Schiffer Publishing, Ltd., 2012.

Chancey, Jill R. *By Native Hands*. Laurel, MS: Lauren Rogers Museum of Art, 2005.

Clary, Willis. *A Sweet, Sweet Basket*. Orangeburg, SC: Sandlapper Publishing Co., 1986.

Daugherty, Robin Taylor. *Splintwoven Basketry*. Loveland, CO: Interweave Press, 1986.

Davis, Grace, and Forrest Davis. *The Weaver's Friendly Handbook for Pricing and Selling Handmade Baskets*. Bunnell, FL: Simple Things, 1977.

Gruber, Nancy. *Fancy Handles for Decorative Woven Baskets*. Asheville, NC: Jadwick Enterprises, Inc., 1993.

Hoppe, Flo. *Contemporary Wicker Basketry*. Asheville, NC: Lark Books, 1996.

———. *Wicker Basketry*. New York: Sterling, 1999.

Irwin, John Rice. *Basket and Basket Makers in Southern Appalachia*. Atglen, PA: Schiffer Publishing Ltd., 1982.

Jensen, Elizabeth. *Baskets from Nature's Bounty*. Loveland, CO: Interweave Press, 1996.

LaFerla, Jane. *Making the New Baskets: Alternative Materials, Simple Techniques*. Asheville, NC: Lark Books, 1999.

Lonning, Kari. *The Art of Basketry*. New York: Sterling, 2000.

Miller, Bruce W. and Jim Widess. *The Caner's Handbook*. New York: Lark Crafts, 1991.

Navajo School of Indian Basketry. *Indian Basket Weaving*. New York: Dover, 1971.

Raven, Margot Theis. *Circle Unbroken*. New York: Farrar, Straus and Giroux, 2004.

Schaaf, Gregory. *American Indian Baskets I: 1,500 Artist Biographies*. Santa Fe, NM: CIAC Press, 2006.

Siler, Lyn. *The Basket Book*. New York: Sterling, 1988.

———. *A Basketmaker's Odyssey: Over, Under, Around and Through*. Matthew, NY: Word Weavers, Inc., 2002.

———. *Handmade Baskets*. New York: Sterling, 1991.

———. *The Ultimate Basket Book*. New York: Lark Books, 2006.

Teiwes, Helga. *Hopi Basket Weaving: Artistry in Natural Fibers*. Tucson, AZ: The University of Arizona Press, 1996.

Turnbaugh, Sarah Peabody, and William Turnbaugh. *Indian Baskets*. Atglen, PA: Schiffer Publishing Ltd., 1996.

NOTES

Chapter 2

1. Bruce W. Miller and Jim Widess, *The Caner's Handbook* (New York: Lark Crafts, 2000), 17.

2. All About Reed page, http://countryseat.com/basketryreed.htm.

3. Suzanne Moore. Walnut hull dye recipe on package.

Chapter 4

1. Kari Lonning, *The Art of Basketry* (New York: Sterling, 2000), 43.

Chapter 6

1. Nancy Gruber, *Fancy Handles for Decorative Woven Baskets* (Asheville, NC: Jadwick Enterprises, Inc., 1993), 11, 19.

Chapter 7

1. Nancy Gruber, *Fancy Handles for Decorative Woven Baskets* (Asheville, NC: Jadwick Enterprises, Inc., 1993), 20–21.

2. Lyn Siler, *Handmade Baskets* (New York: Sterling, 1991), 80.

INDEX

Adirondack Folk School, 17
Advanced Weaving Level, 68, 118, 126
Arrow, 43–44, 109, 114, 128–129, 145
Arrow Handle Wrap, 65
Arrowmont School of Arts and Crafts, 17
Awl, 25, 120, 163
Back cut, 66, 108
Bargello, 44, 129, 143–145
Bases,
  cross-warp, 119, 125
  double wall, 157, 159
  filled-in, 26–28, 147, 148
  how to prepare, 26–27
  open weave, 26, 70, 134, 137
  plaid, 27, 75
  wood, 26, 29, 30, 101
  twill, 28, 87–88, 96
  yayni, 118–119
Beginner Weaving Level, 68, 69, 74, 133
Bi-spoke, 120–122
Black ash, 21, 153, 156
Blending technique, 102, 127, 130
Breast Cancer Awareness Basket, 111–117
Burden basket, 8, 13, 16
Cable ties, 25
Cane, 6, 19, 20, 63
Catsos, JoAnn Kelly, 21, 153
Cathead, 26, 69–72
Cherokee, 17, 95, 159
Coil, 19, 20
Craft and Folk Art Museum, 17
Crimp, 32, 48, 66, 76, 81, 116
Crows' feet, 27, 28
Decreasing, 83, 84, 123
Diamond, 35, 86, 95–99
Double X, 50, 85, 146
Dyes, 11, 22–23, 66, 118
  commercial, 22
  fiber-reactive, 22
Dyeing,
  procedures, 22–24, 66
  space dyeing, 23
  vinegar rinse, 23, 66
Ear, 56, 83, 146
Embellishment, 13, 17, 53, 117, 154
Filler spokes, 27, 147–148
  paired filler spokes, 147–148
Filling in, 142
Finishing touches, 49, 67
Fishsticks Basketry School, 17, 160
French randing, 37, 149, 163
Gallery, 5, 100, 152, 161
God's eye, 15, 79, 140–141
Gruber, Nancy, 62, 79
Gullah, 6
Handle anchor, 60, 61, 62, 64
Handle wraps, 60–65
  arrow, "V", 65
  braid, 62–64
  checkered, 61
  double braid, 62–64
  plain, 60, 138
  triple braid, 62–64, 76
  twill, 61
Handle wrapper, 60, 65
Handles, 54–59, 72
  add-in, 55, 57, 72, 83, 146
  built-in, 116, 138
  "D", 54, 74
  flat-top, 55, 56
  leather, 58, 138, 147, 151
  pottery, 59, 138, 147
  round-top, 55, 143
  swing, 56, 69, 72, 143, 146
  tulip, 55
  Williamsburg, 55
  wire, 57
Hoop, 57, 140–142
Hopi, 8, 118–125
Hoppe, Flo, 154
Horizontal Bands, 127–128, 137
Increasing, 83, 84, 123
Inside rim, 49, 90
Intermediate Weaving Level, 68, 80, 100, 143, 147
John C. Campbell Folk Art School, 17
Juried baskets, 132, 166
Lasher/Lashing, 49–51, 73
Left-most weaver, 38, 45, 101, 109
Molds, wooden, 69, 153
Nantucket, 20, 156
National Basketry Organization, 100, 154, 158
North Carolina Basket Association, 86, 95, 100, 106, 111, 118, 126
North House Folk School, 17
Notch, 27, 56, 72, 75, 80, 83
Notched handle, 55, 56, 75, 83
Number on baskets, 67
Outside rim, 49, 67, 90, 151
Outside spiral, 42, 81, 82, 108, 130
Overlays, 136, 139, 154
Owens, Billy, 20, 155
Ozark Folk Center, 17
Pack, 35, 36, 71, 73
Pattern break, 34, 86, 89, 95, 97
Penland School of Crafts, 17
Penobscot Basketry School, 17
Personalization, 67, 73, 78, 85
Philodendron, 13, 18, 53, 126, 131
Pickens Museum of Art and History, 69, 70, 100
Pine needles, 6, 7, 18, 21
Plaque, 8, 118–125
Projects,
  Autumn's Dress, 36, 42, 126–131
  Becoming Blue Skies, 100–105
  Chasing Diamonds, 35, 65, 86–94

- Cotton Basket, 136–139
- Cozy Wine Cradle, 35, 80–85
- Diamonds All Around, 35, 95–99
- Double Handle Plaid Carryall, 27, 34, 62, 74–78
- Hopi-Inspired Grand Canyon and Rain Clouds Plaque, 118–125
- Oval Bargello Basket, 143–146
- Rectangle Sampler, 36, 147–151
- Ribbons to Remember, 45, 52, 111–117
- Seagrass Egg Basket, 140–142
- Shaker Cathead Basket, 26, 69–73
- Spirals Change, 42, 106–110
- Wren House Williamsburg Basket, 133–135

Quadrant, 30, 81, 101, 107, 112, 144
Qualla Arts and Crafts Mutual, Inc., 17
Rattan, 6, 18, 19, 163
Reed, 6, 18, 19, 66, 154
- flat, 19, 163
- flat oval, 19, 67, 71
- half round, 19
- oval oval, 19
- right/wrong side, 66
- round, 19, 31, 106, 111, 118, 126
- size, 19
- smoked, 8, 20
- storage, 20, 67

Reverse spiral, 42, 43, 108, 109
Rib, 140–142
Ribbed basket, 15, 57, 140–142
Ribbons, 52, 111–117
Right-most weaver, 39, 43, 109, 128
Rim, 47, 49, 67, 73, 99
Rim border techniques,
- cable stitch, 51, 151
- double lashed, 50, 73, 78, 135
- fold and no-tuck, 52, 115–116
- one-way, 49–51
- round reed, 124

Rim filler, 20, 48, 49, 90
Rim row, 47, 72, 77
Rivercane, 6, 10
Scarf, 67, 90, 110
Seagrass, 20, 140–142
Shaker tape, 59, 164
Shaping baskets, 66, 71, 72, 109, 144
Sievers School of Fiber Arts, 17
Single spiral, 45, 109, 112–114
SC State Museum, 69, 95, 100, 106, 143, 147
Spiral, 42
Spoke, 22, 27, 47
Spoke weight, 70, 96, 148
Stain, 67, 73, 164
Starting Spoke, 32, 36–39
Step-up, 39, 42, 44, 108
Sweetgrass, 6, 15, 16
Tapestry needle, 50, 53
Taylor, Nathan, 20, 156
Template, 30, 81, 101, 107
Tessler, Kathy, 21, 157
Ti-Twine, 37, 149–150
Tommey, Matt, 21, 158
Tools, 25
Turnback, 84, 122–125, 138
Twill, 34, 61, 86
Twining, 31, 38. 47, 66, 97
Upsett, 32, 33, 71
Urethane, 23, 29, 30, 127
Upper South Carolina Basketmakers Guild, 136, 147
Waling techniques, 38
- double three rod wale, 40, 149–150
- five rod wale, 45, 46, 100, 102
- four rod wale, 45, 148
- reverse three rod wale, 44, 108–109, 113, 128, 145
- three rod wale or triple twine, 38, 101, 112–113
- triple three rod wale, 40, 41, 84

Walnut hull stain, 22, 23, 24, 67, 73
Waxed linen, 50, 53, 87, 90, 99, 126, 131
Weaver, 66
- start, 33, 66
- end, 33, 66
- overlap, 33

Weaving techniques,
- bargello, 44, 143–145
- blending, 46, 100, 102–103, 127
- braid, 36, 150, 151
- chain, 33, 72
- chase, 32, 44, 81–82, 107, 120
- continuous, 32, 35, 36, 82, 101, 107, 119
- decreasing, 83–84, 123–124
- double braid, 36, 128
- doublewoven, 159
- French randing, 37, 149
- increasing, 83–84
- over and under start and stop / plain, 33, 71, 76, 134, 144
- plaid, 34, 76–77
- ti-twine, 37, 149–150
- twill, 34, 35, 82, 88, 97, 98
- twining, 31, 38, 66

Wedding baskets, 13, 14
Wicker, 111, 118, 126
Wood bases, 29–30
- divided, 29
- holes in, 29
- oval, 29
- racetrack, 29, 80
- rectangle, 29
- round, 29, 30
- square, 29

Wood feet, 86, 90
Yayni, 118, 119
Zanger, Laura Lee, 34, 159
Zugish, Judy, 160

ABOUT THE AUTHOR

An avid collector of Native American baskets, Pati English is Resident Artist on the Approved Artist Roster, South Carolina Arts Commission, and a juried artisan with art centers in the Southeast, where she has earned numerous awards. English teaches many of her basket patterns incorporating materials that are hand-dyed in her studio. Her baskets have been featured in national publications, and she has appeared on ETV and RFD-TV. Active with several guilds, English teaches and works to keep the art of basketry alive in the twenty-first century.

THE PHOTOGRAPHER

Kelly Hazel is a graduate of Greenville County Fine Arts Center and South Carolina Governor's School for the Arts. She has developed a deep appreciation for the process and challenges of expressing the beauty of a sculpture, basket, piece of jewelry, or other three-dimensional visual art through the two-dimensional art of photography. She lives in South Carolina with her husband and their son where she owns and operates Kelly Hazel Photography, specializing in photography of artist portfolios, small products, photographic illustrations, and architecture. She also works as an artist herself through drawing and fine art photography.